TRAUMA AND SELF

TRAUMA AND SELF

Edited by Charles B. Strozier and Michael Flynn

Rowman & Littlefield Publishers, Inc.

ROWMAN & LITTLEFIELD PUBLISHERS, INC.

Published in the United States of America
by Rowman & Littlefield Publishers, Inc.
4720 Boston Way, Lanham, Maryland 20706

3 Henrietta Street
London WC2E 8LU, England

British Cataloging in Publication Information Available

Library of Congress Cataloging-in-Publication Data

Trauma and self / edited by Charles B. Strozier and Michael Flynn.
p.   cm.
Includes bibliographical references and index.
1. Psychic trauma.   2. Self.   I. Strozier, Charles B.   II. Flynn,
Michael, 1962–
BF175.5.P75T74   1996   155.9'35—dc20   96-1354   CIP

ISBN 0-8476-8228-5 (cloth : alk. paper)
ISBN 0-8476-8229-3 (pbk. : alk. paper)

Printed in the United States of America

∞ ™ The paper used in this publication meets the minimum requirements of
American National Standard for Information Sciences—Permanence of
Paper for Printed Library Materials, ANSI Z39.48—1984.

For Robert Jay Lifton

Contents

After the Survivors Are Gone

I tried to imagine the Vilna ghetto,
to see a persimmon tree after the flash at Nagasaki.
Because my own tree had been hacked,
I tried to kiss the lips of Armenia.

At the table and the altar
we said some words written ages ago.
Have we settled for just the wine and bread,
for candles lit and snuffed?

Let us remember how the law has failed us.
Let us remember the child naked,
waiting to be shot on a bright day
with tulips blooming around the ditch.

We shall not forget the earth,
the artifact, the particular song,
the dirt of an idiom—
things that stick in the ear.

—Peter Balakian

Acknowledgments

We would like to thank Jon Sisk, Steven Wrinn, and Julie Kuzneski for undertaking the project, their skilled editing, and meeting our difficult publication schedule; Lucy Silva, Robert Lifton's ever-loyal assistant, for her help in putting the book together and good-humored tolerance for the chaos our book sometimes caused; and Richard Koffler for his editorial assistance as we conceptualized the book.

And to Cathy and Yollie, who gave up much for Robert Jay Lifton.

Contributors to this volume have retained copyright of their work, as follows:

"Introduction" © 1996 Charles B. Strozier

"Crime and Memory" © 1996 Judith Lewis Herman

"The Adopted Self" © 1996 Betty Jean Lifton

"Traumatic Departures: Survival and History in Freud" © 1996 Cathy Caruth. Reprinted by permission of the Johns Hopkins University Press

"The Contextual Self" © 1996 Paul L. Wachtel

"Some Reflections on Twentieth-Century Violence and the Soft Apocalypse" © 1996 Todd Gitlin

"Facts, Truth, and Social Responsibility: Reflections of a Developmental Scientist" © 1996 Frances Degen Horowitz

"Thought Reform Today" © 1996 Margaret Thaler Singer

"Robert Jay Lifton and Biology: The Doctor Is In—Knock Twice" © 1996 Lionel Tiger

"Violence, Selfhood, and the Ambiguities of Truth" © 1996 Lillian Feder

"Socialism and Human Nature, Once Again" © 1996 Norman Birnbaum

"Erik Erikson and Robert Lifton: The Pattern of a Relationship" © 1996 Lawrence J. Friedman

"Mélusine as Feminist: Shape-Shifting in Surrealism" © 1996 Mary Ann Caws.

"The Protean Woman: Anxiety and Opportunity" © 1996 Cynthia Fuchs Epstein

"A Quest of Eternal Life" © 1996 John S. Dunne

"The Second Scar" © 1996 Richard Sennett

"The Japanese Psyche: Myth and Realty" © 1996 Takeo Doi. Previously presented as a lecture to the Japan Society, New York, on May 2, 1989.

"Symbolic Immortality in Modern Japanese Literature" © 1996 David G. Goodman

Introduction

Charles B. Strozier

This book works at many levels. It is, first and foremost, a remarkable collection of essays on the deeper meanings of the broken connections of our lives *and* the transformative potential of the self in a dark time. In its various parts, the book moves from aspects of trauma and other fundamental breaks in human continuity into a varied discussion of the psychological and psychiatric, historical, religious, literary, and scientific aspects of the self.

These wide-ranging themes have a conceptual and ethical unity in the work of Robert Jay Lifton, who has a special relationship to this book. Any investigation of violence, trauma, and survival that moves below the surface will soon encounter Lifton. He helped awaken a whole generation to the psychological meanings of nuclear threat (*Death in Life*, *Indefensible Weapons*). His study of the Holocaust redefined the historical issues of that tragic eruption of twentieth-century violence and introduced into the culture new ideas about genocide in general (*The Nazi Doctors*, *The Genocidal Mentality*). He has long been a major theoretical voice in American psychology (*The Broken Connection*). His groundbreaking interviewing of Hiroshima survivors taught us about victimization and psychological renewal (*Death in Life*). His pioneering work on the psychological effects on veterans of the Vietnam war was the crucial empirical basis for what was later called PTSD *and* directly influenced current thinking about trauma (*Home From the War*). His "formative" theory of the self and the life-death continuum has helped explain the human cost of living with the scientific potential of ultimate endings (*The Life of the Self*, *The Broken Connection*). His method that adapts the psychoanalytic interview has proven vital for qualitative researchers, especially when the subject is human distress in extreme situations (*Thought Reform and the Psychology of Totalism*; *Death in Life*). But for all his focus on death and mass violence Lifton has always sought to define principles of transformation within the context of a psychology of the self (*The Protean Self*). That yearning to keep hope alive has remained a constant *and* brought him into an active leadership role in the peace movement opposing wars from Vietnam to the Gulf. He also takes great pride in his role as a key figure in the anti-nuclear movement and the revitalization of Physicians for Social Responsibility in the early 1980s and the creation of the IPPNW (the extension of PSR allied with Russian medical colleagues that won the Nobel Peace Prize).

This book, in fact, began as a volume of honorary essays for Lifton, a "*Festschrift*" in weighty German terms. It seemed to me and my colleague, Michael Flynn, that Lifton's work had introduced a number of unique perspectives on violence that deserved broader investigation. And so we asked his many friends and colleagues to think about their work in relation to the intellectual architecture of violence and human survival that Lifton has constructed in his various empirical and theoretical studies. To our surprise 49 distinguished colleagues responded to our request with original essays for the book. Some specifically discuss Lifton's work in relation to their own; some reference their ideas more subtly in the context of the categories of inquiry he has established; and some contend with him vigorously.

What began to emerge, in other words, during the year in which we put this book together, was much larger and more interesting than a simple *Festschrift*. Most such volumes are collections of minor essays by the disciples of great thinkers and quickly gather dust on library shelves. Our book was something very different, a kind of *unfestschrift*, as we began calling it informally. Our contributors honored Lifton's work by moving off from it in their own creative ways. There are no panegyrics to Lifton in this book, and in many cases you won't even find Lifton in the text or the notes. Some disagree with him on issues. And yet all the essays reflect an abiding respect for the questions Lifton has raised about violence and human survival. Such is the truer form of honor accorded a major thinker by his colleagues.

Because of its size and complexity, we decided to bring out the book in two separate but companion volumes. Both *Trauma and Self* and *Genocide, War, and Human Survival* honor Lifton's work in the sequence of themes that link violence and survival. The list of contributors for both volumes is printed in each book, as is my introduction, which makes clear the larger purposes of the project. At the same time, the two books are quite separate and conceptually independent. Each follows its own course and we suspect will interest rather different audiences.

This book begins with four papers on trauma. Few topics have been of keener interest to scholars and the public at large in recent years. As contributors to this book know well, Lifton was a pioneer in carrying out the empirical and theoretical work that helped define the contemporary understanding of trauma, whether shell-shocked war veterans or victims of sexual abuse in the family. There is a psychoanalytic context for the focus on trauma, as two papers make clear. It confronts us psychologically, morally, and legally, as the lead paper argues. And trauma even enters into the adoption experience, as argued by Betty Jean Lifton.

Section Two on "broken connections" extends the context of trauma from the individual and familial to the social and historical. Lifton's point about this link, which is essential to understanding his "formative theory," is that we live psychologically on images and that it is only our capacity to symbolize the self's immortality that gives life meaning. Many things can disrupt that fragile process of symbolization, from abuse in the family, to war, to the ultimate threats to existence with which we live. Trauma results, though it is always psychological and social, personal and political, at the same time. The papers in this section explore these issues from many points of view. Autobiographical reflections on the crisis of the 1960s moves into a discussion of cults. But violence in many other ways can break the continuity of life, which is the underlying theme of the essays about intelligence, Naipaul, and the reflections on the crisis in socialist thinking today.

Finally, in Section Three, the book includes essays that probe issues in the understanding of the contemporary self. Over three decades Lifton wrote and talked about "proteanism" as the defining characteristic of self style in an age of genocide and mass violence, ideas that came together in *The Protean Self* in 1993. Many others pick up on these images on their own. Even "hard" science has long wrestled with commitment and responded to it in interesting ways. Certainly, the self is fluid, whether sometimes empty, or shifting in specifically feminine ways. Comparative perspectives in such a topic can be enormously helpful as the two papers on aspects of Japan show clearly. There is a place in the self for God and eternal life. The self of Israeli doctors suggests the reaches of symbolic immortality, which is also explored in its clinical meanings. Finally, not all are quite so sanguine about the fluidities of the postmodern self, as Gerald Holton and David Riesman argue, though all would concur with the ringing final call for participation of the self in the public space.

If those formal categories describe the organization of the book, there are as well other plots and themes that operate in the book's disparate parts. Trauma is the specific theme of the first section but is as well the subtext of the second set of essays. The meaning of psychoanalysis in contemporary life runs throughout all the sections of the book. Lifton's notion of "symbolic immortality" comes up often and is the point of a number of papers in different sections. The proteanism of self transformation that is the underlying theme of the last section of the book is intended by the editors to serve as healing alternatives to the pain of trauma and broken connections.

There is, however, much respectful disagreement between many authors on key issues. Frances Degen Horowitz and Lionel Tiger sharply diverge on the question of nature vs. nurture. John Dunne, the theologian, addresses the immortal side of symbolic immortality (in contrast to Lifton's stress on the symbolic) and in the process makes it his own. Holton notes the enormous value of "pliancy" in science, while personally separating himself from such an orientation.

It is all a great feast of learning and passion that we hope you will enjoy.

Part I
Trauma

1

Crime and Memory

Judith Lewis Herman

What happens to the memory of a crime? What happens to the memory in the mind of the victim, in the mind of the perpetrator, and in the mind of the bystander? When a person has committed or suffered or witnessed atrocities, how does he manage to go on living with others, in a family, in a community, and how do others manage to go on living closely with him?

This is the question I propose to explore. Consider, as a starting point, a case reported by Dan Bar-On, an Israeli psychologist who has investigated the generational impact of the Nazi Holocaust. Bar-On has done extensive interviews not only with children of Holocaust survivors, but also with children of the of the Nazi SS. In fact, for some years now, he has been conducting workshops in which he brings members of these two groups together. In these workshops, the children of victims and the children of perpetrators disclose to one another the stories of the crimes that their families kept secret. Such encounters represent the highest form of therapeutic endeavor, for they carry the potential for both personal and social healing.

During the mid 1980s, Bar-On interviewed forty-eight men and women whose fathers (and in one case, a mother) had participated either directly or indirectly in extermination activities during World War II. He asked them to recall whether their parents had ever discussed wartime experiences at home, and whether they had shown any signs of guilt, regret, or moral conflict. Recognizing that to address such questions would be emotionally stressful both for his subjects and for himself, he took care to build rapport and trust with his subjects, and to maintain his own institutional, collegial and personal support. No one can do this kind of work alone.

The adult children of Nazi criminals could not initially remember

3

any discussion whatsoever in their families, either of the extermination program in general, or of their parents' participation. They also reported that they saw little evidence of distress or moral conflict in their parents. Repeatedly they insisted: "We had a very normal family life." Some constructed their own version of historical events from small bits of information they had gleaned from various sources, minimizing the role their fathers had played.

One man explained that his father had been a train driver during the war but only drove ammunition transports, and had never personally transported Jews to the death camps. When Bar-On expressed skepticism, on the basis of well-established historical evidence, this man agreed to ask his father for more information. For the first time in his life he asked his father direct questions about the past; a few days later he recounted their conversation to Bar-On. At first he reiterated the original story: his father denied any involvement in transports of Jews, and had not known anything about them. On further inquiry, he said that his father had admitted hearing from others at the time about the transports. Just as the interview was about to end, he suddenly added: "And this time, my father told me of another matter. He was on duty when they took a big group of prisoners of war and shot them on the platform in front of his eyes."

"How terrible!" Bar-On exclaimed. "It must have been very difficult to keep that hidden all these years."

"This was the first time he spoke to me about it," the son replied, matter-of-factly. "He never told anyone about it."

A year later, Bar-On re-interviewed the same informant. The memory that had been recovered in the previous interview was gone. The man did not remember his father's disclosure, nor that he had in turn repeated the story to Bar-On. Reflecting on this case, Bar-On invoked the image of a double wall erected to prevent acknowledgement of the memory of crime. The fathers did not want to tell; the children did not want to know.[1]

The ordinary human response to atrocities is to banish them from consciousness. Certain violations of the social compact are too terrible to utter aloud: this is the meaning of the word *unspeakable*. Atrocities, however, refuse to be buried. As powerful as the desire to deny atrocities is the conviction that denial does not work. Our folk wisdom and classic literature are filled with ghosts who refuse to rest in their graves until their stories are told, ghosts who appear in dreams or visions, bidding their children, "Remember me." Remembering and telling the truth about terrible events are essential tasks both for the healing of individual victims, perpetrators, and families, and for the restoration of the social order.

The conflict between the will to deny horrible events and the will to proclaim them aloud is the central dialectic of psychological trauma. Perpetrators, victims and witnessess are all subject to this dialectic, which forms and deforms the memory of the events.

What do perpetrators remember? Here our professional ignorance is almost perfect. We know so very little about the inner lives of people who commit atrocities that relatively sophisticated investigations, such as studies of memory, are utterly beyond our current capability. We know so little about perpetrators first of all, because they have no desire for the truth to be known; on the contrary, all observers agree on their deep committment to secrecy and deception. Perpetrators are not generally friendly to the process of scientific inquiry (though they are quite willing to invoke the authority of science when it suits their purposes). Usually they are willing to be studied only when they are caught (which is not very often), and under those circumstances they tell us whatever it is they think we want to know. In general, we have wanted to know very little. The dynamics of human sadism have almost entirely escaped our professional attention. Our diagnostic categories do not comprehend the perpetrators; they present an appearance of normality, not only to their children, but also to us.

By contrast, we now know a fair amount about what victims remember. It seems clear that close-up exposure, especially early and prolonged exposure, to human cruelty has a profound effect on memory. Disturbances of memory are a cardinal symptom of post-traumatic disorders. They are found equally in the casualties of war and political oppression: combat veterans, political prisoners, and concentration camp survivors, and in the casualties of sexual and domestic oppression: rape victims, battered women, and abused children.

These disturbances have been difficult to comprehend because they are apparently contradictory. On the one hand, traumatized people remember too much; on the other hand, they remember too little. They seem to have lost authority over their memories.[2] The memories intrude when they are not wanted, in the form of nightmares, flashbacks, and behavioral re-enactments. Yet the memories may not be accessible when they are wanted. Major parts of the story may be missing, and sometimes an entire event or series of events may be lost. We have by now a very large body of data indicating that trauma simultaneously enhances and impairs memory. How can we account for this? If traumatic events are (in the words of Robert Jay Lifton) indelibly imprinted,[3] then how can they also be inaccessible to ordinary memory?

When scientific observations present a paradox, one way of resolving the contradiction is selectively to ignore some of the data. Hence we find some authorities even today asserting that traumatic amnesia can not possibly exist because, after all, tramatic events are strongly remembered. Fortunately for the enterprise of science, empirical observations do not go away simply because simplistic theories fail to explain them. On the contrary, some of our most important discoveries arise from attempts to understand apparent paradoxes of this kind. I would like to offer two theoretical constructs that may help us clarify and organize our thinking in this area. The first is the concept of state-dependent learning; the second is the distinction between storage and retrieval of memory.

The common denominator—the A criterion—of psychological trauma is the experience of terror. Traumatic events are those that produce "intense fear, helplessness, loss of control, and threat of annihilation."[4] People in a state of terror are not in a normal state of consciousness. They experience extreme alterations in arousal, attention, and perception. All of these alterations potentially affect the storage and retrieval of memory.

The impact of hyperarousal on memory storage can be studied in the laboratory with animal models. McGaugh and his colleagues have demonstrated in an elegant series of experiments that high levels of circulating catecholamines result in enhanced learning that stubbornly resists subsequent extinction. This is an animal analogue, if you will, of the "indelible imprint" of traumatic events on memory.[5] Building on McGaugh's concept of overconsolidated memory, Pitman and his colleagues have demonstrated that activation of trauma-specific memories in combat veterans with PTSD produces highly elevated physiologic responses that fail to extinguish even over periods of half a lifetime. They interpret their findings as evidence for overconsolidation of memories laid down in a biologic state of hyperarousal.[6]

When people are in a state of terror, attention is narrowed and perceptions are altered. Peripheral detail, context, and time sense fall away, while attention is strongly focused on central detail in the immediate present. When the focus of attention is extremely narrow, people may experience profound perceptual distortions, including insensitivity to pain, depersonalization, derealization, time slowing and amnesia. This is the state we call dissociation. Similar states can be induced voluntarily through hypnotic induction techniques, or pharmacologically, with ketamine, a glutamate receptor antagonist.[7] Normal people vary in their capacity to enter these altered states of consciousness.

Traumatic events have great power to elicit dissociative reactions. Some people dissociate spontaneously in response to terror. Others may learn to induce this state voluntarily, especially if they are exposed to traumatic events over and over. Political prisoners instruct one another in simple self-hypnosis techniques in order to withstand torture. In my clinical work with incest survivors, again and again I have heard how as children they taught themselves how to enter a trance state.

These profound alterations of consciousness at the time of the trauma may explain some of the abnormal features of the memories that are laid down. It may well be that because of the narrow focusing of attention, highly specific somatic and sensory information may be deeply engraved in memory, while contextual information, time sequencing and verbal narrative may be poorly registered. In other words, people may fail to establish the associative linkages that are part of ordinary memory.

If this were so, we would expect to find abnormalities not only in storage of traumatic memories, but also in retrieval. On the one hand, we would expect that the normal process of strategic search, that is, scanning autobiographical memory to create a coherent sequential narrative, might be relatively ineffective as a means of gaining access to traumatic memory. On the other hand, we would expect that certain trauma-specific sensory cues, or biologic alterations that reproduce a state of hyperarousal, might be highly effective. We would also expect that traumatic memories might be unusually accesible in a trance state.

This is, of course, just what clinicians have observed for the past century. The role of altered states of consciousness in the pathogenesis of traumatic memory was discovered independently by Janet and by Breuer and Freud 100 years ago. The concepts of state-dependent memory and abnormal retrieval were already familiar to these great investigators. Indeed, it was Janet who first coined the term "dissociation."[8] More recently, civilian disaster studies, notably those by Spiegel and his colleagues, have demonstrated that people who spontaneously dissociate at the time of the traumatic event are the most vulnerable to develop symptoms of PTSD, including the characteristic disturbances of memory retrieval: intrusive recall and amnesia.[9]

Abnormal memory retrieval in post-traumatic disorders has also now been demonstrated in the laboratory. This is a very fertile and exciting area of current investigation. For example, Bremner and his colleagues have been able to induce flashbacks in combat veterans with PTSD using a yohimbine challenge; the same effect could not be produced in veterans who did not have PTSD.[10] Studies of traumatized people now demonstrate that some have abnormalities not only in trauma-specific memory but also in general memory. McNally and his colleagues have noted that combat veterans with PTSD have difficulty retrieving specific auto-biographical memories, especially after being exposed to a combat videotape.[11] These investigators were struck by the fact that the men who showed the greatest disturbances in autobiographical memory were those who still dressed in combat regalia twenty years after the war. They remembered nothing in words, and everything in action.

Thus, contemporary researchers have rediscovered what was already well known to the great nineteenth-century clinical investigators, namely that traumatic memories could manifest in disguised form, as somatic and behavioral symptoms. Janet attributed the symptoms of hysteria to "unconscious fixed ideas."[12] Breuer and Freud wrote that "hysterics suffer mainly from reminiscences."[13]

This puzzling and fascinating phenomenon has been extensively documented in contemporary clinical studies as well. For example, among twenty children with documented histories of early trauma, Lenore Terr found that none could give a verbal description of the events that had occurred before they were two-and-one-half years old. Nonetheless, these experiences were indelibly encoded in memory and expressed non-verbally, as symptoms. Eighteen of the twenty children showed evidence of traumatic memory in their behavior and their play. They had specific fears and somatic symptoms related to the traumatic events, and they re-enacted these events in their play with extraordinary accuracy. A child who had been sexually molested by a babysitter in the first two years of life could not, at age five, remember or name the babysitter. Furthermore, he denied any knowledge or memory of being abused. But in his play he repeatedly enacted scenes that exactly replicated a pornographic movie made by the babysitter. This highly visual and enactive form of memory, appropriate to young children, seems to be mobilized in adults as well in circumstances of overwhelming terror.[14]

In Bessel van der Kolk's phrase, the body keeps the score.[15] Traumatic memories persist in disguised form as psychiatric symptoms. The severity of symptoms is highly correlated with the degree of memory disturbance. Data from numerous clinical studies, including DSM-IV field trials for PTSD, now demonstrate a very strong correlation between somatization, dissociation, self-mutilation, and other self-destructive behaviors, and childhood histories of prolonged, repeated trauma.[16]

Though it is clear by now that abnormalities of memory are characteristic of post-traumatic disorders, they are not seen in all traumatized people, even after the most catastrophic exposure. For example, in a community study of refugee survivors of the Cambodian genocide, Carlson found that 90% reported some degree of amnesia for their experiences but 10% did not.[17] In childhood abuse survivors, we now have several clinical studies and two community studies. Memory disturbances seem to fall on a continuum, with some subjects reporting that they always remembered the traumatic events, some reporting partial amnesia with gradual retrieval and assimilation of new memories, and some reporting a period of global amnesia, often followed by a period of intrusive and highly distressing delayed recall. The percentage of subjects falling into this last category ranges from 26% to 19%.[18] Degree of amnesia may be correlated with the age of onset, duration and degree of violence of the abuse. Further research is needed to clarify both the determinants of the memory disturbance and the mechanism of delayed recall.

The nineteenth-century investigators not only documented the role of traumatic memory in the pathogenesis of hysterical symptoms, but also found that these symptoms resolved when the memories, with their accompanying intense affect, were re-integrated into the ongoing narrative of the patient's life. These discoveries are the foundation of modern psychotherapy. "Memory," Janet wrote, "like all psychological phenomena, is an action; essentially it is the action of telling a story. . . . A situation has not been satisfactorily liquidated . . . until we have achieved, not merely an outward reaction through our movements, but also an inward reaction through the words we address to ourselves, through the organization of the recital of the event to others and to ourselves, and through the putting of this recital in its place as one of the chapters in our personal history."[19]

Throughout the next century, with each major war, psychiatrists who treated men in combat rediscovered this same therapeutic principle. They found that traumatic memories could be transformed from sensations and images into words, and that when this happened, the memories seemed to lose their toxicity. The miliatry psychiatrists also rediscovered the power of altered states of consciousness as a therapeutic tool for gaining access to traumatic memories. American psychiatrists in World War II pioneered the use of hypnosis[20] or sodium amytal[21] to treat acutely traumatized soldiers. They understood, however, that simple retrieval of memory was not sufficient in itself for successful treatment. The purpose of therapy was not simply catharsis, but rather integration of memory.

Those of us who treat civilian casualties of sexual and domestic violence have had to rediscover these same principles of treatment. Retrieval of traumatic memory in the safety of a caring relationship can be an important component of recovery, but it is only one small part of the "action of telling a story." In this slow and laborious process, a fragmented set of wordless, static images is gradually transformed into a narrative with motion, feeling, and meaning. The therapist's role is not to act as a detective, jury or judge, not to extract confessions or impose interpretations on the patient's experience, but rather to bear witness as the patient discovers her own truth. This is both our duty and our privilege.

So far in this review of the current state of the field, I have said nothing about the accuracy or verifiability of traumatic memories. It has been widely presumed that traumatic memories, especially those retrieved after a period of amnesia, might be particularly prone to distortion, error or suggestion. In fact, a careful review of the relevant literature yields the conclusion that traumatic memories may be either more or less accurate than ordinary memories, depending on which variables are studied. For example, such memories may be generally accurate, or better than accurate, for gist and for central detail. They may be quite inaccurate when it comes to peripheral detail, contextual information, or time sequencing.[22]

On the matter of verifiability, we have some fascinating single case reports of traumatic memories from childhood retrieved after a period of dense amnesia and later confirmed beyond a reasonable doubt.[23] These anecdotal reports prove only that such memories can turn out to be true and accurate; they do not permit us to draw any conclusions about how reliable such memories might be in general. I know of only two systematic studies in which subjects were asked whether they knew of evidence to confirm their memories of childhood trauma. The first is a clinical study I and my colleague Emily Schatzow conducted with fifty-three incest survivors in group therapy. The majority of these patients undertook an active search for information about their childhood while they were in treatment. As a result, 74% were able to obtain some form of verification. More recently, Feldman-Summers and Pope conducted a nationwide study of 330 psychologists. Of these 23.9% gave a history of childhood physical or sexual abuse, a figure consistent with general community surveys. Exactly half of these subjects reported that they had some independent source of information corroborating their memories.[24] In these two studies, the subjects who reported amnesia and delayed recall did not differ from those with continuous memory in their ability to obtain confirming evidence. The limitations of these studies should be noted, however; since these were not forensic investigations, the researchers did not independently confirm the subjects' reports.

Finally, I know of no empirical studies indicating that people who report histories of trauma are any more suggestible, or more prone to lie, fantasize or confabulate, than the general population. Nevertheless, whenever survivors come forward, these questions are inevitably raised. In the absence of any systematic data, those who challenge the credibility of survivors' testimony repeatedly resort to argument from anecdote, overgeneralization, selective omission of relevant evidence, and frank appeals to prejudice. The cry of "witch hunt" is raised, invoking an image of packs of irrational women bent on destroying innocent people. When this happens, we must recognize that we have left the realm of scientific inquiry and entered the realm of political controversy.[25]

This brings us to the question: when a crime has been committed, what do bystanders remember? For we are the bystanders, called upon to bear witness to the many crimes that occur, not far away in another time and place, but in our own society, in normal families very much like our own, perhaps in our own families. Like the son of the man who drove the trains in wartime, we have been reluctant to know about the crimes we live with every day. We have sought information only when prodded to do so, and once we have acquired the information we have been eager to forget it again as soon as possible. We can see the phenomenon of active forgetting in operation as it pertains to crimes against humanity carried out on the most massive scale of organized genocide. It operates with the same force in the case of those unwitnessed crimes carried out in the privacy of families.

When we bear witness to what victims remember, we are inevitably drawn into the conflict between victim and perpetrator. Though mental health professionals may strive for therapeutic neutrality, it is impossible to maintain moral neutrality. To clarify the difference: therapeutic neutrality means remaining impartial with regard to the patient's inner conflicts, respecting his or her capacity for insight, autonomy and choice. This is a cardinal principle of all psychotherapy, and is of particular importance in the treatment of traumatized people, who are already suffering as the result of another's abuse of power. Moral neutrality, by contrast, means remaining impartial in a social conflict. When a crime has been committed, moral neutrality is neither desirable nor even possible. We are obliged to take sides. The victim asks a great deal of us; if we take her side we will inevitably share the burden of pain and responsibility. The victim demands risk, action, engagement, and remembering. The perpetrator asks only that we do nothing. He appeals to the universal desire to see, hear, and speak no evil, the desire to forget.

In order to escape accountability for his crimes, the perpetrator will do everything in his power to promote forgetting. Secrecy and silence are the perpetrator's first lines of defense, but if secrecy fails, the perpetrator will aggressively attack the credibility of his victim, and anyone who supports her. If he cannot silence her absolutely, he will try to make sure that no one listens or comes to her aid. To this end, he marshalls an impressive array of arguments, from the most blatant denial to the most sophisticated rationalizations. After every atrocity one can expect to hear the same apologies: it never happened; the victim is deluded; the victim lies; the victim fantasizes; the victim is manipulative; the victim is manipulated; the victim brought it upon herself (she is masochistic); the victim exaggerates (she is histrionic), and in any case it is time to forget the past and move on. The more powerful the perpetrator, the greater will be his prerogative to name and define reality, and the more completely his arguments will prevail.

This is what has happened in the mental health professions. In the past we have been only too ready to lend our professsional authority to the perpetrator's version of reality. For decades we taught that sexual and domestic crimes are rare, when in fact they are common; for decades we taught that false complaints are common, when in fact they are rare. At times, we have been willing to see what happens to men assaulted on the battlefield, and women and children assaulted in the home. But we have been unable to sustain our attention for very long. The study of psychological trauma has had a discontinuous history. Periods of active investigation have alternated with periods of oblivion, so that the same discoveries have had to be made over and over again.

Why this curious amnesia? The subject of psychological trauma does not languish for lack of scientific interest. Rather, it provokes such intense controversy that it periodically becomes anathema. Throughout the history of the field, dispute has raged over whether patients with post-traumatic conditions are entitled to care and respect or deserve contempt, whether they are genuinely suffering or malingering, whether their histories are true or false, and, if false, whether imagined or maliciously fabricated. In spite of a vast body of literature empirically documenting the phenomena of psychological trauma, debate still centers on the most basic question: whether these phenomena are credible and real.

It is not only the patients but also the investigators of post-traumatic conditions whose credibility has been repeatedly challenged. Clinicians and researchers who have listened too long and too carefully to traumatized patients have often become suspect among their colleagues, as though contaminated by contact. Investigators in this field have often been subjected to professional isolation. Most of us are not very brave. Most of us would rather live in peace. When the price of attending to victims gets to be too high, most of us find good reasons to stop looking, stop listening, and start forgetting.

We find ourselves now at an historic moment of intense social conflict over how to address the problem of sexual and domestic violence. In the past twenty years, the women's movement has transformed public awareness of this issue. We are now beginning to understand that the subordination of women is maintained not only by law and custom, but also by force. We are beginning to understand that rape, battery and incest are human rights violations; they are political crimes in the same sense that lynching is a political crime, that is, they serve to perpetuate an unjust social order through terror.[26] The testimony of women, first in the privacy of small groups, then in public speakouts, and finally in formal epidemiologic research, has documented the fact that these crimes are common, endemic and socially condoned. Grass-roots activists pioneered new forms of care for victims (the rape crisis center and the battered women's shelter), and advocated for legal reforms that would permit victims to seek justice in court. As a result we now find ourselves in a situation where for the first time perpetrators face the prospect of being held publicly accountable.

I should emphasize the fact that the odds still look very good for perpetrators. Most victims still either keep the crime entirely secret or disclose only to their closest confidantes. Very few take the risk of making their complaints public. The most recent data we have indicate that though the reporting rate for rape may have doubled in the last decade, it is still only 16%.[27] For sexual assaults on children, the rate is even lower, ranging from 2–6%.[28] These numbers are further reduced at each step along the way to trial. Victims of sexual and domestic crimes still face an uphill battle in court. Besides the strong constitutional protections which all defendants enjoy (and which no one is proposing to abrogate), perpetrators are also aided by the widespread bias against women that still pervades our system of justice. Nevertheless, even the prospect of accountability is extremely threatening to those who have been accustomed to complete impunity.

When people who have abused power face accountability they tend to become very aggressive. We can see this in the political experience of countries emerging from dictatorship in Latin America or in the former Soviet bloc. In many cases the military groups or political parties that were responsible for human rights violations retain a great deal of power, and they will not tolerate any settling of accounts. They threaten to retaliate fiercely against any form of public testimony. They demand amnesty, a political form of amnesia.[29] Faced with exposure the dictator, the torturer, the batterer, the rapist, the incestous father all issue the same threat: if you accuse me I will destroy you, and anyone who harbors or assists you.

This social conflict over accountability has reached a peak of intensity just at the same moment that we in the mental health professions are struggling to relearn and integrate the fundamental principles of diagnosis and treatment of traumatic disorders. We professionals are just now feeling the backlash that grass roots workers in women's and children's services have already endured for quite some time. Just as mental health professionals are starting to figure out how to treat survivors, (often by trial and error), we sudddenly find ourselves and the work we do under very serious attack. These attacks are not restricted to the realm of intellectual argument, but may also include anonymous threats, pickets in front of homes or offices, entrapment attempts, legal harassment and other intimidation tactics.

In the face of this onslaught, we have three choices. We can ally with, and become apologists for, accused perpetrators, as some distinguished authorities have done. We can back away from the whole field of traumatic disorders, as has happened many times in the past.[30] Or we can determine not to give in to fear, but rather to continue our work: in the laboratory, in the privacy of the consulting room, and ultimately in public testimony.

We need to be clear about the nature of the work that we do. The pursuit of truth in memory takes different forms in psychotherapy, where the purpose is to foster individual healing; in scientific research, where the purpose is to subject hypotheses to empirical tests; and in court, where the purpose is to mete out justice. Each setting has a different set of rules and standards of evidence, and it is important not to confuse them. It is no more appropriate to apply courtroom procedures and standards of evidence in the consulting room or the laboratory than to apply therapeutic or laboratory procedures and standards of evidence in the courtroom. But if we pursue the truth of memory in scientific and therapeutic settings, then we will inevitably have to defend our work in the courtroom as well. For our work places us in the role of the bystander, bearing witness to the memory of crimes long hidden.

Some of our patients will eventually choose to seek justice. Our stance regarding this decision should be one of technical neutrality. Nowhere is the principle of informed choice more important. When I am consulted I always suggest that patients think long and hard about the consequences of taking this step; it is not a decision to be made impulsively. But when, after careful reflection, some of our patients choose to speak publicly and to seek justice, we will be called upon to stand with them. I hope we can show as much courage as our patients do. I hope that we will accept the honor of bearing witness, and stand with them when they declare: we remember the crimes committed against us. We remember, we are not alone, and we are not afraid to tell the truth.

Notes

1. Dan Bar-On, "Holocaust Perpetrators and Their Children: A Paradoxical Morality," *Journal of Humanistic Psychology* 29(1989):424–43.
2. Mary Harvey and Judith Herman, "Amnesia, Partial Amnesia and Delayed Recall Among Adult Survivors of Childhood Trauma," *Consciousness and Cognition* 3(1994): 295–306.
3. Robert Jay Lifton, "The Concept of the Survivor," *Survivors, Victims and Perpetrators: Essays on the Nazi Holocaust,* ed. J. E. Dimsdale (New York: Hemisphere, 1980), 113–26.
4. Nancy C. Andreasen, "Posttraumatic Stress Disorder," *Comprehensive Textbook of Psychiatry* 4th edition, ed. Harold I. Kaplan and Benjamin J. Sadock (Baltimore: Williams and Wilkins, 1985), 918–24.
5. James L. McGaugh, "Affect, Neuromodulatory Systems, and Memory Storage," *The Handbook of Emotion and Memory,* ed. Sven Ake Christiansen (Hillsdale, NJ: Erlbaum, 1992), 245–68.
6. Roger K. Pitman and Scott P. Orr, "Psychophysiology of Emotional Memory Networks in Post-Traumatic Stress Disorder," *Proceedings of the Fifth Conference on the Neurobiology of Learning and Memory,* University of California, Irvine CA, October 22–24, 1992 (Oxford: Oxford University Press, in press).
7. John H. Krystal, et al., "Subanesthetic Effects of the Noncompetitive NMDA Antagonist, Ketamine, in Humans: Psychotomimietic, Perceptual, Cognitive and Neuroendocrine Responses," *Archives of General Psychiatry* 51(1994):199–214.
8. Pierre Janet, *L'automatisme psychologique: essai de psychology experimentale sure les formes inferieures de l'activite humaine* (Paris: Payot, 1973 [1889]).
9. Cheryl Koopman, Christine Classen, and David Spiegel, "Predictors of Posttraumatic Stress Symptoms Among Survivors of the Oakland/Berkeley California Firestorm," *American Journal of Psychiatry* 151(1994): 888–94.
10. J. Douglas Bremner, et al., "The Neurobiology of Posttraumatic Stress Disorder," *Reviews of Psychiatry* (American Psychiatric Press, 1993), vol. 4.
11. S. B. Zeitlin and Richard J. McNally, "Implicit and Explicit Memory Bias for Threat in Post-traumatic Stress Disorder," *Behavioral Research And Therapy* 29 1991):451–57.
12. Pierre Janet, "Etude sur un cas d'aboulie et d'idees fixes," [1891] Trans-

lated and cited by Henri Ellenberger, *The Discovery of the Unconsicous* (New York: Basic Books, 1970), 365–66.

13. Joseph Breuer and Sigmund Freud, *Studies on Hysteria* [1893–95], *Standard Edition of the Complete Psychological Works of Sigmund Freud*, Volume 2, translated by James Strachey (London: Hogarth Press, 1962).

14. Lenore Terr, "What Happens to Early Memories of Trauma? A Study of Twenty Children Under Age Five at the Time of Documented Traumatic Events," *Journal of the American Academy of Child and Adolescent Psychiatry* 27 (1988):96–104.

15. Bessel van der Kolk, "The Body Keeps the Score: Memory and the Evolving Psychobiology of Post-traumatic Stress Disorder," *Harvard Review of Psychiatry* 1 (1994):253–65.

16. Bessel van der Kolk, Susan Roth, David Pelcovitz, Francine Mandel, "Complex Post-traumatic Stress Disorder: Results From the DSM-IV Field Trial for PTSD," *Post-Traumatic Stress Disorder: Psychological and Biological Sequaelae* (Washington, D.C.: American Psychiatric Press, 1993).

17. Eve B. Carlson, Rhonda Rosser-Hogan, "Cross-cultural Response to Trauma: A Study of Traumatic Experiences and Posttraumatic Symptoms in Cambodian Refugees," *Journal of Traumatic Stress* 7(1994):43–58.

18. Judith L. Herman and Emily Schatzow, "Recovery and Verification of Memories of Childhood Sexual Trauma," *Psychoanalytic Psychology* 4(1987):1–14; and Elizabeth F. Loftus, Sarah Polonsky, and Mindy T. Fullilove, "Memories of Childhood Sexual Abuse: Remembering and Repressing, *Psychology of Women Quarterly* 18 (1994):67–84.

19. Pierre Janet, *Psychological Healing* [1919], vol. 1, translated by E. Paul E and C. Paul (New York: Macmillan, 1925), 661.

20. Abram Kardiner and Herbert Spiegel, *The Traumatic Neuroses of War* (New York: Hoeber, 1947).

21. Roy Grinker and John Spiegel, *Men Under Stress* (Philadelphia: Blakeston, 1945).

22. Sven Akê Christianson and Elizabeth Loftus, "Remembering Emotional Events: The Fate of Detailed Information," *Cognition and Emotion* 5 (1991):81–108; and A. Burke, Frederick Heuer, and David Reisberg, "Remembering Emotional Events," *Memory and Cognition* 20 (1992):277–90.

23. N. M. Szajnberg, "Recovering a Repressed Memory and Representational Shift in an Adolescent," *Journal of the American Psychoanalytic Association* 42 (1993):711–27.

24. Shirley Feldman-Summers, S. K. S. Pope, "The Experience of 'Forgetting' Childhood Abuse: A National Survey of Psychologists," *Journal of Consulting Clinical Psychology*, vol. 62, (1994):636–39.

25. Judith Herman, "Presuming to Know the Truth, *Nieman Reports* 48 (1994):43–45.

26. Susan Brownmiller, *Against Our Will: Men, Women, and Rape* (New York: Simon & Schuster, 1975).

27. Jeanne G. Kilpatrick et al., *Rape in America: A Report to the Nation* (Arlington, VA: National Victim Center, 1992).

28. Dana E. Russell, *Sexual Exploitation: Rape, Child Sexual Abuse, and Sexual Harassment* (Beverly Hills: Sage, 1984).

29. Laurence Wechsler, "The Great Exception": Part I: "Liberty," *New Yorker*, April 3, 1989, 43–85; Part II: "Impunity," *New Yorker*, April 19, 1989, 85–108.

30. Judith Herman, *Trauma and Recovery* (New York: Basic, 1992).

2

The Adopted Self

Betty Jean Lifton

In the beginning, before I became a psychologist, I was a children's writer and journalist. My husband, Robert Jay Lifton, was the one involved with trauma—on a massive scale—from brainwashing in China, to the survivors of Hiroshima, to the veterans of the Vietnam War, to the Nazi doctors.

Even as I wrote about the war-wounded, orphaned, and traumatized children of Hiroshima, Vietnam and the Holocaust, I did not allow myself to see that my own experience as an adopted child growing up in the closed adoption system had a place in the field of trauma—that it may have contributed to my empathy for children who experienced grief and loss.

I remember that when I first confessed my dread status as an adoptee to Robert, he shrugged it off as of no importance. He didn't see me as a changeling, or any different from anyone else. The psychology of the adopted had not been included in his training. Freud had not been adopted. The adoptive family had managed to "pass" until then, and it still remains, for the most part, an unexplored constellation that has escaped psychological detection.

During the long course of our marriage, in which he accompanied and supported me on my journey through search and reunion, Robert came to appreciate the unique identity problems of adopted people, cut off as they are from their origins. Not only did he recognize adoption as a trauma, but one of "disconnection and imposed inauthenticity that is thrust upon the child."

In my writing, I have been faced with the problem of how to make the link between adoption and trauma acceptable. Far from being regarded as traumatic, adoption is still widely viewed as fortunate for the child who is rescued from homelessness, and for the adoptive parents who are rescued from childlessness. And in most cases, as was mine, it is. But what is overlooked is that it is unnatural for members of the human species to grow up separated from and without knowledge of their natural clan; that such a lack can have a negative influence on a child's psychic reality and relationship with the adoptive parents.

My first book on adoption, *Twice Born, Memoirs of An Adopted Daughter* (in which Robert was a main character), was an attempt to give form to my adoption experience. Rather than freeing me as a writer to go on to other subjects, however, it was to plunge me even deeper into the mysteries of the adopted psyche.

I was inundated with letters from adopted men and women telling me that my book had told the story of their lives and that they wanted to understand what it was we shared. Why did so many of us feel alienated, unreal, invisible to ourselves and others? How had we been able to cut off the primal subject of who our parents were? Or to put it another way: How does a child's mind close down when it senses danger, and stay closed until some life event or crisis inadvertently jars it open? What traumatic effects does this have on the child's growing sense of self? And—a central mystery—why do adoptees feel they have no self?

The Divided Self

Of course, everyone has some kind of self. The adoptee born psychologically into the closed system and shaped by its myths, secrets and taboos from first conscious memory, and even before, has a unique self, an adopted self. But this fragile self has a basic inner division brought about by the need for denial that is built into the closed adoption system.

When I began my trauma research, I was primarily interested in how secrecy affects the formation of the adoptee's self. I saw it as emotional abuse (of which adoptive parents are unaware) that traumatizes the child. I came to realize, however, that it is not just secrecy that causes the trauma, but that there are a series of traumas. This "cumulative adoption trauma" begins when adoptees are separated from the mother at birth; builds when they learn that they were not born to the people they call mother and father; and is further compounded when they are denied knowledge of the mother and father to whom they were born.

We know that children cannot form a healthy sense of self if they must disavow reality. Yet, this is what adopted children are asked to do from the moment they are told they are adopted. They are asked to collude in the fiction that their genetic and historical heritage are disposable. They get the message from their adoptive parents: We will love you unconditionally—under the condition that you live *as if* you are really our own. It is a Faustian bargain. The adoptee is expected to step out of his own narrative and into the narrative of the adoptive parents.

The child is in a survival bind. Already abandoned by his birth parents, he must now abandon them and, by so doing, abandon his real self. A child forced to give up the real self cannot develop feelings of belonging. There is instead a feeling of basic anxiety, of being isolated and helpless.

D. W. Winnicott and R. D. Laing both used the terms True Self and False Self to describe the split in the human psyche that many children make. I call the split in the adopted child the Artificial Self and the Forbidden Self, neither of which is completely true or completely false.

The Artificial Self becomes almost selfless in its desire to please. Wanting to fit in at any cost, it will deny its own needs for the sake of others. It is afraid to express its real feelings of sadness or anger, for fear of losing the only family it has. It cuts the natural parents off from consciousness until they are no longer available, except in daydreams or fantasy.

The Artificial Self may behave like the perfect child but knows itself to be an impostor. Having cut off a vital part of the self, it may experience an inner deadness.

The Forbidden Self holds on to the self that might have been had it not been separated from its mother. Refusing to disavow reality, it goes underground for vitality and authenticity, harboring a jumble of fantasies about the birth parents and the life that might have been. It keeps itself hidden in order not to be flushed out and destroyed, or acts out in anti-social ways.

The Ghost Kingdom

Over time, the birth parents become little more than ghosts to the adopted child. I call the spectral place in which these ghosts reside the Ghost Kingdom. It is an awesome sphere—forbidden and forbidding—located only in the adoptee's psychic reality. If we can grasp the unreality of the realm wherein adoptees perceive their most real selves to reside, we will understand the adopted person's own sense of unreality, and how, at any age, conscious thoughts of reunion with the birth mother back in the womb, which the Ghost Kingdom represents, can bring with them terrifying images of disintegration into nothingness.

Adoptees may go in and out of the Ghost Kingdom even as they go back and forth between the Artificial Self and the Forbidden Self at different stages of their lives. They may be compliant as children, and then as adolescents struggle for authenticity, rebel against the adoptive parents, whom they see as inauthentic and a barrier between them and their authentic self.

Fantasy as Structure for the Self

Adopted children spend an inordinate amount of psychic time in fantasy. They may seem to be sitting quietly at home or in the classroom, when really they are deep in the Ghost Kingdom imagining scenarios that might have been or still might be. I believe that adoptee fantasies, both positive and negative, are an essential part of the building blocks of the developing self. We could say that they are the fragile center beam around which the edifice of the adopted self is built. They are the mother replacement; the comfort zone that the mother did not provide. They are also a form of grieving, of conjuring up the lost mother.

Adoptee fantasies can also be seen as an attempt to repair one's broken narrative, to dream it along. They enable the children to stay magically connected with the lost birth mother, whom they may alternately see as a famous movie star or a whore. (They suspect the latter). But situated as they are in the Ghost Kingdom, these fantasies cannot connect with the outer world, or become integrated into reality. They run the danger of becoming pathological when they interfere with the child's function in everyday life.

Stuck in the Life Cycle

The mystery of who they are becomes especially poignant when adoptees reach adolescence. If your personal narrative doesn't grow and develop with you, with concrete facts and information, you run the danger of becoming emotionally frozen. You cannot make the necessary connections between the past and the future that everyone needs to grow into a cohesive self.

According to Erik Erikson (who never knew his own father), young people who are confused about themselves have "identity hunger." I like this term because it suggests the starved part of the adoptee's psyche—the part that hungers for the nourishment that the mystery of their heritage has denied them. Who am I?, the adopted adolescent asks. Who do I look like and act like? What religion and nationality am I?

Florence Clothier, a Boston psychiatrist, felt this hunger in her patients. "The child who does not grow up with his own biological parents, who does not even know them or anyone of his own blood, is an individual who has lost the thread of family continuity," she wrote. "A deep identification with our forebears, as experienced originally in the mother–child relationship, gives us our most fundamental security. Every adopted child, at some point in his development, has been deprived of this primitive mother. This trauma and the severing of the individual from his racial antecedents lie at the core of what is peculiar to the psychology of the adopted child."

In Great Britain, psychiatrist Erik Wellisch noticed that his adolescent patients showed signs of "geneological bewilderment." He realized that everyone, including himself, took the presence of others with similar physical characteristics for granted because they had grown up surrounded by relatives who resembled them. He warned that being deprived of knowledge of their heritage could lead children to irrational rebellion against their adoptive parents and the world as a whole, and eventually to delinquency.

Anger that adoptees have built up over the years can erupt as uncontrollable rage. There is the unexpressed anger that they are adopted; anger that they are different; anger that they cannot know who they come from; anger that they cannot express their real feelings in a family climate of denial. When this anger is allowed to build in a child over the years, it can eventually erupt with tragic consequences.

For some time there has been a disproportionate number of adolescent adoptees in residential treatment centers and hospital adolescent wards. Their symptomatology includes lying, stealing, running away, setting fires, sexual promiscuity, substance abuse, and extreme antisocial behavior that often gets them in trouble with the law. Their personalities are characterized by impulsivity, low frustration tolerance, manipulativeness, and deceptive charm that covers over a shallowness of attachment. Long Island psychologist David Kirschner believes they fall into the category of the "Adopted Child Syndrome."

There are professionals who are uncomfortable with the concept of a syndrome because it implies pathology, but whatever one wants to call the constellation of disturbed behaviors displayed by adoptees, they should be seen on a continuum: from mild to serious to pathological. My own work with nonclinical adoptees who have grown up in the closed adoption system reveals that virtually all of them exhibit some depression and anxiety.

The Adult Child

On the surface, many adult adoptees seem to lead successful lives. Adoption is an invisible trauma, and so few can guess an adoptee's basic insecurity about coping with life or sustaining a relationship with others.

Adults, unlike adolescent adoptees, are not overrepresented in mental health facilities—but there are no statistics to tell us the number who seek private therapy or support groups for alcohol or drug addiction, eating disorders, depression, or who commit suicide.

Adult adoptees often describe themselves as shy loners or floaters, lacking self confidence. They may change jobs often and have problems with control and power, intimacy and commitment. Many are self-negating, and suffer from feelings of shame, inner badness, and defectiveness. They fear homelessness, betrayal, disintegration, and going mad. But, most of all, they fear abandonment.

The message most adoptees give to friends and spouses is: "Do anything you want to me, but don't abandon me."

The Search

I am often asked why some adult adoptees search and others don't. A Zen answer might be that inside every searcher is a nonsearcher, and inside every nonsearcher is a searcher. The difference between those who search and those who don't lies in how they have formed their defense structures as children: how much they have denied, repressed, and split off.

We could say that from the time they are separated from their birth mothers, all adoptees are consciously or unconsciously in search. Each time an adopted child wonders whose tummy she was in, what her mother looked like, why she was given up; each time he has a fantasy or a dream, looks on the street for someone who looks like him, the adoptee has taken a small step toward becoming a searcher.

Adoptees think of searching when they are in touch with their unconscious, when they have access to the feelings they have sealed off. The dissociation, which has worn thin in places, like the ozone layer, no longer protects them from the ultraviolet rays of reality. This may happen when they are jolted by a life crisis—the death of a parent, the end of a marriage, the loss of a job—and find themselves suddenly falling through a trapdoor of the self. Everything that was neatly arranged and nailed down in the psyche comes undone and flies through the trapdoor with them.

Still, the decision to search is not made in one impulsive moment, but is arrived at over a period of time as the self gradually evolves from one level of consciousness to another.

I see adoptees who search as on the mythic Hero's Journey. It is their heroic attempt to bring together the split parts of the self. It is an authentic way of being born again. It is a rite of passage from one state of consciousness to another. It is the quest for connectedness and a coherent sense of self. It is a way of modifying the past, of living out the script that might have been. It is a way of taking control of one's own destiny, of seizing power.

Yet, as Campbell warned, the hero must go into a dark forest where he will be confronted with a series of trials that challenge his courage and ingenuity. The hero can never let down his guard: the glorious road to transformation and growth is strewn with death encounters and survivorlike experiences.

So, too, is the adoptee's journey fraught with perils.

Adoptees are in peril because they are breaking the taboos inherent in the closed adoption system.

They are in peril because they could lose their fantasy mother who is more real, and in some ways more vital to them, than the real woman whom they seek.

They are in peril because that real woman could reject them.

They are in peril because they could lose their own magical self that was fused with the fantasy birth mother.

They are in peril because they could lose their adoptive parents, who were their only providers and protectors.

They are in peril because they could lose the self that grew up adopted, and no matter how imperfect it might be, it is the only self they have ever known.

They are in peril because they are not in control of the outcome.

They are in peril because the search uncovers their psychic split, beneath which lies the threat of fragmentation and disintegration, which they had built defenses to ward off.

The Regressed Self

As the adoptee in search returns to the beginning of time, time curves back on itself. One is on a "pilgrimage back to the womb," as one adoptee put it, moving toward one's original mother. Actually, one is moving toward two mothers: the fantasy mother, frozen in time, whom one has internalized, and the actual mother, whose life has moved on without her child in the real world.

While the adoptee regresses, he or she is becoming two people: the ambivalent adult who returns and the traumatized baby who was left behind.

The adoptee is moving between two time zones: the past and the future. And between two selves: the self one was and the self one will become. And between two realities: the reality one has always known and the alternative reality into which one is about to cross over.

Reunion

We cannot speak of reunions as successful or unsuccessful. All of them, no matter whom one finds, are successful in that adoptees feel grounded in the human condition, feel in control of their own lives.

The types of reunion experiences are as varied as the types of people who search. No two are alike, and yet in a sense everyone finds the same mother—a woman who has survived the trauma of giving up a baby. The way the mother receives the adoptee is directly related to how she handled that original trauma.

The birth mother may have some resistance to reunion if she felt abandoned by the birth father; if she has rewritten her history; or if she has changed her perception of herself from the fallen woman to the church-going den mother and doesn't want to be thrown back to that earlier self. The adoptee who returns is both the beloved lost baby for whom the mother once pined and the dangerous enemy who wreaked havoc on her life once and could do it again. The mother cannot embrace one without confronting the other.

This is true for the adoptee, too. Although the adoptee's adult psyche is bound up with the lost mother as profoundly as the fetus's archaic psyche was bound up with her in utero, the mother is perceived as both goddess and witch, representing both life and death. The adoptee cannot embrace one without confronting the other. Mother and child cannot help but react to the psychological fallout of their traumas. "All my anguish is because of you," is the unspoken message that lies between them.

I have come across reunions that have ended after one meeting and others that are still holding fast, despite ups and downs, after ten years or more. They run the gamut from the adoptee being welcomed back by the birth mother and her family to the rare cases where the adoptee is denied any contact. I have seen adoptive families and birth families blend into an extended family for the sake of the adoptee, just as I have seen the two families orbit separately around the adoptee, without ever interacting. But in all of these scenarios, even the seemingly negative ones, the adoptee feels a sense of grounding and renewal.

Becoming Whole

Adoptees are often perplexed after reunion: they thought that the mere sight of the birth mother or father would render them whole. Instead, they may feel more fragmented than ever, overwhelmed with grief, anger, and depression. They have lost the self they started off with and have not yet found the self they will become.

Reunion, then, is not the end of the adoptees' journey, but just another station along the way. It is not one moment, but a lifelong process.

Adopteees must still manage to heal the split in the divided self. They must weave a new self-narrative out of the fragments of what was, what might have been, and what is.

They must integrate the internal and external birth mother (the fantasy and the actual one) into a composite mother, just as they must integrate the internal and external adoptive mother into a composite one. They must integrate the birth father and the adoptive father in the same way.

Adoptees must accept that they cannot be fully the birth parents' child any more than they could be fully the adoptive parents' child. They must claim their own child, become their own person, and belong to themselves.

It takes a long time for adoptees to heal. Once when we were discussing why this was so, Robert had the insight that it is because they have no "pre-traumatic self." By this he means that the adoptee, who experienced separation and loss early in life, usually at birth, has no previous self from which to draw strength.

To overcome this lack, adoptees must search for ways to find empowerment and reconnection with the same energy they used in searching for their origins. Eventually, they come to realize that the healing had already begun when they took control of their own lives by making the decision to search, and it continued with each victory along the way: each name, address or telephone number.

Some adoptees need professional assistance in this reordering of the self. A perceptive therapist can help the adoptee to integrate the Artificial and Forbidden selves, so that an authentic core self can take over. During this period, when it seems that no self is in charge, the adoptee may despair that the emotional chaos will never end. But gradually, the adoptee's core self will emerge—one that retains a sensibility for the needs of others that the Artificial Self so carefully honed, along with the ability to express one's own needs and to assert oneself. The goal for the adoptee is to feel that he has a right to exist, and to stake the claims that come with such entitlement.

Adoptees empower themselves by joining one of the hundreds of support groups that have sprung up across the country. They can express the emotions that have been bottled up, and validate each other. They also empower themselves by engaging in political action to open records in their state legislatures.

A major step in the healing process takes place when adoptees are able to accept that what happened happened; it cannot be undone. It was their existential fate to be surrendered by one mother at birth and raised by another: they cannot annul that fact.

Through it all, the adoptee must keep integrating and growing and living in the present, dipping back now and then to recapitulate, accepting that the grief, anger, and depression are never completely resolved: they just get recycled and reapppear when you least expect them.

"Organisms and people do what they can," Robert once said when we were discussing this.

I like that.

We are, after all, part of the organic microcosm. We are limited in our abilities and, adopted or not, we try to go on. We do what we can.

3

Traumatic Departures: Survival and History in Freud

Cathy Caruth

> What happened on that day?
> What happened?
> Yes. What happened.
> I didn't die.
> *The Pawnbroker*

In recent years psychiatry, psychoanalysis, and neurobiology have shown an increasing insistence on the direct effects of external violence in psychic disorder. This trend has culminated in the study of "post-traumatic stress disorder," which describes an overwhelming experience of sudden, or catastrophic events, in which the response to the event occurs in the often uncontrolled, repetitive occurrence of hallucinations and other intrusive phenomena.[1] As it is generally understood today, post-traumatic stress disorder reflects the direct imposition on the mind of the unavoidable reality of horrific events, the taking over of the mind—psychically and neurobiologically—by an event that it cannot control. As such, PTSD seems to provide the most direct link between the psyche and external violence and to be the most destructive psychic disorder. I will argue in what follows that trauma is not simply an effect of destruction but also, fundamentally, an enigma of survival.[2] It is only in recognizing traumatic experience as a paradoxical relation between destructiveness and survival that we can also recognize the legacy of incomprehensibility at the heart of catastrophic experience.

The centrality and complexity of trauma in our century is first most profoundly addressed in two important and controversial works by Freud, *Beyond the Pleasure Principle* and *Moses and Monotheism*. These two pieces, written during the events surrounding World War I and World War II, respectively, have been called upon by contemporary critics as

showing a direct relation between Freud's theory of trauma and historical violence, a directness presumably reflected in the theory of trauma
he produces.³ I will suggest that these two works, read together, represent Freud's formulation of trauma as a theory of the peculiar incomprehensibility of human survival. It is only by reading the theory of individual trauma in *Beyond the Pleasure Principle* in the context of the notion of
historical trauma in *Moses and Monotheism* that we can understand the
full complexity of the problem of survival at the heart of human experience.

Beyond the Pleasure Principle indeed opens with Freud's perplexed observation of a psychic disorder that appears to reflect the unavoidable
and overwhelming imposition of historical events on the psyche. Faced
with the striking occurrence of what were called the war neuroses in the
wake of World War I, Freud is startled by the emergence of a pathological condition—the repetitive intrusion of nightmares and relivings of
battlefield events—that is experienced like a neurotic pathology and yet
whose symptoms seem to reflect, in startling directness and simplicity,
nothing but the unmediated occurrence of violent events. Freud thus
compares these symptoms to those of another long-problematic phenomenon, the accident neurosis. The reliving of the battle can be compared, he says, to the nightmare of the accident:

> Dreams occurring in traumatic neuroses have the characteristic of repeat-
> edly bringing the patient back into the situation of his accident, a situation
> from which he wakes up in another fright. This astonishes people far too
> little. . . . Anyone who accepts it as something self-evident that dreams
> should put them back at night into the situation that caused them to fall ill
> has misunderstood the nature of dreams.⁴

The returning traumatic dream perplexes Freud because it cannot be
understood in terms of any wish or unconscious meaning, but is, purely
an inexplicably, the literal return of the event against the will of the one
it inhabits. Unlike the symptoms of a normal neurosis, whose painful
manifestations can be understood, ultimately, in terms of the attempted
avoidance of unpleasurable conflict, the painful repetition of the flashback can only be understood as the absolute inability of the mind to
avoid an unpleasurable event that has not been given psychic meaning
in any way.⁵ In trauma, that is, the outside has gone inside without any
mediation. Taking this literal return of the past as a model for repetitive
behavior in general, Freud ultimately argues, in *Beyond the Pleasure Principle,* that it is traumatic repetition, rather than the meaningful distortions

of neurosis, that defines the shape of individual lives. Beginning with the example of the accident neurosis as a means of explaining individual histories, *Beyond the Pleasure Principle* ultimately asks what it would mean for history to be understood as the history of a trauma.

Freud's comparison of the war experience to that of the accident introduces another element as well, however, which adds to the significance of this question. For it is not just any event that creates a traumatic neurosis, Freud indicates, but specifically "severe mechanical concussions, railway disasters and other accidents involving a risk to life" (p. 12). What Freud encounters in the traumatic neurosis is not the reaction to any horrible event but, rather, the peculiar and perplexing experience of survival. If the dreams and flashbacks of the traumatized thus engage Freud's interest it is because they bear witness to a survival that exceeds the very claims and consciousness of the one who endures it. At the heart of Freud's rethinking of history in *Beyond the Pleasure Principle*, I would thus propose, is the urgent and unsettling question: *What does it mean to survive?*

The intricate relation between trauma and survival indeed arises in this text not, as one might expect, because of a seemingly direct and unmediated relation between consciousness and life-threatening events, but rather through the very paradoxical structure of *indirectness* in psychic trauma. Freud begins his discussion of trauma by noting the "bewildering" fact that psychological trauma does not occur in strict correspondence to the body's experience of a life threat—that is, through the wounding of the body; a bodily injury, Freud notes, in fact "works as a rule *against* the development of a neurosis" (p. 12, emphasis added). Indeed, survival for consciousness does not seem to be a matter of known experiences at all. For if the return of the traumatizing event appears in many respects like a waking memory, it can nonetheless only occur in the mode of a symptom or a dream:

> [People] think the fact that the traumatic experience is constantly forcing itself upon the patient even in his sleep is a proof of the strength of that experience: the patient is, as one might say, fixated to his trauma. . . . I am not aware, however, that patients suffering from traumatic neurosis are much occupied in their waking lives with memories of their accident. Perhaps they are more concerned with *not* thinking of it. (p. 13)

If a life threat to the body and the survival of this threat are experienced as the direct infliction and the healing of a wound, trauma is suffered in the psyche precisely, it would seem, because it is *not* directly available to experience.⁶ The problem of survival, in trauma, thus emerges specifically as the question: what does it mean for *consciousness* to survive?

Freud's speculation on the causes of repetition compulsion in relation to the origins of consciousness can indeed by understood as attempting to grasp the paradoxical relation between survival and consciousness. Freud suggests that the development of the mind seems, at first, to be very much like the development of the body: consciousness arises out of the need to protect "the little fragment of substance suspended in the middle of an external world charged with the most powerful energies," which "would be killed by the stimulation emanating from these if it were not provided with a protective shield against stimuli" (p. 27). Unlike the body, however, the barrier of consciousness is a barrier of sensation and knowledge that protects the organism by placing stimulation within an ordered experience of time.⁷ What causes trauma, then, is a shock that appears to work very much like a bodily threat, but is in fact a break in the mind's experience of time:

> We may, I think tentatively venture to regard the common traumatic neurosis as a consequence of an extensive breach being made in the protective shield against stimuli. This would seem to reinstate the old, naive theory of shock . . . [It] regards the essence of the shock as being the direct damage to the molecular structure . . . of the nervous system, whereas what *we* seek to understand are the effects produced on the organ of the mind. . . . And we still attribute importance to the element of fright. It is caused by lack of any preparedness for anxiety. (p. 31)

The breach in the mind—the conscious awareness of the threat to life—is not caused by a pure quantity of stimulus, Freud suggests, but by "fright," the lack of preparedness to take in a stimulus that comes too quickly. It is not simply, that is, the literal threatening of bodily life, but the fact that the threat is recognized as such by the mind *one moment too late.* The shock of the mind's relation to the threat of death is thus not the direct experience of the threat, but precisely the *missing* of this experience, the fact that, not being experienced *in time,* it has not yet been fully known.⁸ And it is this lack of direct experience that, paradoxically, becomes the basis of the repetition of the nightmare: "These dreams are endeavoring to master the stimulus retrospectively, by developing the anxiety whose omission was the cause of the traumatic neurosis" (p. 32). The return of the traumatic experience in the dream is not the signal of the direct experience, but, rather, of the attempt to overcome the fact that it was *not* direct, to attempt to master what was never fully grasped in the first place. Not having truly known the threat of death the past, the survivor is forced, continually, to confront it over and over again. For consciousness then, the act of survival, as the experience of trauma, is the repeated confrontation with the necessity and impossibility of grasping the threat to one's own life. It is because the mind cannot confront the possibility of its death directly that survival becomes for the human being, paradoxically, an endless testimony to the impossibility of living.

From this perspective the survival of trauma is more than the fortunate passage past a violent event, a passage that is accidentally interrupted by reminders of it, but rather the endless *inherent necessity* of repetition, which ultimately may lead to destruction.[9] The examples of repetition compulsion that Freud offers—the patient repeating painful events in analysis, the woman condemned repeatedly to marry men who die, the soldier Tancred in Tasso's poem wounding his beloved again[10]—all seem to point to the necessity by which consciousness, once faced with the possibility of its death, can do nothing but repeat the destructive event over and over again. Indeed, these examples suggest that the shape of individual lives, the history of the traumatized individual, is nothing other than the determined repetition of the event of destruction. In modern trauma theory as well, there is an emphatic tendency to focus on the destructive repetition of the trauma that governs a person's life. As modern neurobiologists point out, the repetition of the traumatic experience in the flashback can itself be retraumatizing; if not life-threatening, it is at least threatening to the chemical structure of the brain and can ultimately lead to deterioration. And this would also seem to be the case with the high suicide rate of survivors, for example survivors of Vietnam or of concentration camps, who commit suicide only *after* they have found themselves completely in safety. As a paradigm for the human experience that governs history, then, traumatic disorder is indeed the apparent struggle to die. The postulation of a drive to death, which Freud ultimately introduces in *Beyond the Pleasure Principle*, would seem only to realize the reality of the destructive force that the violence of history imposes on the human psyche, the formation of history as the endless repetition of previous violence.

If we attend closely, however, to Freud's description of the traumatic nightmare of the accident, we find a somewhat more complex notion of what is missed, and repeated, in the trauma. In the description of the accident dream, indeed, Freud does not simply attribute the traumatic fright to the dream itself, but to what happens upon waking up: "Dreams occurring in traumatic neuroses have the characteristic of repeatedly bringing the patent back into the situation of his accident, a situation *from which he wakes up in another fright."* If "fright" is the term by which Freud defines the traumatic effect of not having been prepared in time, then the trauma of the nightmare does not simply consist in the experience *within* the dream, but in *the experience of waking from it.* It is the experience of *waking into consciousness* that, peculiarly, is identified with the reliving of the trauma. And as such it is not only the dream that surprises consciousness but, indeed, the very *waking itself* that constitutes the surprise: the fact not only of the dream but of having passed beyond it. What is enigmatically suggested, that is, is that the trauma consists not only in having confronted death, but in *having survived precisely, without knowing it.* What one returns to, in the flashback, is not the incomprehensibility of one's near death, but the very incomprehensibility of one's own survival. Repetition, in other words, is not simply the attempt to grasp that one has almost died, but more fundamentally and enigmatically, the very attempt *to claim one's own survival.* If history is to be understood as the history of a trauma, it is a history that is experienced as the endless attempt to assume one's survival as one's own.

It is this incomprehensibility of survival, I would suggest, that is at the heart of Freud's formulation of the death drive. Freud describes the origin of the drive as a response to an awakening not unlike that of the nightmare:

> The attributes of life were at some time awoken [wurden . . . erweckt] in inanimate matter by the action of a force of whose nature we can form no conception. . . . The tension which then arose in what had hitherto been an inanimate substance endeavored to cancel itself out. In this way the first drive came into being; the drive to return to the inanimate state. (p. 38 translation modified)

At the beginning of the drive, Freud suggests, is not the traumatic imposition of death, but rather the traumatic "awakening" to life. Life itself, Freud says, is an awakening out of a "death" for which there was no preparation. The origin of the drive is thus precisely the experience of having passed beyond death without knowing it. And it is in the attempt to master this awakening to life that the drive ultimately defines its historical structure: failing to return to the moment of its own act of living, the drive departs into the future of a human history.

Indeed, it is the historical complexity of the story of departure and return that lies at the heart of Freud's most famous example of repetition compulsion, the game of the child playing "fort" and "da" with his spool.[11] Freud says that he observed the strange game of a child (his grandson) who repeatedly threw a wooden spool on a string into his cot, uttering the sound "o-o-o-o," then retrieved it, uttering "a-a-a-a." Freud interprets these sounds as meaning "fort" ["gone"] and da" ["here"], and suggests that the child is reenacting the departure and return of his mother, which he had just recently been forced to confront.[12] While Freud offers the game as part of his search for evidence of the repetition compulsion, what is most striking is not so much the meaning of the game itself, its exemplification or nonexemplification of repetition compulsion, as the way in which Freud presents the example, that is, his curious wavering, as the example unfolds, on the question of whether the game is a game of departure or of return:

> I eventually realized that it was a game and that the only use he made of any of his toys was to play "gone" with them. . . .
>
> This, then, was the complete game—disappearance and return. As a rule one only witnessed its first act, which was repeated untiringly as a game in itself, though there is not doubt that the greater pleasure was attached to the second act. . . .
>
> It may perhaps be said . . . that [his mother's] departure had to be en-acted as a necessary preliminary to her joyful return, and that it was in the latter that lay the true purpose of the game. But against this must be counted the observed fact that the first act, that of departure, was staged as a game in itself and far more frequently than the episode in its entirety, with its pleasurable ending. (pp. 15–16)

What strikes Freud as he tells the story of the fort-da is that the game of departure and return is ultimately, and inexplicably, a game, simply, of departure.[13] I would suggest that if this game is resonant in *Beyond the Pleasure Principle* it is not only because of how the child's play does or does not provide evidence of repetition compulsion. It is rather because the symbolized pattern of departure and return brings into prominent view a larger conception of historical experience, a conception Freud was grappling with and trying to bring into focus in the writing of *Beyond the Pleasure Principle*.[14] This historical pattern, moreover, will indeed be thought out more explicitly in a later work that is also about the story of a departure and a return, the story of the history of the Jews in *Moses and Monotheism*. In the game of the fort-da, that is, we already see what is implicit in the curious movement from the example of combat-trauma to the death drive, the fact that the theory of trauma, as a historical experience of a survival exceeding the grasp of the one who survives, engages a notion of history exceeding individual bounds. To grasp the rethinking of individual trauma as an experience of departure—of a leaving-behind of the event in *Beyond the Pleasure Principle*—means to have already arrived in the history—the collective, transgenerational, and religious—of *Moses and Monotheism.*

In *Moses and Monotheism* Freud argues that the history of the Jews can be explained through the occurrence of a traumatic event—the murder of Moses—during Moses' return of the Hebrews from Egypt to Canaan. After the murder the Jews repressed it and took on a second leader, also named Moses, who was eventually assimilated to the first Moses who had been murdered.[15] The belated experience of the murder and the return of the repressed Mosaic religion through Jewish tradition, Freud argues, ultimately established Jewish monotheism and determined the subsequent history of the Jews. A brief look at Feud's explanation of the history of the Jews in *Moses and Monotheism* will show how Freud's understanding of history as survival, in *Beyond the Pleasure Principle,* ultimately extends beyond the confines of the individual psyche and delineates the structure of Jewish historical experience.

The history of the Jews in *Moses and Monotheism* indeed resonates in significant ways with the theory of trauma in its attempt to understand the actual experience of the Jews—their historical development—in terms of an experience they cannot fully claim as their own: the passing on of the monotheistic religion. This passing on of monotheism is the experience of a determining force in their history that makes it not fully a history they have *chosen,* but precisely the sense of *being chosen by* God, the sense of chosenness that, Freud says, is what has enabled the Jews "to survive until our day."[16] Jewish monotheism, as the sense of chosenness, thus defines Jewish history around the link between survival and a traumatic history that exceeds their grasp.

The sense of chosenness, Freud argues, was originally taught to the Hebrews by Moses. But it was not truly part of a Jewish monotheistic religion, Freud suggests, until after Moses' death. As a consequence of the repression of the murder of Moses and of the return of the repressed that occurs after the murder, the sense of chosenness returns not as an object of knowledge but as an unconscious force, a force that manifests itself in what Freud calls "tradition." Thus Freud argues that the point of *Moses and Monotheism* is not to explain monotheism as a doctrine, but precisely to explain its peculiar *unconscious force* in shaping Jewish history: "The religion of Moses exercised influence on the Jewish people *only when it had become a tradition.*" (p. 154; pp. 127–28, emphasis added). Arguing that monotheism is truly operative in Jewish history only as a "tradition," Freud suggests that the sense of being chosen is precisely *what cannot be grasped* in the Jewish past, the way in which its past has imposed itself upon it *as* a history that it survives but does not fully understand. Linking this formation of tradition to the traumatic murder of Moses, Freud implicitly argues that the structure of monotheism—the emergence, after the return of the repressed murder of Moses, of the sense of being incomprehensibly chosen by God to survive—is very similar, in certain respects, to the curious nature of the survival of trauma. Monotheism, in shaping Jewish history, turns out to function very much like what is described, in *Beyond the Pleasure Principle*, as the death drive. The question that governs the story of the individual in *Beyond the Pleasure Principle*— *What does it mean to survive?*—thus becomes, in the history of the Jews, the crucial and enigmatic query: *What does it mean to be chosen?*[17] The traumatic structure of monotheism at the heart of this question signifies a history of Jewish survival that is both an endless crisis and the endless possibility of a new future.

The argument that Freud presents is complex, but the basic problem that underlies the meaning of this question can be understood in terms of the nature of what it is, in the traumatic history of the Jews, that remains, precisely, ungrasped and endlessly returning in the passing on of monotheism. On the one hand, Freud seems to suggest that what is central to Jewish history is the complex configuration of love, hatred and loss that occurs during the traumatic murder of the father figure Moses. Using as his model the traumatic experience of the castration threat and its consequences in the development of the child, Freud suggests that the repression of the monotheistic religion following the murder of Moses and the subsequent return of his religion in tradition is like the repression and return of the repressed following the castration threat.[18] When the religion of Moses returns, it comes back in the form of an unconscious identification with the father. Thus we might say, on the basis of the understanding of traumatic repetition that Freud outlines in *Beyond the Pleasure Principle*, that the murder of Moses, suffered as the traumatic separation from the father, ultimately leads to a belated attempt to return to the moment before the murder, to Moses' doctrine of chosenness. This attempt to return always confronts again the act of violence—the moment or cause of separation—in the form of later violence directed against the Jews: specifically, Freud, argues, the Oedipal rivalry that others feel toward the Jews, most notably the rivalry and hatred of the Christians. The separation from the father figure in the murder is thus an endlessly incomprehensible violence that is suffered, repeatedly, both as the attempt to return to the safety of chosenness, and as the traumatic repetition of the violent separation, a return occurring through the violence imposed by the Christians. The history of chosenness, as the history of survival, thus takes the form of an unending confrontation with the returning violence of the past.[19]

But we can understand the emergence and power of the Jewish sense of chosenness in monotheism in another way, an interpretation that is made possible by Freud's use, in the explanation of trauma in this text, not only of the model of Oedipal trauma but of the example, familiar from *Beyond the Pleasure Principle,* of the accident:

> It may happen that someone gets away, apparently unharmed, from the spot where he has suffered a shocking accident, for instance a train collision. In the course of the following weeks, however, he develops a series of grave psychical and motor symptoms, which can be ascribed only to his shock or whatever else happened at the time of the accident. He has developed a "traumatic neurosis." This appears quite incomprehensible and is therefore a novel fact. The time that elapsed between the accident and the first appearance of the symptoms is called the "incubation period." . . . As an afterthought we observe that—in spite of the fundamental difference in the two cases, the problem of the traumatic neurosis and that of Jewish monotheism—there is a correspondence in one point. It is the feature which one might term latency. There are the best grounds for thinking that in the history of the Jewish religion there is a long period, after the breaking away from the Moses religion, during which no trace is to be found of the monotheistic idea . . . until . . . [tradition] . . . succeeded in waking to life the religion which Moses had instituted centuries before. (p. 84; pp. 67–68)

In the occurrence of the accident, Freud seems to compare the traumatic history of the Jews, the breaking away from the Moses religion, to the murder of Moses and his return in the form of Jewish monotheism. But the event of the accident, as Freud describes it here, consists not only, as Freud puts it, in the "shock or whatever happened at the time of the accident," but also, we might argue, in the fact that the person "walks away from it apparently unharmed." The leaving of the accident, that is, is not only the unexperienced event of the crash, but the non-experiencing of the fact that the person has indeed remained "unharmed." I would propose that what returns in monotheism—the monotheistic idea that comes back after the latency of the Jewish people—is not simply the missed event of the violent separation, but the incomprehensible sense, precisely, of having violently separated from Moses *and survived.* If monotheism for Freud is an "awakening," it is not simply a return of the past but of the fact of having survived it, a survival that, in the figure of the new Jewish god, appears not as an act chosen by the Jews, but as the incomprehensible fact of *being chosen for* a future that remains, in its promise, yet to be understood. Chosenness is thus not simply a fact of the past but the experience of being shot into a future that is not entirely one's own. The belated experience of trauma, in Jewish monotheism, suggests that history is not only the passing on of a crisis, but also the passing on of a survival that can only be possessed within a history larger than any single individual or single generation.[19]

Freud's understanding of survival will only be fully grasped, I think, when we come to understand how it is through the peculiar and para-doxical complexity of survival that the theory of individual trauma con-tains within it the core of the trauma of a larger history.[20] One might perhaps, of course, attempt to understand Freud's own theory of trauma in *Beyond the Pleasure Principle* and in *Moses and Monotheism*, and his move-ment from one text to the next, through the many survivals and suffer-ing he was forced to face in World War I, World War II, and in be-tween—the loss of his daughter Sophie, of his grandson, the threat to his son, and finally his forced departure from Vienna.[21] Rather than attempt such a task, however, I will point toward another kind of sur-vival—more like what Freud refers to in *Moses and Monotheism* as the survival of "tradition"—the survival Freud conceived as the very theory, the future tradition, of psychoanalysis. World War I, Freud believed, was less a threat to his life or his family than to psychoanalysis itself. And it is of psychoanalysis as a kind of survival that he writes in 1924 to Ferenczi:

> I have survived the Committee that was to have been my successor. Perhaps I shall survive the International Association. It is to be hoped that psycho-analysis will survive me. But it gives a somber end to one's own life.[22]

Freud suggests that psychoanalysis, if it lives on, will live on not as the straightforward life of a known and understood theory, but as the end-less survival of what has not been fully understood. If psychoanalysis is to be continued in its tradition, it is paradoxically in what has not yet been fully grasped in its survival that its truest relation to its insight must be found. I would suggest that trauma theory is one of the places today where this survival is precisely taking place, not only in the assuredness of its transformation and appropriation by psychiatry, but in the creative uncertainties of this theory that remain, for psychiatry *and* psychoanaly-sis, in the enigma of trauma as both destruction *and* survival, an enigma that lies at the very heart of the Freudian insight itself.

Notes

1. "Post-traumatic stress disorder" is the name given by the American Psy-chiatric Association in the *Diagnostic and Statistical Manual of Mental Disorders* III

(1980) to what had previously been called shell shock, combat neurosis, and traumatic neurosis, among other names given at various times in the nineteenth and twentieth centuries. The definitions in DSM III, III-Revised and IV contain the same basic symptoms that Freud described in his later work on trauma, including what he called the "positive symptoms" (flashbacks and hallucinations) and the "negative symptoms" (numbing, amnesia and avoidance of triggering stimuli).

2. Trauma theory often divides itself into two basic trends: those which focus on trauma as the "shattering" of a previously whole self, and those which also emphasize the survival-function of trauma as allowing one to get through an overwhelming experience by numbing to it. In the former camp see, for example, Jonathen Cohen, "Structural Consequences of Psychic Trauma: A New Look at *Beyond the Pleasure Principle*," *International Journal of Psychoanalysis* 61 (1980), and Abram Kardiner, *War Stress and Neurotic Illness* (New York: Paul B. Heber, 1941, 1947); and the self-psychological approach expressed in the essays in Richard B. Ulman and Doris Brothers, *The Shattered Self: A Psychoanalytic Study of Trauma*; in the latter see Robert Jay Lifton, "Survivor Experience and Traumatic Syndrome," in *The Broken Connection: On Death and the Continuity of Life* (New York: Basic Books, 1979), and Charles Marmar, "The Dynamic Psychotherapy of PTSD," lecture at "Psychological Trauma in Times of War and Peace: Intervention and Treatment," Boston, June 7–8, 1991.

3. Many writers have pointed to the relation between these texts and the events of the wars. The conclusions concerning this relation tend to differ; for the most part, Freud's wartime writing is seen as showing an inevitable tendency towards destruction that is linked directly to what Freud saw around him in Europe. The fact that *Beyond the Pleasure Principle* and *Moses and Monotheism* are simultaneously seen as fantastical or mythical accounts of history is significant; in order to understand either text as simply and directly referential, one must ignore its mythical side, or put differently, the referential theory finds itself inscribed in what appears to be a mythical or figurative theory.

4. All quotations from *Beyond the Pleasure Principle* refer to *The Standard Edition of the Complete Psychological Works of Sigmund Freud*, Volume 18. This reference is to page 13.

5. The full impact of this notion of trauma can be understood when we look at it in terms of the inside/outside model of the psyche implied in the theory of the pleasure principle, which implicitly suggests that what is inside the psyche is a mediation of the outside through desire, repression, and so on. In trauma, there is an incomprehensible outside of the self already gone inside without the self's mediation, hence without any relation to the self—and this consequently becomes a threat to any understanding of what a self might be in this context.

6. The relation between intrusion and amnesia reemerges in the recent work on trauma in both psychiatric and neurobiological contexts; see Mark S. Greenberg and Bessel A. van der Kolk, "Retrieval and Integration of Traumatic Memories with the 'Painting Cure,' " in Bessel A. van der Kolk, *Psychological*

Trauma (Washington: American Psychiatric Press, 1987), and John Krystal, "Animal Models for Posttraumatic Stress Disorder," in Earl L. Giller, Jr., ed., *Biological Assessment and Treatment of Post-traumatic Stress Disorder* (Washington: American Psychiatric Press, 1990).

7. Freud actually offers two models that are not clearly differentiated: a model of quantity (the stimulus barrier protects the organism from "too much stimulus" coming from the outside) and a model of time as well, in the following paragraph. When he goes on to define trauma in terms of fright, or lack of preparedness for anxiety, the emphasis lies on time rather than quantity, which ultimately, it could then be argued, marks the difference between the nature of bodily and mental barriers.

8. Freud's temporal definition of trauma in *Beyond the Pleasure Principle* seems to be an extension of his early understanding of the trauma as not being locatable in one moment alone but in the relation between two moments. What the two models share is the description of the traumatic experience in terms of its temporal unlocatability. The original and striking reading of this two-scene model is to be found in Jean Laplanche, *Life and Death in Psychoanalysis*, translated by Jeffrey Mehlman (Baltimore: Johns Hopkins University Press, 1976).

9. The repetitive dimension of trauma is only possible to explain when one takes its constitutively temporal aspect into account.

10. See the introduction to Cathy Caruth, *Unclaimed Experience: Trauma, Narrative and History* (Baltimore: Johns Hopkins University Press, 1996).

11. Sam Weber indeed interprets the passage on the origin of the drive as a "fort." See his *The Legend of Freud* (Minneapolis: University of Minnesota Press, 1982), 139. It is important to note here that the originary status of the drive in a departure can be understood not simply as a universalizing move (all drives originating in trauma) but as a way of indicating once again the unlocatability of any particular traumatic experience: it could always have been merely a repetition of an earlier one.

12. To be precise, Freud says that the child uttered the sounds "o-o-o-o," which he interpreted as "fort," and the word "da"—he eliminates in his presentation the sounds "a-a-a-a" and immediately assumes their interpretation. Clearly the movement from sound (or letter, in the text) to word to meaning would bear some analysis, and has received some in the literature on this passage. See for example Jacques Derrida, "Spéculer—sur 'Freud'," in *La carte postale: de Socrate à Freud et au delà* (Paris: Flammarion, 1980).

13. It is interesting to note in this context that the very introduction of the fort-da example is framed as an apparent "departure" from the theme of the traumatic neurosis ("Ich mache nun den Vorschlag, das dunkle and dustere Thema der traumatischen Neurose zu verlassen"). The game of course is nonetheless determined as a kind of traumatic play at the end of the next chapter (Chapter Three). For the resonances of *verlassen* (leaving, departing) in Freud's writing on trauma, see *Unclaimed Experience*, ch. 1.

14. The vertiginously self-reflexive qualities of the example of the fort-da have

received much attention from literary critics. See in particular *La carte postale* and *The Legend of Freud.*

15. It is not clear in Freud's text whether the second Moses is named that because of his assimilation to the first, or whether there was coincidentally a second leader named Moses who became assimilated to the first, which would suggest an element of accident in the process of assimilation.

16. Quotations from *Moses and Monotheism* are taken from Sigmund Freud, *Moses and Monotheism,* translated by Katherine Jones (New York: Vintage Books, 1939). Page numbers in the text refer first to this edition, then to the corresponding passages in the *Standard Edition,* Volume 23. Other passages emphasizing the history of the Jews as a history of survival can be found on pp. 23, 116, and 176.

17. The nature of chosenness thus resonates with the sense of being possessed by one's past that is part of traumatic experience.

18. Throughout his work, Freud suggests two models of trauma that are often placed side by side: the model of castration trauma, which is associated with the theory of repression and the return of the repressed, as well as with a system of unconscious symbolic meanings (the basis of the dream theory in its usual interpretation), and the model of traumatic neurosis (or, let's say, accident trauma), which is associated with accident victims and war veterans (and, as some would argue, with the earlier work on hysteria—see Judith Herman, *Trauma and Recovery* [New York: Basic Books, 1992], and which emerges within psychoanalytic theory, as within human experience, as an interruption of the symbolic system and is not linked to repression, unconsciousness and symbolization but rather to a temporal delay, repetition and literal return. Freud generally placed his examples of the two kinds of trauma side by side (for example in *Beyond the Pleasure Principle* in Chapters Two and Three, and in *Moses and Monotheism*), and admitted, in the *Introductory Lectures on Psychoanalysis* of 1916, that he was not sure how to integrate the two. Jacques Lacan, in *The Four Fundamental Concepts of Psychoanalysis* (Seminar XI), could be seen as attempting to reread the received understanding of repression theory through trauma theory, as do Jonathan Cohen and Warren Kinston in "Repression Theory: A New Look at the Cornerstone," *International Journal of Psychoanalysis* 65 (1984).

19. This understanding of trauma thus corresponds to the deterministic model of the repetition of violence that constituted the first interpretation of the traumatic nightmare above.

20. That is, by being described in terms of a possession by the past that is not entirely one's own, trauma already describes the individual experience as something that exceeds itself, that brings within individual experience as precisely its most intense sense of isolation the very breaking of individual knowledge and mastery of events. It also acknowledges that it is quite possible that the witnessing of the trauma may not be able to occur within the individual at all, that it may only be in future generations that "cure" or at least witnessing can take place. On the intergenerational structure of trauma see Martin S. Berg-

mann and Milton E. Jucovy, eds., *Generations of the Holocaust* 9, (New York: Columbia University Press, 1982), and Nadine Fresco, "Remembering the Unknown," *The International Review of Psychoanalysis* 11 (1984).

21. The point is not to see group trauma or historical trauma (or intergenerational trauma) on the analogy with individual trauma (which is what Freud explicitly claims to be doing), but to understand how historical or intergenerational trauma is in some sense presupposed in the theory of individual trauma, which is what I believe is happening implicitly in Freud's texts.

22. See *Unclaimed Experience*, ch. 1. This is, of course, not to suggest a simple reduction of the psyche to biographical experience but to show how experience and text are linked, in trauma, around what is not known or not fully experienced. Regarding the writing of *Beyond the Pleasure Principle*, as many have noted, Sophie did not die until shortly before Freud had finished writing his text. However, the role of survival as the survival of one's child seems to permeate the text in a more complicated manner than a simple reference or lack of reference to Freud's life; on this matter see Derrida, *La carte postale*. On the events surrounding the writing of *Beyond the Pleasure Principle* and *Moses and Monotheism* see Peter Gay, *Freud: A Life for Our Time* (New York: Doubleday, 1989).

4

The Contextual Self

Paul L. Wachtel

The "self" is a rather modern concept, though of course the experience of selfhood—in some manner or other—is virtually coterminous with the evolution of our self-reflective species. It is perhaps the qualifying phrase—*in some manner or other*—that is uniquely modern. That is, ours is perhaps the first era in which we have become aware not only of selfhood but of selfhood as a fact, as an object of study. Our era represents a departure as well in our appreciation of the quite significant ways in which the experience of selfhood has *varied* from era to era. Histories of the self and efforts to situate varying self experiences in varying historical circumstances are a uniquely modern enterprise.

Although the numerous writers in recent years who have directed their attention to the historical evolution of the experience of selfhood have each given a somewhat different spin to the story, a common thread is not difficult to discern. Most have noted in one way or another the emergence of an increasingly individualistic experience of self, beginning at the time of the Renaissance and accelerating with the development of capitalism and industrialism. From selfhood as rooted in place, family, community, and tradition—a self marked by continuity, connectedness and embeddedness—there has emerged an experience of self that is highly individual and individuated. In some ways this has been a salutary experience, yielding a degree of awareness, differentation, and articulation of experience that enriches life. But in other ways this same tendency has been responsible for a sense of isolation, loss of moorings and meanings, and a host of destructive movements that can be understood as desperate efforts to replace what was lost. In recent years there has been a tendency for theorists of the self to highlight a further transformation within the vector of the modern individualized self. Philip Cushman has described this as a shift from a conception of

45

the individualized self as bounded, masterful, and subjective to conceptions, emphasizing instead the self as empty and fragmented.[1]

Within this line of psychohistorical inquiry, Robert Lifton's contribution has been distinctively affirmative. Lifton too notes the ways in which the singular coherent self, grounded in stable community and enduring assumptions, has become increasingly rare. But rather than simply lamenting this change, and portraying a one-dimensional vector of decline, he introduces the idea of the protean self, a new self structure and self process that he sees as an adaptive response to the circumstances of the contemporary world. Proteanism, marked by fluidity and many-sidedness, he suggests, is "appropriate to the restlessness and flux of our time." Although the roots of the protean self lie in "confusion [and] the widespread feeling that we are losing our psychological moorings," the new structure of self has turned out to be "surprisingly resilient" and the new form of self experience and self structure he describes is "a self of many possibilities, one that has risks and pitfalls, but at the same time holds out considerable promise for the human future."

Lifton's conception is clearly a more optimistic one than that offered by many other critics. But it is not an optimism based on screening out the dark side of human experience. A man who has studied the holocaust, nuclear terror, thought reform, and virtually every other major evil of our century does not come to his optimism easily or blithely. Rather, Lifton shares with his mentor Erik Erikson what one might call a *grounded* optimism, rooted not in denial or sentimentality but in attention to the ongoing struggle human beings engage in to find meaning and order amidst the chaos of their lives.

What enabled both Erikson and Lifton to develop views that were at once hard-headedly realistic and cautiously optimistic was an attention to the ways in which identity or the sense of self evolve throughout the life span *in relation to the world around us.* I wish here similarly to emphasize the relational and contextual nature of selfhood and to highlight as well the ways in which some of the most influential conceptions of selfhood have been hampered by being largely *a*contextual, by portraying the self in terms that are excessively "internal" and hermetic.

Psychoanalysis and the "Archaic"

The place I wish to begin in seeking to understand this acontextual bias and its implications is with Freud. Although there were certainly other important sources of this tendency in our intellectual life—I shall consider below ways in which the very foundations of our social system pull for highly individualistic, context-erasing conceptions of human experience and action—Freud's vision for so long dominated intellectual discourse on matters psychological that even as alternative views have emerged both within and outside of psychoanalysis, they have incorporated more of Freud's grounding assumptions than we tend to realize.

Interestingly, the first route toward the compellingly acontextual formulations Freud bequeathed us lay in observations that, at first glance, seemed to highlight rather than disregard the impact of actual life events. Freud's earliest theories of hysteria and other "defense neuropsychoses," as he then called what he would later call psychoneuroses, were in one sense anything but acontextual. Hysterics and obsessional neurotics, Freud suggested, were victims of real circumstances encountered in childhood. As he elaborated the consequences of those circumstances, however, he laid down the groundwork for a theory which would become increasingly acontextual. The simple rediscovery of the real interpersonal and social world would be a decades-long struggle, and even when the struggle was concluded, the formulations that preceded it would cast a shadow from the past over many of the conceptualizations that might seem at first glance to have transcended them.

In attempting to understand the consequences of the early traumas he thought his patients had undergone, as well as why only some of them became ill, Freud attributed a central causal role to the process of repression. The dimension of this process that entails rendering thoughts or memories unconscious is, of course, widely known and understood. But another aspect of Freud's formulation, perhaps even more weighty with consequence, is much less frequently noted and appreciated: When Freud was able, through the method he had developed, to recover the memories of these repressed events, the recollections were characterized by what he called a remarkable freshness. Unlike ordinary memories, that seem to undergo a kind of wearing away over time, these memories remained as vivid, as laden with feeling, as "fresh" as the day they were laid down. Thus they lay in the psyche not as a moldering anomaly but as a ticking bomb, ever ready to explode and ever requiring effort to prevent their ripping the psyche apart.

When, for a variety of reasons, Freud later decided he had erred in assuming that the traumatic events had really happened, and concluded that in fact his patients' "memories" were actually the residues of wish-fulfilling fantasies, the theoretical structure already laid down was largely preserved. Instead of actual memories preserved in their original form, Freud now posited that *wishes* and *fantasies* were thus preserved.

Relegated to a dark corner of the psyche, these repressed wishes could not partake in the growth and maturity that characterized those portions of our mental life of which we are more aware (and which benefit from their access to and modifiability by new input and new experience). Rather they remained "infantile," "primitive," "archaic."

The image that this model of the psyche has suggested to me is that of the woolly mammoths that are occasionally discovered buried beneath the Arctic ice. Like the archaic, paleolithic impulses postulated by psychoanalysis, these archaic beasts have been preserved in their original form—hair, flesh, and all—by the ice that, like the barrier of repression, cuts them off from the influences of the outer world that would otherwise cause their wearing away. Thus, like the memories Freud first thought he had discovered, they are as "fresh" as the day they were buried, indeed even edible for anyone with a taste for the primitive.

Contemporary psychoanalytic formulations often look rather different from the depictions of instinctual drives and defenses against them that dominated psychoanalysis for so many years. Instead of emphasizing forces and energies and peremptory strivings after bodily pleasure, the newer formulations tend to focus on primitive internalized images of self or other and on powerful fantasized images of desired or feared relationships and attachments. But in their deepest core, they retain the crucial features of the "woolly mammoth" model: depictions of parts of our psychic life cut off from maturation and modulation and from influence by the outer world, "primitive" or "archaic" parts of the psyche that disrupt our lives and, while impervious to revision by what transpires in our daily experience, cast a fateful shadow over those experiences—for one way in which all of these hypothesized mental processes differ from the buried mammoths is that they do not lie still and lifeless but rather trumpet loudly in the psyche, casuing a ruckus that would do a fully live mammoth proud.

Put differently, all of these theories postulate that something that remains primitive in the psyche persists in spite of what is going on around us. Because these "early" fantasies, images, objects, or what have you have been split off from the evolving ego, the part of the psyche that is in touch with perceptual reality and responsive to its ever-changing indications, they do not change as circumstances change nor do they learn from experience. In that sense, they are divorced from the context, have little or nothing to do with the person's life as it is actually being lived—except to disrupt it from their invulnerable bunker, firing potshots at reality but impervious to its influence.

Theorizing of this sort has been highly influential not only among practitioners of psychotherapy but among literary theorists and writers attempting to explore the links between the world of subjective experience and the world of economic and political forces. The appeal of such theories is not hard to understand; they seem to offer an unusual "depth," to point us to the very roots of human experience and to subtleties and hidden connections to which more commonsense psychologies are blind. But in fact, notwithstanding their appeal to intellectuals from Frankfurt to Big Sur, such theories have severe limitations for the work of illuminating the impact of our social and economic arrangments on our experience of the world (and thus for understanding the insidious processes whereby the system permeates the psyche and renders alternatives to itself virtually invisible). Through its lens, only those parts of the real world that directly affect how parents treat their children in the first years of life seem to have much chance of getting "in."

But there is another way of understanding these seemingly "primitive" or "infantile" psychological manifestations that pays full attention to both their subtleties and their power yet has vastly different implications. Closer inspection suggests that these apparently archaic and anomalous manifestations persist not in spite of, but precisely because of, the way the person is living his or her life. Although seemingly unrealistic and out of touch with reality, they are in fact rather closely linked to the conditions and experiences of everyday life.

Consider, for example, that almost quintessential character type of contemporary urban life, the so-called narcissistic personality.[2] Individuals who exhibit this character structure may frequently manifest overweening grandiosity, but it is readily apparent to the astute observer that this grandiosity is an attempt to conceal deep-seated feelings of inadequacy and insigificance or to counter a disturbing sense of fragmentation and insubstantiality. However arrogant and irritatingly self-important such individuals may sometimes be, they usually suffer substantially even as they make life uncomfortable for others. Psychoanalytic accounts of this character structure usually stress the impact of events in the very earliest years of life in generating it, and the dynamics described entail descriptions of "inner" struggles and of deficient structures resulting from developmental deficits remaining from years past. Little is usually said about how the person lives now, except as a *reflection* of this inner deficit, as a symptomatic expression of a state of affairs that was set long ago and that will yield to no corrective experiences in the present save for the possibility that analysis might eventually provide what mother did not.

Such an account, from a point of view that is labeled as psychody-

namic, is curiously static. There is little description of the ceaseless interplay between the individual and his environment, between his sufferings
and attempts to relieve them and his interactions with the other people
who inhabit his daily life.[3] From the vantage point of the most influential
contemporary theories of narcissistic difficulties, the problem may have
arisen from the interaction with others—especially with his mother—but
it has long ceased to be really about human interaction at all; it is "inside" him, a character trait *of* him.

If one brackets the overly internal assumptions of the woolly mammoth model, however, and pays close attention to the actual details of
living of such a person—both by observing, as a therapist, how he inter-
acts in the sessions and by carefully listening and inquiring into the details of his interactions with others—one sees a quite different picture.
Through this latter lens the problem looks no less severe and in certain
respects no less difficult to resolve. It appears, in certain ways, no less
difficult to resolve, no less "deep-seated." But it is revealed as much
more dynamic and context-related. What one sees is that daily life for
such a person is replete with repetitions of a vicious circle that may have
originated in the past but is *perpetuated* by what happens day after day. The
feelings of inner doubt, hollowness, and fraudulence that lie behind the
grandiosity end up, ironically, generating behaviors that have precisely
the effect of fueling the doubts and vulnerabilities still further. For each
time the person attempts to cover over the painful feeling by puffing up
and showing off, he grounds his contacts with others on a false picture
of himself. And whether he puts people off by his apparent arrogance
and disdain—thereby heightening his sense that the world does not
really regard him very favorably—or, rather, "succeeds" in impressing
people, but in a way that at some level he knows is not rooted in who he
really is, his sense of fraudulence or vulnerability is rekindled. And
when, in turn, he attempts to deal with this new resurgence of the distressing feeling of baselessness via still more of the same defensive behavior, the stage is set for still another step in the painful circle.

The character traits that seem to be so deeply ingrained, we thus may
see, are not the simple result of some "inner" property deposited years
before, but rather a product of a dynamic—and continuing—
interaction with the world around him. Their origins may indeed lie in
quite early experiences, but we do not understand these characteristics
very well if we do not see how they are continuously reproduced by the
very way of life they serve to perpetuate. Moreover, we do not understand them well if we do not see the crucial role of *other* people's participation in the pattern. The complexities of that participation are beyond

the scope of this brief chapter, but it should be clear that sycophantic admiration, competitive challenging, and a tendency for others to exaggerate their talents and accomplishments in response to the "narcissist's" own lily gilding all are responses that such an individual is more likely to encounter than most of us and that, in direct or indirect fashion, are likely to contribute to maintaining his difficulties. Indeed, so important is the reciprocal participation of others as one looks closely into this or other patterns of difficulty, that I have come to the conclusion that "every neurosis requires accomplices" and have come to believe that efforts to help people change through psychotherapy are enormously enhanced by identifying the accomplices in people's lives and the nature of their participation.

Notice that this is not a simple "environmental" or "behavioristic" account. It is not a matter of the individual simply responding to a stimulus or being shaped by his or her environment. Understanding the pattern requires understanding the complex inner dynamics and conflicts, the ways in which we ward off uncomfortable feelings and in doing so may successfully enough banish them that, although they continue to dominate our lives, they are but rarely a part of our conscious experience. Moreover, adequate understanding requires appreciation of the ways in which the environment that we encounter is not simply something that happens to us but is, equally, a product of our own behavior and our own previous choices.

Nonetheless, it should be apparent that the picture I am describing here is one in which context is crucial. In contrast to theories characterized by the "woolly mammoth" model, this perspective emphasizes how even the seemingly most "primitive" or "inner" characteristic is not just something that emerges from the depths but a product of our continuing interaction with the world. The implications for therapeutic practice of this recontextualizing of the depth inquiries of psychoanalysis are profound, but the significance of the shift is not limited to the consulting room. In applying psychoanalytic insights to the larger social and political arena, the implications of moving from the "woolly mammoth" model to a more contextual one are equally notable.[4]

The Contextual Self and the Larger Social Order

In their neglect of context in understanding human behavior, the theories I have been discussing parallel a key feature of the social order in which they developed and in which they have further evolved. Central to both the moral and the analytical foundations of capitalist societies is a view that systematically excludes the context within which individual decisions are made. The influence of the larger social context is obscured in a number of ways. First, in addressing the moral implications of our social organization and the distributions of wealth and status it yields, everything is reduced to the decisions of two parties, buyer and seller. According to the just-so story that undergirds our system, it is a system in which every economic event is an improvement. Buyer and seller decide to trade because the buyer is better off with the product than the money and the seller is better off with the money than the product. Each gains, and no one loses. Moreover, it is not only a *gain* for each, it is the very best they could possibly achieve, for if either could do better, he would promptly do so. Such is the beauty of the "free market"

Since over and over all we do is trade what we have for something we prefer still more, it would seem through this lens that life in such a system must keep getting better and better. If we turn away from buying and selling to human experience, however—something economists practically forbid themselves to do—it is plain, both from formal surveys of the sense of well being and from simply observing oneself, one's neighbors, or the evening news, that this is scarcely the case.

The source of the fallacy becomes evident as one looks more closely at how the assumptions of market advocates compare to the real world. Robert Frank, one of the relatively few prominent economists who has been able to look reflectively at the model that guides his profession, notes that "In setting up formal models of economic behavior, economists almost always assume at the outset that a person's sense of well-being, or utility, depends on the absolute quantities of various goods he consumes, not on how those quantities compare with the amounts consumed by others." Frank adds, however, that in the real world, in contrast to the models of economists, "abundant evidence suggests that people do in fact care much more about how their incomes compare with those of their peers than about how large their incomes are in any absolute sense." He notes with pleasure Mencken's definition of wealth as "any income that is at least one hundred dollars more a year than the income of one's wife's sister's husband."

Frank has also argued insightfully and persuasively that economists operate under a highly misleading picture of what people really want because they do not take into account the way in which the very operations of the market, which exclude *collective* decisions, force people into choices that resemble the Prisoner's Dilemma. The model of "choice" that is hawked by economists and other defenders of the market system is—to return more overtly to the central theme of this essay—a radically acontextual one. In truth, my purchases are *not* just a matter of a decision between me and the seller. The purchases and economic decisions each of us make profoundly influence many other people in many other ways, from parents feeling helpless to deny their kids overpriced sneakers they really can't afford because "all the other kids at school are wearing them," to the effects of my purchase of an automobile on your lungs.

Now in principle, economists take such matters into account; the concept of "externalities" is designed to acknowledge the impact of a particular exchange on those who were not parties to it. But the existence of externalities is most often acknowledged in the abstract and ignored in the daily operations of the market economy. Moreover, as I have discussed elsewhere,[5] even if externalities were to be attended to with much greater rigor and diligence, the economists' conception does not even come close to addressing the degree to which our lives are interdependent and our choices both constrained and intertwined.

Another component of the justifying mythology that rationalizes our inequalities and our despoliation of the environment is the idea that our choices are not only separate and independent but also witting. The economist's model, as Nobel economics laureate Herbert Simon has put it with wry skepticism, assumes that every person has

> a complete and consistent system of preferences that allows him always to choose among the alternatives open to him; he is always completely aware of what his alternatives are; there are no limits on the complexity of the computations he can perform in order to determine which alternatives are best.[6]

In a similar vein, Israeli economist Shlomo Maital notes that the "economic man" of mainstream economic theory is a virtually flawless paragon of rationality who "[matches] subjective value and objective price right at the precipice of his budget line, along which he or she skates with Olympian precision."[7]

To such a view, psychoanalysis is clearly a challenge. Psychoanalytic theories—of *all* sorts, including the alternative version I implicitly sketched above—especially highlight the ways in which we *deceive* ourselves about our wants (as well as the *conflict* between wants that can make what we *seem* to want the enemy of what we want and feel more deeply). To extricate ourselves from the prevailing idolatry of market worship and the myriad social and ecological problems such idolatry yields, it is essential to be clear how far from the truth is the claim that ours is a system in which what people end up with is what they want. For the economist, using the methodology of so-called "revealed preferences," the answer to what we want is astoundingly simple—look at our Mastercard statements. If with our purchases we have also bought a hole in the ozone layer or toxins in our soil and water, well, that package of goods and damages must be what we witting, rational, utility-maximizing consumers wanted; in a clearheaded way, we have decided to trade off precisely the amount of environmental degradation we have borne for the precisely anticipated pleasure provided by the goods we have chosen. Thus, virtually by definition, any other "tradeoff" would leave us worse off. Clearly, a psychoanalytic perspective addresses such matters rather differently, and it provides an invaluable foundation for questioning whether in fact the "preferences" we reveal in our daily forays into the marketplace should be taken as the last word about what will maximize our well being.

But if psychoanalysis helps to uncloak some of the justifying myths of the religion of the market—those that portray us as knowing exactly what we want, as making witting choices based on a lucid understanding of our needs and of what brings us satisfaction—it partly parallels and reinforces the prevailing mythology in another respect: The efforts by John Kenneth Galbraith and others to point out how our "wants" and "needs" do not just issue spontaneously from the deepest wellsprings of our being, but rather are products of ceaseless messages and manipulations—messages and manipulations, indeed, that may lure us further and further *away* from our true selves—have met with extraordinary resistance from an economics and political community committed to a respect for the choices exercised by consumers that does not seem matched by a respect for any other values. We thus still urgently need an effective and comprehensive critique of consumer desires. Psychoanalysis, as the science of desire par excellence, seems a natural foundation for such a critique. But the widespread emphasis in psychoanalytic thought on desire as welling up from within, and on a true self hidden beneath—and largely impervious to—the world of daily life, interferes with this potential. For although in principle such a view of true and false selves could lend itself to explicating how our overt choices often do *not* reflect our deepest natures, its cutting edge is dulled by a failure to be clear about how our desires and our very image of self are shaped by continuing interactions in the world around us. Desire is not a one-way street running from "inside" to "out." It is a product of our continuing transactions with the social world.

Virtually the only depth conceived of in the flat, psychologically opaque model of the economist is the mysterious space from which our desires magically arise. Those desires, economists insist, must never be questioned, never be related to the ceaseless stimulation and manipulation of daily life in a culture in which the failure to have more each year than the year before is the only human tragedy acknowledged. To this relentlessly, and even cruelly, superficial view of human life—a point of view that, while celebrating individual choice, has an extraordinarily impoverished understanding of the individuals who are doing the choosing—psychoanalysis potentially offers an alternative. But in order to achieve that potential, psychoanalysis will have to move beyond its proclivity toward hermetic interiorization to illuminate the connections between the experiences of daily life and the fears and desires of the people living it. Depth, it turns out, is not a matter of how far "inside" we look, but rather of how profoundly we understand that inside and outside are one.

Notes

1. Although important and valuable, it must also be acknowledged that much of this description contains more than a touch of hyperbole. Surely the experience of self in the Middle Ages was never as lacking in the sense of individual identity as many of the descriptions imply. The fact that *individuals* are born, die, and feel pain ultimately alone—that however much the community may have participated in these experiences in different ways from today, they are ultimately experiences that individuals bear separately and that cannot be fully shared—must have enabled a quite considerable appreciation of separate selfhood even in the most thoroughly embedded community. Similarly, however much we may experience isolation and separateness today, not only are we more interdependent than we tend to acknowledge, but we are as well more connected than *the critics* acknowledge; that is, the tension between the poles of embeddedness and isolation, a tension that is the very heritage of a self-conscious species, cannot be abrogated. The relative strengths of these two poles can differ—and, I agree, *has* differed—from era to era and society to society in important ways; but the tension always remains, and must always in some way be reflected in people's experience.

2. I say so-called both because, like so many of the terms in fashion in contemporary psychoanalytic discourse, it is an insult masquerading as a helpful diagnostic term and because, appearances notwithstanding, self-love is the very last thing that characterizes such individuals.

3. In this discussion of the "narcissistic personality," I will use the male pronoun because it is a pattern that, although it can entrap both men and women,

is discussed much more often in its male version and represents to some degree an exaggeration of the male role and style as it is conceived of in our society.

4. For a more detailed discussion of those implications, and of the theoretical perspective implicit in the foregoing discussion—a perspective I have called "cyclical psychodynamics" because of its emphasis on the role of cyclical interactions between the "internal" and the "external" world—see, for example, Paul Wachtel, *The Poverty of Affluence: A Psychological Portrait of the American Way of Life* (Philadelphia: New Society Publishers, 1989) and *Therapeutic Communication* (New York: Guilford Press, 1993).

5. Paul L. Wachtel, "Overconsumption: Lessons from Psychology for Politics and Economics. In D. Bell, L. Fawcett, R. Keil, and P. Penz, eds., *Political Ecology: Global and Local Perspectives* (Montreal: McGill-Queens-University Press, in press).

6. Herbert A. Simon, *Models of Man* (New York: John Wiley & Sons, 1957), xxiii.

7. Shlomo Maital, *Minds, Markets, and Money* (New York: Basic Books, 1982), 147.

Part II
Broken Connections

5

Some Reflections on Twentieth-Century Violence and the Soft Apocalypse

Todd Gitlin

1

During the last bitter days of 1969, it seemed the most natural thing in the world to read Robert Jay Lifton's *Death in Life.* Nine years into New Left politics, I felt stale, trapped. Political passions seemed futile, a weight on the heart. In my corner of the political universe, what was the reward? Like virtually everyone I knew in the no-longer-New Left, I felt, I *was* overwhelmed by the unstoppable Vietnam War. Four years of protest seemed unavailing. I say *seemed* because the movement was, in fact, a pressure against still more barbaric military escalations than the ones taking place, but this sort of accomplishment was almost undetectable. Everything conspired against the knowledge that we were in fact having an effect, and I was not much for faith. For all the movement's bravado, Nixon was in command, and with him, awesome state violence. Unlike virtually everyone I knew, I saw no way out—not the drug way, not the revolutionary way, not the religious or therapeutic way. The movement itself was self-carnivorous, fatuous, gripped by reckless revolutionary fantasies, thrashing about in search of someone to blame for its miseries, ripping itself apart. Isolated, dead-ended, burdened by the political intellectual's characteristic fantasy that knowledge is supposed to be power, I was trying to think my way out of the impasse, but the better I understood how this once-promising movement had harbored even in its fresh days the go-it-alone arrogance which prepared the later self-immolation, the more hopeless the situation looked. In this dispirited state, I spent hours reading Robert Lifton's description of the unending horrors visited upon the survivors of the atomic bomb attacks in Japan.

The capital-B Bomb, that product of human ingenuity in the pursuit of hubris—the Bomb was where I had come in. It was against the Bomb that, as a sophomore at Harvard, I had been drawn into political activity in 1960. I was a mathematics major. While a senior at the Bronx High School of Science, a year earlier, I had been courted by the Office of Naval Research, so I needed no fancy theory to tell me that the chief sponsors of mathematics in America were the institutions which harnessed research to the purposes of war. So much for the freedom of pure mathematics against all taint of the practical, a freedom that sang in my blood when I read praise for otherworldly abstraction in the loving memoirs of mathematicians like the Englishman G. H. Hardy! So much for the pleasures of doing mathematics, the promise of moments spent happily at play in the sphere of Platonic Forms! I read obsessively, awed and repelled, about the atomic scientists, who had converted their knowledge into power, their power into sin, and in the case of the most conscience-stricken, their sin, eventually, into protest. Foremost among the intellectuals I admired was David Riesman, one of the faculty advisers of our anti-bomb group Tocsin, and through Riesman I had met others in his little circle of countercyclical intellectuals, including Robert Lifton.

Death in Life has been, ever since, linked in my mind with the rock concert at Altamont in December of 1969. I was living in San Francisco, at the end of continental America, where everyone I knew seemed at the end of one or another sort of tether. Altamont had been promoted as the West Coast's echo of the Woodstock jubilee. It turned out to be an ending to all kinds of illusions about the new society supposedly aborning. Altamont had been organized around the Rolling Stones, and there were a lot of technical snafus, and a last-minute change of site— did anyone realize how close the eventual site turned out to be to the nuclear research laboratory at Livermore?—and the moronic decision to let the Hell's Angels serve, or reign, as security guards. But a lot more than logistics was wrong with Altamont. The vibes, as we said, were awful. Far from a resurrection of the beloved community, the scene felt more like some kind of slow crucifixion. It was a bright, warm day, but without much cheer. Surliness was in the air. Some people were getting stomped for getting in other people's line of sight. Wandering around, I ran into an old movement friend, stoned on LSD, who said he was convinced that everyone was dead. In the sense of the spirit, he was absolutely right. My girlfriend and I left early, without waiting for the Rolling Stones to come on, hitched a ride back to our car, drove back to San Francisco. I felt dulled, depleted.

I sat that night in an old beat-up armchair and read in *Death in Life*, about bodily pain, psychic numbing, survivor guilt in Japan. How much misery was a reader expected to bear, and toward what end? If contemporary societies had inflicted the high technology of inferno upon the world, was it not incumbent upon sane people to know everything they could bear to know? What the victims had to bear, others could surely bear to know about. But there were realities the mind could not hold—not my mind, at any rate. The more I read, the bleaker and less alive I felt. "We have talked our extinction to death," Robert Lowell had written, and that was in 1961, hundreds of bull sessions and demonstrations earlier. How many more dues was a person obliged to pay for the dubious privilege of living in the twentieth century? Death in life, indeed. How absurd, or worse, to liken oneself to the victims of absolutely unmetaphorical burn and radiation. I am not recommending it, only reporting that, as best I can remember, these were the sort of thoughts that flooded me.

When I heard the radio report later that night about the young Altamont concert-goer who had pulled a gun, waved it in Mick Jagger's direction, and been stabbed to death by a Hell's Angel, I wasn't surprised in the least. There are times when a single murder plays like a social murder. The spiritual nihilism of the scene in the winter-browned hills had been headed in the direction of murder all day. Perhaps what was surprising was that nobody else had been murdered, given how little attachment anyone had felt toward anyone else. This was not a community, it was an aggregation of strangers who composed, for a day, a city of anomie. How perfect, in fact, that the festival of pleasure should culminate in idiotic death! A giant rock concert for hundreds of thousands of dazed spectators was yet another spectacle for the consumer society. The so-called counterculture had sentimentalized itself, from the start, as the camp of the saved, the refutation of violence. America was a bummer for which the only remedy was secession. Tune in, turn on, drop out, etc. But you did not get peace by declaring that peace had come. You got distraction, America's chief activity. If the war was the embodiment of instrumental reason gone mad, then Altamont was a celebration of ignorant fun, the counterrational, a different kind of helplessness. Altamont was no kind of a living refutation of the Vietnam War, it was more like an auxiliary.

Killing, organized killing, is what the whole misbegotten twentieth century is best at—the underground tributary of much of its imagination, the well of inventions and rituals, the music of mobilization, the cement of nations. The savagery began improvisationally, with slaughter at a few yards' distance, a camp-out in the muddy trenches of Europe, and progressed, that is, regressed, to the Enola Gay. To think about the essential political question of our time as anything other than the understanding of the organization of mass violence is pure sentimentality. And one of the dirty little secrets about war is how much the warriors relish the electricity of their experience. It is much better form to express regret, to reminisce about the flood of terror and the anguish of loss when they "go off to war," and no doubt those memories are sincere, but there is also a suppression of the pure sensory experience—an experience that gets interpreted, especially as filtered through movies, as a rite of manhood. One of the wounds in the psyches of many young men who survive their injuries—Dalton Trumbo expressed it in his pacifist novel, *Johnny Got His Gun*, and Ron Kovic in his memoir, *Born on the Fourth of July*—is the knowledge that they had started out craving the very war that left them maimed.

The thought of killing on an immense scale inevitably brought up thoughts about the mass murder of the Jews. Was that full horror going to be muffled, now, because mass murder, now and forever an ineradicable fact in the dreadful history of the human race, had been in a certain way banalized by the Bomb? It seemed that what the Nazis had done would be extremely hard to do again. After 1945 (thank the second half of the twentieth century for small favors!), it had become extremely bad form to classify any people into subhuman status or to advocate, let alone build, advanced machinery for annihilating them. But thanks to the routinization of the Bomb, the brandishing of the Bomb, the matter-of-fact build-up of Bomb upon Bomb, the annihilation of the Jews of Europe could now appear as something more than a uniquely terrible episode in history. It would always be unique, yes—the sheer intentionality of setting out to eradicate a people, the insistence on proceeding with the diabolical work ("Arbeit Macht Frei") even at great cost to the Germans' military defense. But with the Bomb there was pressure to think: yes, the Nazis were unique, yes, yes, *but.* . . .

The *but* was problematic, could even be shameful. It was badly wrong, could even be vile, to talk away the uniqueness of the torture and death of the Jews. But set alongside this uniqueness—one could not exactly say *against* it—was the fact that, for all the anti-Semitism that was Nazi state policy, indeed, state obsession, the Nazis had hidden their death camps. Reports were published in the Allied countries, enough to alert anyone who was prepared to be alerted, but public knowledge in the twentieth century rests upon photographs, and the full magnitude of the archipelago of death had never been made public in real time in the form of photos. That was why the newsreels after the war were especially shattering. "We didn't know" was the routine postwar alibi of the Germans. "We didn't know it could be that bad" was the response of virtually everyone else. But now, everyone knew—*human beings can do such things.* After such knowledge, what pride in humanity? (But then had pride in humanity ever been more than a ridiculous conceit erected on ignorance?)

The nuclear arms build-up demonstrated that the threat to slaughter millions of people was now an instrument of state policy. Citizens were now born into a peculiar status: hostages to the designs of their statesmen. Henceforth, this was an essential aspect of what it would be like to live in a nuclear state. To put it this way is not to diminish the uniqueness of the Nazi design for the extermination of a people. If the nuclear arms race was very far—*very* far—from the equivalent of Auschwitz, they shared something important: the absolute depersonalization of the Other, combined with the capacity for obliteration. To deter the Soviet Union (or the United States) by threatening to obliterate whole populations—this was "nothing personal" against any particular Russians, no proof that they were subhuman, it was simply, well, too bad. Too bad, and quite routine. The twentieth century was not only what Raymond Aron called "the century of total war," it was the century of dissociation. Out there, the horrors of public events; in here, home sweet home, business as usual. This rupture of worlds seemed novel. The strangeness of the Bomb was that it coexisted with peace, the muffled, dazed peace of the consumer society which in principle offered everything to everyone, apparently, along with the faint itch to have more.

The strangeness of the Bomb. . . . The Cuban missile crisis of October 1962 had brought home, literally *home,* that the Bomb was in the world precisely so that its use might be made credible. When Kennedy arranged a rapprochement with Khrushchev, and East-West détente resulted, the Bomb faded from the national radar screen—even from the screens of the ban-the-bombers. But, contrary to collective delusion, the Bomb had never gone away. In 1969, as in 1959 and 1949, the Bomb was—the thousands of Bombs were—very much still in the world. Those Bombs had been eclipsed, for a time, by the lower-case bombs falling on actual human beings in Vietnam. With Vietnam burning away in the foreground of any sensitive person's thinking, the Bomb had receded into the background. The Bomb was not predestined to fall within the next year, or decade, or century, but what kind of reassurance was that, when the future was a long time, and with more nations insisting on building these Bombs, insisting that they were membership cards in the club of important states, sooner or later the chances that one would be used were, well, significant "enough." Enough? The idea of deterrence—brandishing the Bomb in order to keep the Bomb from being used—remained a crackpot rationalization. The proprietors of the Bomb were holding hundreds of millions of citizens hostage to their ideas about foreign policy and military organization. However small the chances that a nuclear weapon would be detonated somewhere in the world in a given year, the risks were cumulative and not infinitesimal. The risks were real. Think about them and you would go mad. Fail to think about them and they were still real. Try not to think about a pink elephant.

I put down *Death in Life* and went to bed. I don't remember what I was thinking but I remember exactly what happened next. There was a split second in which I felt my mind trying to blast out of my body. It was a physical sensation: the mind, in here, wants to go out there, wants to leave. I sat bolt upright and cried for help. I swallowed hard. I think I was shuddering. I concentrated on pulling my mind back, stuffing it back into my cranium—or that is how I put it, what I thought I was doing, knowing at the same time that to put it that way made no sense. I would learn that this spasm was called an anxiety attack. The technical label was supposed to be reassuring. Labels are good for that. They also denature the experiences they name. What happened to me that night had, in fact, felt like pulling my mind back to my body. (I have sometimes wondered: What if I *had* let it go? Or was that in my power?) What followed was the fear that it would happen again, a fear that dogged me intensely for days and lingeringly for years. But perhaps, however fearful, this was my moment of illumination. Whoever promised that illumination would be pleasant?

Over the years that followed, I came to understand, or half-understand, this moment in various ways. Moments of fear, moments of truth—are they different? That moment, in any event, spurred me to change my life. My mind wanted to exit from the twentieth century, and in particular from the lunatic maelstrom and the guilt machine that "the movement" had become. The movement had become an elaborate contrivance for numbing. The crude slogans, the mindless left-wing "discourse," all of it was a drug against the actuality—including the actual violence—of the world. What I experienced that night was nothing I recommend, nor anything from which I derive an uplifting moral, but it had its personal meanings—and uses. A while later, I read with a shock of recognition, in Erik H. Erikson's *Young Man Luther*, a reference to a decisive moment when Luther "half-realizes that he is fatally overcommitted to what he is not." I knew that this half-realization is what had happened to me the night of the Altamont disaster. In the course of the decade, against my better judgment, I had become overcommitted to political fantasies: to apocalyptic expectations that everything was going to be new. Now the revolutions of consciousness—pseudorevolutions, actually—were over for me. Altamont was the end of all that, and I wasn't the only one who knew it. What exactly this realization had to do with reading *Death in Life* I cannot be sure. But perhaps, inadvertently, the book was reminding me of the stakes that drive people to numb themselves against abominable facts. Numbing is a central experience in the twentieth century. Numbing gives good value. You don't come down from the numbing without pain.

2

I don't want to claim too much for this experience of mine. It was what it was, private, a moment in an individual life. But perhaps there are aspects that refer to something larger. I want to ruminate about what that might be.

Altamont was a psychic numbing that failed. "Gimme Shelter;" that was the way Mick Jagger screamed his personal appeal for protection. A few years earlier, the Rolling Stones had mocked "Mother's Little Helpers"—the tranquilizers on which the middle class relied to get them through the day. The counterculture, wrapped in a soft haze of transcendence talk, had turned into a market for the latest, more efficient—and more dangerous—little helpers. But the Stones, who had learned to pump up their rough-tough act in order to sell tickets, were more typical of the entertainment machine than they fancied themselves, for the vast entertainment machine is, among other things, an industry for numbing.

One aspect of this numbing today is the homeopathic flirtation with violence. Routine brutality is the norm throughout popular culture. It is not a question simply of the quantity of murders and rapes, but rather, of the way they combine two apparently discordant features: grotesqueness and casualness. The depiction of damaged flesh has become a degraded craft of its own, thanks partly to competition in the use of technology with which to depict wounds, blood spurts and spatters, tortured flesh, explosions, and the rest. Individual victims will frequently not do, but planeloads, trainloads, even planets full of human beings must be blown sky-high by the bad guys. Video games feature cute decapitations, stylized bloodiness, casual when they are not trading in the offhand apocalypse of planetary demolition. There are sonic and video equivalents in heavy metal, gangsta rap, and their variants, sometimes designed to overpower, other times to bemuse, sometimes both. Technological improvements cannot by themselves explain the sheer quantity of this routine harshness. The depiction of threat has flourished along with the depiction of damage. The arousal of a sense of jeopardy was always an element of the movies. Now, with the phasing out of censorship, the "action movie" genre, newly named, flourishes as never before.

This style proves appealing for film producers who want to draw to the cineplex that part of the population most interested in leaving the house and going out to a movie: adolescents. The visit to the latest action movie has become a normal ritual of adolescence throughout at least the industrialized world. Each film is produced with a market motive, of course. But the market motive succeeds—at least just often enough to keep the genre flourishing. This is what has to be faced: no one forces anyone to attend the slasher movie. Peer pressure itself needs to be explained. I would interpret it as training for the cool and the hard. The movie is an exercise in anesthesia. The shock of the moment is followed by a cooling and hardening, so that, the next time, a higher dose will be required to produce an effect. (This raising of the threshold for sensation is the way of all drugs.) These executions frequently are devoid of moral implications. It is hard to equip them with ideological meanings. They are neither exactly realistic nor tragic, since they do not arouse pity. Mainly, they do not take place on a human scale. The human beings who die never really lived. They are occasions for the eruption of death. They can be "blown away" so painlessly because they were insubstantial in the first place. Life is fluff, and such is the way of the world: such is the message.

In other words, there takes place every day a sort of lightweight Altamont, a soft apocalypse, an endless rehearsal of the endgame. Entertainment has, as one of its central purposes, the muffling of the knowledge of mortality, and the paradox today is that the knowledge of mortality can be muffled by a certain way of representing mortality. So-called action movies, heavy metal, gangsta rap, and the like express the common experience of the weightlessness of existence. The lesson is that life is cheap. This mortality kitsch is an expression that, indeed, in Robert Lifton's terms, our connections with posterity are broken. *1984* was the wrong dystopia, *Brave New World* is more the case. To watch the images of humans routinely "blown away" or "taken out" is to become inured to a world of casual violence and murky threat.

Habituation: this is not the way most Americans think about the relationship between violence and the media. The presumption of the easy crusades of recent years is that the movies, television, videos and video games are dangerous because the thousands of murders, bashings, chain-saw cuts, explosions, car crashes, and cartoon pulverizations that are the routine stuff of the contemporary screen inspire murders, bashings, etc. in the real world. They are supposed to do so either directly, by inspiring imitation, or indirectly, by arousing aggression. The evidence for this proposition, as I read it, is poor to mixed. The style of Stallone, Willis, Seagal, Schwarzenegger & Co. plays on big screens virtually everywhere on earth with a coarsening effect, to be sure, but without generating epidemics of carnage outside the United States—if for no other reason than that guns are hard to procure. But demon Hollywood is a handy issue for politicians who dare not deal with palpable social failure: poverty, inequality, guns. To blame human wickedness on images is the moralistic recourse of a society that is unwilling to condemn trash on aesthetic grounds. Since the market expresses the only value worth valuing, moral condemnation is untenable unless trash is supposed to have dire consequences. In order to *be* bad, it has to *do* bad. It isn't bad enough that the movies, noise, etc. are ugly. Bodies have to pile up as a result.

The new anti-violence Puritans are not, in general, curious as to why anyone would find pleasure in dreadful images and high-decibel noise. The censorious impulse is not, in general, known for its curiosity. It does not inquire into the uses of anesthesia. Nor does it wonder why so many people—not only Americans, not only teenagers—might take pleasure in skimming the surface of death. It strikes me that there is something deeply American about this passion for mortality, this lizard-skin rapture in the face of the beautiful harshness of life. On the one hand, the Disney machine, American popular culture expertly packaging images of the smoothest innocence; on the other hand, the not-so-noble savagery of the muscular thug. But what has enabled these styles to triumph in the United States also enables them to be popular everywhere else.

The taste for the kitsch of slow-motion apocalypse has more than one root, in other words. It is hard to say what *isn't* one of its roots. Start with the fact that the sense of an ending is a constant during the waning days of a century—all the more so, it would seem, during the countdown to the millennium. The Bomb has survived the Cold War. Moments of acute fear will alternate with periods of obliviousness, but one way or another the Bomb will perennially certify that the danger of nonexistence is more than figurative. Ecological catastrophe has also taken up residence in the collective imagination. Rituals of renewal and replenishment are scarce. On the ground, youth are flooded by practical fears of unemployment, insecurity, violence. Not only is a sense of disconnection from the past built into modernity, but a sense of disconnection from the future is built into the technological onslaught, and coupled with a sense of disconnection from family, city, profession, and frequently from nation. "I'm a loser, baby, why don't you kill me?" goes one popular song. This fatalism is the other side of our contemporary habituation to endgame.

George Orwell's *1984*, with its drone society intimidated into submission in part by the televised spectacle of perpetual war, was mistaken. True, we did a few weeks' taste of that sort of the rapture of submission during the Nintendo days of the Gulf War, when a fantasy video game, rigged by Pentagon managers and video impresarios, passed for truth in the bedazzled eyes of the multitude. But the endless mobilization of *1984* proved too clunky a forecast, at least outside Iran and Iraq. After Vietnam we're too squeamish for too much real death on camera. So when American culture slipped past the eponymous date without Big Brother shutting down the multiplex or the video arcades, the sigh of relief was audible—but premature.

In the mall-to-mall world of the American spectacle, the more accurate dystopia turns out to be Aldous Huxley's *Brave New World*. Catastrophe is a logo. If Tom Brokaw can speak of "the matchups in the Gulf" on the brink of war, why shouldn't the *Terminators* and *Die Hards* be the stuff of fun? Destruction as distraction: Now *there's* an idea for a theme park. Unlike the war movies of yore, at least the kitsch of apocalypse doesn't serve for recruitment. It shows the limits of heroism—a concept hopelessly uncool. If history is a nightmare, at least it comes with theme music.

Violent kitsch is what we have instead of a serious reckoning with mass violence in the twentieth century. The culture of collective amnesia gives us action movies. Titillation is our form of numbing, leaking out the edges of the culture of collective amnesia. The repressed returns with special effects. *Isn't that horrible?* yields to *Isn't that cool?* This is extremity's cunning, the logic of acquiescence. The banality of apocalypse is the consumer society's revenge on history—but that is too apocalyptic a way to put it. Rather, action movies, video games, heavy metal and the rest of the show are the banal shadow of history. They are the means by which the young, flattened into their seats, learn how to get with the program. In the recycled apocalypse, history repeats itself, first as slaughter, then as a video game.

6

Thought Reform Today

Margaret Thaler Singer

Many persons wrote about totalitarian regimes, such as Defoe, Orwell, Zamyatin, Huxley, London, and Hofer, predicting how they thought totalistic regimes would psychologically impact individuals. Robert Lifton had the opportunity to actually study individuals who had been so subjugated. At the end of the Korean War he chose to carefully study the personal experiences of a series of Westerners and Chinese intellectuals who had been exposed to the Chinese thought reform programs both in prisons and in "revolutionary universities." Lifton delineated the techniques and methods of the Chinese thought reform program and revealed in telling detail through case studies its impact on the mind, emotions and social behavior of its victims in his 1961 book, *Thought Reform and the Psychology of Totalism: A Study of Brainwashing in China.*[1]

In his preface to the 1989 reprinting of that book Lifton stated that he sees his book as "less a specific record of Maoist China and more an exploration of what might be the most dangerous direction of the twentieth-century mind—the quest for absolute or 'totalistic' belief systems." He commented that he was especially pleased by the extent to which his volume on thought reform has remained central to literature on cults and on totalism in general. Lifton adds: "We can speak of cults as groups with certain characteristics: first, a charismatic leader, who tends increasingly to become the object of worship in place of more general spiritual principles that are advocated; second, patterns of 'thought reform' akin to those described in this volume, and especially in Chapter 22 (Ideological Totalism); and third, a tendency toward manipulation from above with considerable exploitation (economic, sexual, or other) of ordinary supplicants or recruits who bring their idealism from below."[2]

Cultic groups continue to increase and apply their variants of thought reform. As this century draws to a close we are seeing hordes of millenni-alists and ecofatalists gathering groups about them to set up the elite whom they claim will survive. These groups appear to be putting into place totalistic regimes with leaders claiming that they alone have the one answer for all. Lifton's seminal work on how totalism constricts the human mind, and requires victimization is, as this century draws to a close, going to be more useful than ever, because we are already seeing a new wave of totalism not only in cults, but in the burgeoning millenni-alist and ecofatalist movements.[3]

Thought reform is not mysterious. It is the systematic application of psychological and social influence techniques in an organized program-matic way within a constructed and managed environment. The goal is to produce specific attitudinal and behavior changes that management wants. The changes occur incrementally without it being patently visible to those undergoing the process that their attitudes and behavior are being changed a step at a time according to the plan of those directing the program.

In society there are numerous elaborate attempts to influence atti-tudes and modify behavior. However, thought reform programs can be distinguished from other social influence efforts because of their totalis-tic scope and their sequenced phases aimed at destabilizing participants' sense of self, sense of reality, and values. Thought reform programs rely on organized peer pressure, the development of bonds between the leader or (trainer) and the followers, the control of communication, and the use of a variety of influence techniques. The aim of all this is to promote conformity, compliance, and the adoption of specific attitudes and behaviors desired by the group. Such a program is further charac-terized by the *manipulation* of the person's total social environment to stabilize and reinforce the modified behavior and attitude changes.

Thought reform is accomplished through the use of psychological and environmental control processes that do *not* depend on physical coercion. Today's thought reform programs are sophisticated, subtle, and insidious, creating a psychological bond that in many ways is far more powerful than gun-at-the-head methods of influence. The effects generally lose their potency when the control processes are lifted or neutralized in some way. That is why most Korean War POWs gave up the content of their prison camp indoctrination programs when they came home, why the Westerners thought reformed in China, with rare exceptions, dropped the effects and contents, and why many cultists leave their groups if they spend a substantial amount of time away from the group or have an opportunity to discuss their doubts with an non-member who understands the thought reform process.[4]

Contrary to popular misconceptions, a thought reform program does not require physical confinement or physical coercion and does not produce robots. Nor does it permanently capture the allegiance of all those exposed to it. In fact, some persons do not respond at all to the programs, while others retain the contents and behavior for varied periods of time. In sum, thought reform should be regarded as "situationally adaptive belief change that is *not* stable and is environment dependent."

At the end of the Korean War, I worked at the Walter Reed Army Institute of Research in Washington, D.C., along with Lifton and others studying the thought reform and indoctrination programs the Chinese and North Koreans had used to reshape attitudes and behaviors in revolutionary universities, prisons, and prisoner of war camps. Besides working with material from prisoners of war, I interviewed a number of priests who had been interned in China and subjected to thought reform efforts.

By the late 1960s I became aware of the cult phenomenon in our society and began to interview cult members, ex-cultists and families of cultists. I soon discovered that the basic properties of thought reform as outlined by Lifton were alive and well right here in the United States and becoming one of our least desirable exports to other countries.

The burgeoning of the cult phenomenon caused me to return to using Lifton's work and that of my colleagues from the Walter Reed years. Relying on those seminal contributions, I have continued studying thought reform as Lifton described it in 1961 and its evolution since then. At this point leaders of cults and groups using thought reform processes have taken in and controlled millions of persons to the detriment of their welfare.

In my work studying how cults and groups with totalistic views are applying their current versions of thought reform programs, I have termed such programs on occasion "coordinated programs of coercive influence and behavior control" or "exploitative persuasion." This was done in an effort to make more understandable the thought reform process to those unfamiliar with the concepts and history of thought reform. During this period thought reform has been called by various names, as shown in Table 1.

Having returned to an interest in thought reform programs as I was noting their use by cults, I found a colleague with interests in social influence and we began to write about "second generation of interest" thought reform programs.[5] The first generation of interest was that which Lifton had delineated. The newer programs, even though they do not have the power of the state behind them, such as was present in

TABLE 1
Terms Used to Identify Thought Reform

Term	Originator
Thought struggle (*ssu-hsiang tou-cheng*)	Mao Tse-tung (1929)
Brainwashing (*hse nao*)	Hunter (1951)
Thought reform (*ssu-hsiang kai-tsao*)	Lifton (1956)
Debility, dependency, and dread (DDD syndrome)	Farber, Harlow, and West (1957)
Coercive persuasion	Schein (1961)
Mind control	Unknown (about 1980)
Systematic manipulation of psychological and social influence	Singer (1982)
Coordinated programs of coercive influence and behavioral control	Ofshe and Singer (1986)
Exploitative persuasion	Singer and Addis (1992)

China, appear more efficient, effective and also often more psychologically risky for participants than the earlier ones. Lifton noted that the managers of the Chinese programs attempted to closely monitor subjects so that when they reached the brink of decompensation, pressures could be reduced. The current programs do not monitor individuals in their thought reform programs, and thus produce a certain number of psychiatric casualties.[8]

We compared the thought reform programs being used by cults and some of the New Age so-called "awareness" programs with Lifton's original work. Not only were the current programs speeding up the process, but they were intensifying the psychological and social pressures without monitoring the individual's responses to the pressures put on them. The newer applications attempt to gain conformity more rapidly than did the earlier programs, and attack not just the person's political self, but appear designed to destabilize a person's overall sense of self and reality.

Most of the current cultic and New Age thought reform programs make the Chinese programs appear more interested in re-cycling persons by monitoring their ability to tolerate stress during thought reform programs, while the current groups appear to rely on replacing with new recruits those who break from the stresses. A colleague and I termed what we were seeing "the second generation of interest thought reform programs" and wrote of our ongoing study of psychiatric casualties from these programs as they are being carried out currently.[6]

The impact of cult life, which by its very structure tends to be totalistic, has been such that many psychiatrists and mental health professionals have discussed the behavior, attitude changes, and decompensations noted in former cult members and efforts have evolved to properly classify the residual effects of thought reform stresses. In 1980 the *Diagnostic and Statistical Manual of Mental Disorders* (DSM III), published by the American Psychiatric Association, cited "thought reform" as a contributing factor to Atypical Dissociative Disorder (a diagnosis frequently noted in former cult members).[7] Thought reform and its synonyms brainwashing and coercive persuasion were also noted in DSM-III-Revised (1987), as a contributing factor to Dissociative Disorder Not Otherwise Specified, as well as appearing in widely recognized medical texts.[8] Most recently, in 1994 the new DSM-IV again cites thought reform as contributing to the same type of dissociative disorder. Thus the psychiatric and psychological world has come to note the impacts the stresses, conflicts, and procedures of thought reform programs have on individuals' functioning.

Lifton's work in Hong Kong interviewing repatriated Westerners and Chinese intellectuals was his first major contribution to what has become a series of works by him centering on human responses to extreme stress, the production of victims, and his interests in the broader implications of totalism and its alternatives. He has also offered the concept of proteanism and "open" instead of "closed" methods of education and personal change as the hope of the future, apparently kindled by his work on thought reform.

Lifton formulated eight themes characterizing a totalistic environment which makes ideological totalism possible. By ideological totalism he meant "the coming together of immoderate ideology with equally immoderate individual character traits—an extremist meeting ground between people and ideas." The totalist environment seeks to re-educate participants into submission and conformity, not creative individual participation in society.

Lifton found eight themes predominating in the social milieu in which human zealotry and thought reform programs grow. He concluded: "In combination they [the eight themes] create an atmosphere which may temporarily energize or exhilarate, but which at the same time poses the gravest of human threats." Below, for brevity, I am abbreviating and paraphrasing Lifton's eight themes which characterize a thought reform milieu. Quoted material if from Lifton's book on thought reform.

1. Milieu control: Human communication is controlled by many means. External information and inner reflection are so controlled and managed by the system that the ordinary member becomes unable to test reality and experience a sense of identity separate from the environment. Communication is further controlled through the use of loaded jargon by the group. All information generated about persons, including any secrets they reveal to anyone, must be passed upward to authorities and then used to make the leader seem omniscient. Thus people cannot trust one another and develop support systems within the milieu.

2. Mystical manipulation: After controlling the milieu and communication, extensive personal manipulation occurs. Patterns of behavior and emotion are elicited in ways to make them appear to have arisen spontaneously from within the environment. Having been manipulated from above without realizing it, a person becomes sensitive to cues, and merges himself with the flow of the group to avoid continuing pressures being put upon him. He now adopts the psychology of the pawn. He drops self expression and independent actions and joins in the manipulation of others.

3. Demand for purity: A two-valued world is set in place. There is good and evil, pure and impure. The emotional levers of guilt and shame can applied to manipulate and control people especially playing upon existential guilt in which a person is made aware of his own limitations and his unfulfilled potential. Denouncing others, the outside world, and "projection" is encouraged. This leads to mass hatreds, purges of heretics, and to political and religious holy wars. "For there is no emotional bondage greater than that of the man whose entire guilt potential—neurotic and existential—has become the property of ideological totalists."

4. Cult of confession: The demand for absolute purity in the totalist environment leads to massive and varied uses of confession. "In totalist hands, confession becomes a means of exploiting, rather than offering solace." People can be led to falsely confess to deeds they did not do, and to falsely accuse, and through confession experience a sense of purification. Lifton noted two ends were achieved through confession: this seeming "purging milieu" only enhances the totalists hold on followers guilt and at the same time accomplishes a symbolic self-surrender in which the person feels he is merging with the environment. A sense of intimacy is created and the followers merge into the Movement. Lifton and Camus noted the perpetual confessor easily becomes the "judge-

penitent," that is, the more I accuse myself, the more I have a right to judge you.

5. Sacred science: The totalist world is the ultimate moral vision. "To dare to criticize it, or to harbor even unspoken alternative ideas, becomes not only immoral and irreverent, but also 'unscientific.' In this way, the philosopher kings of modern ideological totalism reinforce their authority by claiming to share in the rich and respected heritage of natural science." Lifton saw a composite of counterfeit science added to supposedly sacred ideas promulgated by the leaders of totalist groups as one more theme and pressure that pushes a person in a totalist environment toward total personal closure—that state of feeling an all-or-nothing emotional alignment with the immoderate ideology.

6. Loading the language: The language in the totalist environment is loaded with thought-terminating cliches and ultimate terms. "Totalist language is repetitively centered on all-encompassing jargon, prematurely abstract, highly categorical, relentlessly judging, and to anyone but its most devoted advocate, deadly dull: in Lionel Trilling's phrase 'the language of nonthought.' "

7. Doctrine over person: Ideological totalism overrides personal human experiences. What you as a person experience must be subordinated to the claims of the doctrine. Totalist doctrine engages in history revision in order to justify the regime's present stance. Individual memory can be overridden and distortions imposed. "The underlying assumption is that the doctrine—including the mythological elements—is ultimately more valid, true and real than is any aspect of actual human character or human experience."

8. Dispensing existence: A totalist environment divides people into two groups—those with a right to existence and those without such a right. Lifton noted that totalist environments even when not using physical abuse, stimulate in followers a fear of extinction and annihilation. Existence depends on obeying and merging with the totalist environment.

Lifton concluded: "The more clearly an environment exercises these eight psychological themes, the greater its resemblance to ideological totalism; and the more it utilizes such totalist devices to change people, the greater its resemblance to thought reform [or 'brainwashing']."

Thus Lifton's careful observations from his study of repatriates from the Chinese thought reform milieu laid the foundation for evaluating environments in which thought reform is the change agent used to control the expressed behavior of people.

In addition to Chinese exposed to thought reform in revolutionary universities, Lifton studied Westerners subjected to thought reform in prison settings and especially paid attention to seeing if there was sequencing in the thought reform programs they had experienced. Lifton noted there was indeed a general sequence of psychological pressures, twelve in number, put upon each person, even though they had been in separate prisons, far removed from one another, and with different staff and surroundings. The psychological steps he labeled: (1) the assault on identity, (2) the establishment of guilt, (3) the self-betrayal, (4) the breaking point, total conflict and the basic fear, (5) leniency and opportunity, (6) the compulsion to confess, (7) the channeling of guilt, (8) re-education: logical dishonoring, (9) progress and harmony, (10) the final confession: the summing up (11) rebirth, (12) release, transition and limbo.

Helping persons who have left current cultic groups by going over this sequence of psychological steps is especially useful. By so doing, these persons see and feel that common properties exist between what Lifton found decades ago and what they have experienced. What Lifton termed the two basic identities of thought reform, the repentant sinner and the receptive criminal, are among the most bothersome induced roles cultists battle after leaving their groups. To learn that these are roles almost uniformly induced by thought reform programs, regardless of age, nationality, education, and social class, helps to alleviate the guilt, self doubt, self abnegation, and loss of trust in the self that the current cult thought reform programs induce.

Lifton studied in carefully documented detail what in fact has emerged as one of the most powerful efforts at human manipulation ever undertaken. It led him to call attention to "closed" versus "open" approaches to human change—the thought reform methods used in a closed, totalist society versus the methods of human change used in open societies in which education, choice, individual responsibility, reflective thought are the means of seeking human change.

My work and that of colleagues studying cults and newer uses of thought reform programs has necessitated adding some orientation about the differences between a thought reform program backed by state power, as in China, and a thought reform program as seen in modern cultic groups. We also have tended to translate Lifton's concepts and findings into simple terms for youth and nonprofessional audiences. Lifton's themes, steps, and findings that thought reform could be carried out effectively in nonprison settings, as well as his many insights about human responses to totalist programs, stand as he wrote them. Cult apologists work to hide the fact that Lifton clearly commented that neither a prison setting nor physical coercion was required for thought reform to work. The same apologists tend to ignore all the rest of the literature on thought reform and decades of study of influence by social psychologists.

The people Lifton studied had either found themselves immersed in thought reform programs in revolutionary universities or were exposed in prison settings, and were aware that there was an effort to change their political beliefs. However, today, individuals become involved with cultic and other groups that recruit deceptively and are unaware before joining just what will follow. My work and that of others on such groups has found that it is rare that these groups reveal to new members just what they will be exposed to. The new members often know practically nothing of how they are going to be treated, processed, and changed. Thus some modernization such as item 1 below was needed to help other researchers and the general public see the extra mystification that is present in the current scenes in which thought reform is practiced.

After studying the degree to which Lifton's themes are present in a group suggesting a totalist milieu exists, the following six conditions can serve as a brief checklist to evaluate a group's methods. The group:

1. Keeps the person unaware that there is an agenda to control or change the person.
2. Controls time and physical environment (contacts, information)
3. Creates a sense of powerlessness, fear, and dependency
4. Suppresses old behavior and attitudes
5. Instills new behavior and attitudes
6. Puts forth the program in a closed system of logic

With the exception of item 1, these are abbreviated versions of Lifton's themes intended to simplify outlining the thought reform process.

What follows below is again a condensation of the steps he found in a thought reform program. The explanations of the steps have been simplified and used by me and colleagues as we have connected Lifton's work to our current studies of "second generation of interest" thought reform groups.

1. Destabilizing the person: A person's whole sense of self and notion of how the world works are destabilized by group lectures, personal contacts by authorities, rewards, punishments and other exchanges with the group. The person is moved to a point where self-confidence is eroded; he has become more suggestible; and is uncertain about what choices to make.

2. Accepting the solution that the group offers: At this point, the person being thought reformed senses that the solutions offered by the group provide the path to follow. Anxiety, uncertainty and self-doubt can be reduced by adopting the concepts put forth by the group or leader. Newcomers observe the behavior of old timers and begin to model themselves after the examples. Massive anxiety can be reduced by cooperating with the social pressures to conform. The newcomers begin to "talk the talk, and walk the walk" that the thought reform program is instilling.

3. Now you are in: After "the acceptance" has been made, the group reinforces in the newcomers the desired behavior with social and psychological rewards, and punishes unwanted attitudes and behaviors with harsh criticism, group disapproval, social ostracism, and loss of status.

Most of the modern thought reform groups seek to produce non-resistant, hardworking persons who do not complain about group practices and do not question the authority of the guru, leader or trainer. The more followers display the group-approved attitudes and behavior, the more their compliance is interpreted by the leadership as showing that they now know that their life before they belonged to the group was wrong and that their new life is "the way."

Recently Lifton wrote:

I have been preoccupied with questions of totalism from the time of my study of Chinese thought reform in the mid 1950s, and came full circle in returning to the subject when studying Nazi doctors in the late 1970s and early 1980s. Totalism is likely to emerge during periods of historical—or psychohistorical—dislocation, in which there is a breakdown of the symbols and structures that guide the human life cycle. Contributing to this dislocation is the mass media revolution, which creates the remarkable possibility of any one of us, at any moment, having access to any image or idea originating anywhere in the contemporary world or from any cultural moment of the entire human past. Still another powerful influence furthers our dislocation: awareness of our late-twentieth-century technological capacity to annihilate ourselves as a species, and to do so with neither purpose nor redemption. What results from these historical forces are widespread feelings that we are losing our psychological moorings. We feel ourselves buffeted about by unmanageable currents and radical social uncertainties.

"A major response to this confusion has been the contemporary worldwide epidemic of fundamentalism. That movement, broadly understood, drives from a fear of the loss of "fundamentals," giving rise to demand for absolute dogma and a monolithic self—all rendered sacred in the name of a past of perfect harmony that never was.

While the above may sound dire, Lifton, with his ever-present faith in mankind's capacity to choose the "protean self" and the "open" methods of change rather than the constricted, thought reform methods continues to contribute to efforts to insure that freedom of the mind will continue.

Notes

1. Robert Jay Lifton, *Thought Reform and the Psychology of Totalism* (New York: W. W. Norton, 1961).

2. Robert Jay Lifton, *Thought Reform and the Psychology of Totalism* (University of North Carolina Press, 1993). Note also Lifton, "Totalism and Civil Liberties, *The Future of Immortality and Other Essays for a Nuclear Age* (New York: Basic Books, 1987); and Lifton, "Cult formation," *Harvard Mental Health Letter* (1991).

3. Margaret T. Singer, with Janja Lalich, *Cults in Our Midst* (San Francisco: Jossey-Bass, 1995).

4. Stuart A. Wright, *Leaving Cults. The Dynamics of Defection*, Society of the Scientific Study of Religion, Monograph no. 7, Washington, D.C., 1987.

5. Richard Ofshe and Margaret T. Singer, "Attacks on Peripheral Versus Central Elements of Self and the Impact of Thought Reforming Techniques," *Cultic Studies Journal* 3 (1986): 8; and Margaret T. Singer and Richard Ofshe, "Thought Reform Programs and the Production of Psychiatric Casualties," *Psychiatric Annals* 20 (1990):188–93. Richard Ofshe, "Coercive Persuasion and Attitude Change," *Encyclopedia of Sociology*, vol. 1, (New York: Macmillan, 1992), 212–24.

6. Louis J. West and Margaret T. Singer, "Cults, Quacks, and Nonprofessional Psychotherapies," H. I. Kaplan, A. M. Freedman and B. J. Sadock, eds., *Comprehensive Textbook of Psychiatry* III (Baltimore: Williams & Wilkins, 1980).

7. *Diagnostic and Statistical Manual of Mental Disorders, III* (Washington, D.C.: American Psychiatric Association, 1980); Revised, III-R, 1987; and DSM-IV, 1994.

8. Margaret T. Singer, "Group psychodynamics," in R. Berkow, ed., *Merck Manual*, 15th ed. (Rahway, NJ: Merck, Sharp, & Dohme, 1987).

7

Facts, Truth, and Social Responsibility: Reflections of a Developmental Scientist

Frances Degen Horowitz

Robert Jay Lifton cared to understand the social, philosophical and historical context that made it possible for the Nazi doctors to violate the very essence of the oath they had taken to preserve life. In his book, *The Nazi Doctors*, after the human stories were told, after the lives were depicted, after detailing the evil that was done, and after his incisive analysis of what he had discovered, Robert Jay Lifton would not let us escape the necessity to face the profound emotional import of that which was beyond human. In doing so, he made it impossible for the reader to escape confronting the inherent aspects of social responsibility that must be, but often are not, on the agenda of anyone who wants to claim the respect that comes with being credentialed as a professional.

In our society, titled and credentialed professionals are assumed to have knowledge, skills and expertise applicable to particular problems and issues. Most of the time, in the routine exercise of expertise, the professional can ply his or her trade without encountering moral and ethical issues. But not always. In any given instance, the moral and ethical issues may be simple and of small consequence. In other instances, they may involve complex matters and with broad implications.

The twentieth century has certainly produced more than its share of moral dilemmas for professionals of all kinds. In the context of war and for the potential of the sheer force of the destruction of human life, the American counterpart of the moral dilemma faced by the Nazi doctors was that which was faced by the physicists and chemists who signed on to the development of the atomic bomb.

While the condition of a war may well produce the most dramatic instances of these kinds of moral dilemmas, there are many other moral dilemma situations in which experts and professionals, to different de-

81

grees and with varying frequency, are called upon to lend their skills and expertise. Sometimes the decision about lending skills and expertise presents up-front ethical issues: Shall the wildlife specialist serve as a consultant to a real-estate development corporation on the question of natural species habitats that might be threatened by the developers' plans to build a controversial shopping center? At other times moral and ethical issues become apparent only in hindsight—especially when there is strong consensus at the time of cooperation that everyone wants to do "good" and little attention is being paid to the possibilities of unintended consequences.

In this essay I want to examine the impetus for doing good that captured my imagination and the imagination of many of my developmental colleagues during the economic war on poverty that was announced in 1964 by President Lyndon Johnson. I want to consider the way in which facts were used, the way in which truth was fashioned and the way in which a deep sense of social responsibility served to justify lending skills and expertise to help shape public programs and policies that were supposed to overcome the effects of poverty on children's lives. In the end, I want to consider the moral and ethical dilemmas that confront developmental scientists whose research is relevant to current debates about whether human development, human behavior and human achievement are more influenced by environmental experience or by hereditary factors.

A story

Chapter I

Early in the spring of 1965, I received a phone call asking if I would send someone from the faculty to a meeting in Washington to discuss a new federal preschool program. I was the chair of the Department of Human Development and Family Life at the University of Kansas. The department operated the university's laboratory preschool and was responsible for the training of individuals who wished to become certified to teach at the preschool level. I chose one of our faculty (Margaret H.). She was responsible for overseeing the training of preschool teachers and was, herself, a head teacher for one of the laboratory preschool classrooms. In Washington she learned of the intention to mount Head Start, a key component in President Lyndon Johnson's War on Poverty. Head Start was to be an "intervention" in the lives of poor children to provide them with learning opportunities and experiences in the preschool years analogous to the experiences that middle-class parents were providing their children and that seemed to be so effective as a preparation for the school success of middle-class children.

Margaret H. also learned that the intention was to begin the Head Start program in June (it was now April). "June?," I responded, half questioning, half wondering aloud. "Yes." And, furthermore, the initial enrollees were to be poor children who were bound for first-time public-school enrollment in kindergarten or first grade in September. Now I became a bit incredulous, if not wary.

Here it was April. We were being asked to plan a special half-day summer preschool program in our facilities and to enroll children who would be entering the public schools for the first time in September. A six- to eight-week program of "early experience and early intervention" was expected to raise the level of academic achievement of the Head Start participants when they went to school in the fall.

Margaret H. told me that she and others at the meeting shared my concern about initiating a program so quickly. They had questioned the wisdom of expecting that a brief summer intervention program would produce significant increases in intelligence and in the academic performance of children who had lived already five and six years under conditions of poverty. True, the "facts" were available from the animal experimental literature and from some experimental and observational studies of children to suggest that early experience makes a difference in later learning. Still, how could one accept the proposition that such a program would make a permanent difference, to say nothing of having to put the program together in less than two months.

All this was happening at a time when the facts, as we knew them, contributed to a sense of optimism that environmental experience was the key to developmental achievements. Nevertheless, even the most naive and optimistic environmentalist would not claim that a few weeks of intervention prior to school attendance was likely to have a profound and lasting impact on school achievement.

The response to the concerns and the skepticism was, "Well, would you rather do nothing for poor children?" No. We did not want to be in the position of advocating that we do nothing for poor children. We wanted to do good. So we agreed to have a Head Start program in our university preschool facility beginning in June.

Sometime in early May I received another telephone call from Washington. This time it was in response to the budget we had submitted for the first summer of the Head Start program. I was told the budget was too high and we would have to cut it. I explained that our department had run a highly acclaimed preschool for many years and that we knew what was required to put on a quality preschool program for children. The reply at the other end of the telephone produced a response that, again, left me incredulous, "This is Head Start—it is not a quality preschool program. You will have to reduce this budget to fit the financial guidelines for Head Start."

When I began to protest and found no sympathy on the phone, the possibility of cancelling our participation came to mind. But then I imagined an echo response, "Would you rather do nothing for poor children this summer?" I said no more. We revised the budget and ultimately supplemented the federally provided funds with our own university resources. That summer, for eight weeks, we ran the first half-day Head Start program in Lawrence, Kansas.

Chapter II

In recounting the events of the spring of 1965, Robert Cooke has written, "The decision to launch Head Start as a nationwide summer program, rather than a limited pilot effort—either summer or year-round—was controversial. The final decision was a political and fiscal one, not an academic one, but it proved to be proper since it led to intense public interest upon which future Head Start programs capitalized."[1]

It was also decided that an effort should be made to evaluate the effectiveness of the half-day summer programs. A small number of evaluation studies were funded for this purpose. Most of them had a pre-program and a post-program assessment to measure the gains that might be attributed to the summer experience. Control groups would provide a comparison.

In the fall, the first results of these evaluations pronounced Head Start as a success. The children who had the summer Head Start program were, on average, doing better in their first year of school than those who had not had the program. But the program's funding was not assured for the second year. By the time it was, the first year's experience was repeated—late notice in the spring and half-day hurriedly mounted summer programs.

Unlike the program in Lawrence, many of these initial summer Head Start programs were staffed by people with little or no pre-school training (and sometimes not even early primary school teaching experience.) Some of the programs were in relatively make-shift facilities. Still, the quick evaluations suggested they were effective in helping the children do better in school than children who did not have Head Start.

Chapter III

All of the early research on Head Start showed that the children benefitted from the program, but that specific advantages of Head Start on academic achievement faded within a year or two. In 1969, in a monograph based almost entirely on the studies reporting the effects of the first two summer Head Start programs, Arthur Jensen declared Head Start a failure for the purpose of boosting IQ and academic achievement. The failed experiment, he asserted, strengthened the proposition that intelligence was based on genetic endowment and not affected by environmental experience.[2] The argument for early experience, and for environmental effects on school achievement and IQ were dealt an initial blow. It was the opening salvo on the side of "nature" that began to define the current era of the nature-nurture debate.

Within a few years Head Start became a full-year program serving three- and four-year-old children in the two years prior to their entrance into school. Standards were established for personnel and facilities and programmatic content. Head Start became and remained the national commitment to compensatory preschool education for this nation's poor children.

Thirteen Head Start Research and Evaluation Centers were established across the country—one of them at the University of Kansas—to determine the effectiveness of Head Start as an educational intervention program. While designing the evaluation protocols, there were many arguments about the most appropriate measures of the impact of the Head Start experience on poor preschool children. Some of us were against the use of the IQ measure. The counter-argument was that Congress would understand increases in IQ in a way that they would not understand increases in performance, which were based on more obscure measures. And then the, "Would you rather do nothing?" type of question: "Are you so opposed to using the IQ measure that you are willing to risk Congress not funding Head Start because the members of Congress will not understand other measures?" "No." So we agreed to include IQ among the measures.

The first and subsequent evaluations of Head Start and of other preschool early intervention programs have, overall, found that Head Start was beneficial for the participants. On the average, Head Start served to lift performance in the early grades of school to a higher level than would have been achieved in the absence of Head Start. But the effects were also shown to fade over time, leaving Head Start children no further ahead than those who did not have Head Start. In some instances continued special interventions through the elementary school years were able to sustain the effects—and most especially in highly funded programs that were related to university-based research programs. But gone were the high hopes that a Head Start experience, would, by itself, propel a poor child onto the developmental trajectory of the more advantaged middle-class child. And gone were any expectations that a Head Start experience would impact performance on IQ tests.

In reflection, Ed Zigler noted that: "We should never have allowed the IQ score to become the ultimate indicator of compensatory education's success or failure. The goal of Head Start never was to produce a cadre of geniuses to fill the teaching posts at our universities. . . . The goal of Head Start is the production of socially competent human beings."[3]

We all knew that the IQ measure was unlikely to be affected in a dramatic way by a compensatory preschool intervention program when everything else in a child's life of poverty did not change. Not even the most ardent proponents of the now obsolete naive environmentalism claimed that the larger and dominating social context of growing up in poverty—often grinding urban poverty—could be overwhelmed by Head Start. As for long-term effects—why should a two-year preschool program be expected to serve as an inoculation for the "ever afterward" of development when development is a dynamic ongoing process.

Yet, as developmental scientists, we were enthusiastic. We knew the facts and we constructed the truth in a hopeful desire that our efforts would make a difference in the lives of children. And we cooperated eagerly and were proud to share the knowledge that defined the field of child development.

The Macro-social Context

In 1977 the Carnegie Council published a study of the factors affecting the functioning of children and their families. The conclusion was that a "family's economic position is the single most powerful determinant of the opportunities open to families and to children. . . . It is vitally important for children and their parents to have the self-esteem and the wherewithal that a decent job and decent income provide."[4] The most enduring improvements in the lot of disadvantaged children, it was argued, would come only when the parents of these children had access to good jobs that provided incomes sufficient to sustain a family.

These were thoughtful observations. They should have alerted us to consider the interplay of the micro-psychological variables involved in education and the macro-social context of the economy. But they did not. We were excited about what we were doing and sincerely committed to using our knowledge to make a difference.

Some attention was being paid to the macro-social variables affecting the lives of poor children. The "war on poverty," designed to produce the "great society," had equal opportunity economic programs with the goal of stimulating economic gains for the poor that could be translated into jobs with family-sustaining incomes. Programs to empower the parents of Head Start children were developed along with efforts to increase economic sufficiency. The results, for many reasons, were mixed with respect to long-term impact.

The efforts to create new economic realities for the poor have to be seen in the context of the profound restructuring of the American economy that gathered steam in the 1980s and can be expected to continue well past the end of the twentieth century. Driven by globalization and technology, the entry level blue-collar and manufacturing jobs that had been the typical first rung of the economic ladder up out of poverty were fast disappearing. And the structural conditions for joblessness and/or jobs that do not pay family-sustaining wages hardened.

In the 1990s an even larger social context (undoubtedly influenced and perhaps controlled by an economy in the process of dynamic restructuring) has to be considered. It involves the availability of illegal drugs and of guns and an underground, highly dangerous, and very destructive criminally based economy that has taken hold—especially in the inner cities of America, catching the traditionally disadvantaged in its ripple effects. These conditions have come to affect patterns of addiction and the stability of family structure. Joblessness and then homelessness have gotten a grip on the social fabric of significant sections of most of America's large urban areas and also, increasingly, of some of America's small urban areas. As a nation with significant portions of our population having diminished access to the job-related social benefits that support families, our national direction is now exactly opposite of that which the Carnegie Council report deemed necessary for fostering the development of poor children—the availability of stable jobs with family-sustaining wages and benefits. These powerful macro-social variables, if they persist, stand ready to swamp many of the beneficial effects of early intervention programs.

Environmentalism: Point-Counterpoint in the Twentieth Century

While Head Start and the War on Poverty were the result of social and political pressures that gained momentum in the early 1960s, the underlying rationale for these programs—especially Head Start—reflected clearly the prevailing academic and intellectual belief systems about the power of environmental experience to affect developmental outcome.

Such propositions about the power of environmental experience have vied back and forth with hereditarianism for almost the whole of the twentieth century. Through the 1930s, John B. Watson and Arnold Gesell were the principal protagonists. Gesell asserted that nature (heredity) was responsible for individual development; Watson claimed environment as the major factor. Intelligence was the primary focus of the debate, and there is a large corpus of research that was designed to try to determine whether intelligence was influenced more by factors associated with nature (heredity) or more by factors related to nurture (environment).

Gesell showed that children adopted away from their birth mother had intelligence scores that correlated more strongly with the birth mothers than with the adoptive mothers. The environmentalists countered by noting that the actual level of the intelligence of the adopted children was closer to the level of the IQ of the adoptive mothers than to the IQ of the birth mothers. Experiments showing the influence of natural maturational forces were balanced by experiments showing how environmental influences could affect developmental progress.

Common sense seemed to prevail when, in the late 1940s and into the 1950s most people accepted the proposition that nature and nurture interacted to produce developmental outcome and that portions of responsibility were not easily assignable to one or the other factor. And, anyway, the nurture part—environment—was more accessible to manipulation so that an optimistic activist agenda to improve the chances for good developmental outcome had to focus on environment. These common sense inclinations were reinforced by research with animals showing how environmental enrichment and experience contributed to increased problem solving abilities.

An early dent in this optimism occurred with the "cognitive revolution" in the 1960s when it was shown that all manner of human cognitive capabilities appeared to be inborn and not the result of early experience. Piaget's theoretical and empirical claims for universals of cognitive development and Chomsky's assertions about the innate bases for the development of linguistic abilities served to brake some of the environ-mentalist claims.

The environmental position has continued to be under assault and, in recent years, most especially from practitioners in the field of behavior genetics. Though never observing a gene directly, behavior geneticists derive percentages of characteristics that they claim are genetically based. They study the similarities between identical twins and make as-sumptions about shared and nonshared environments and calculate the extent to which a characteristic such as intelligence or a depressive per-sonality is based on genetic inheritance.

Despite many arguments against defining intelligence solely in terms of an IQ score, and despite a considerable body of work showing how the IQ score misses the mark in capturing the larger part of functional human intelligence, the popular aspect of the nature-nurture debate about intelligence has been framed almost entirely in reference to scores on IQ tests, culminating in the publication of *The Bell Curve*.[5]

Here, in *The Bell Curve*, for the 1990s, the issues of poverty, race, envi-ronment, genes and intervention have been joined blatantly and un-abashedly in a more sophisticated way than they were in the 1920s. In the 1920s, in the heyday of hereditarianism, it was claimed that the deaf, delinquents, the "negro," and the foreign born—especially the "races from the south and east of Europe," i.e., Jews, were of inferior intelli-gence, if not retarded, compared to whites and those from northern and western Europe. It was claimed then that all sorts of complex traits, intelligence included, were inherited in the same ways as "purely physi-cal traits."[6] Public and social policies related to immigration and to edu-cation were influenced by these claims just as they would be influenced by the claims of the environmentalists in the 1960s.

In the 1990s, the authors of *The Bell Curve* claim evidence for support-ing the following set of propositions: Intelligence is highly influenced by genetic factors; intelligence determines one's place in the social hier-archy of American society; one's social class is therefore a function of one's genetic inheritance; environmental interventions designed to in-fluence intelligence and thus one's place in the social structure are naive and doomed to fail. Now, marry to this argument the "fact" that Americans of African ancestry, on average, score lower on standardized intelligence tests that yield an IQ score than do those not of African ancestry. (It should be noted that the *standard deviation*, a measure, of variability in a sample, is typically larger for groups of African Ameri-cans. The import of this is never discussed, but it suggests an overall broader spread of scores for African Americans—possibly a function of the greater and more variable influence of concurrent social circumstances.) And add the "fact" that Americans of African ancestry are disproportionately to be found in the lower socio-economic classes in our society. The conclusion that is drawn by the authors is that Americans of African ancestry are in the lower socio-economic classes because of their genetic background even though the reasoning that produces this conclusion is basically faulty. It is faulty because it is a basically circular argument involving arbitrary distal measures. It is faulty because it does not consider the impact of dynamic macro-social variables of opportunity and racism on the development of individual capabilities.

Nevertheless, here, at the end of the twentieth century, the "nature" position has returned in full flower presented in a popularized form. The 1960s small voice of Arthur Jensen asserting the genetic basis of IQ has grown to a chorus, and a more sophisticated one at that.

Many behavioral and developmental scientists have protested against the conclusions in *The Bell Curve*. Reviews of the book by responsible and sophisticated individuals have provided facts and reasons why the conclusions are not justified. They have noted flaws in the studies cited and have contested the premises that underlie the major thesis of the book. The majority of the reviews by competent, *mainstream developmentalists* have been negative.

On the other side, in an attempt to counter or undermine the negative evaluations of the book, a group of individuals who identified themselves as representing "mainstream science on intelligence" issued a signed statement that was published in the *Wall Street Journal* claiming that the critics of *The Bell Curve* "misstate current scientific evidence" on human intelligence.[7] After representing what the signers of the statement claimed were consensus opinions about IQ and intelligence, they offered the centerpiece of their position. Namely, that the evidence supports the assertion that "genetics plays a bigger role than does environment in creating IQ differences among individuals." This claim is based upon a foregoing discussion of the concept of "heritability." Omitted is the fact that heritability estimates from behavior genetics studies apply only to groups and not to individuals. Also, omitted is the fact that the term "genetics" as behavior geneticists use it has nothing to do with genes, but everything to do with inferences from mostly paper and pencil tests of genetically related individuals.

The *Wall Street Journal* statement ended with the assertion that, "The research findings neither dictate nor preclude any particular social policy, because they can never determine our goals. They can, however, help us estimate the likely success and side effects of pursuing those goals via different means."

The *Wall Street Journal* statement was well crafted. The lack of knowledge about brain processes underlying intelligence was acknowledged, as was the fact that many African Americans have mixed ancestry and many of the self-identified ethnic groups are mixed in terms of biological and social backgrounds. Considering the impact of the major focus of the statement, the caveats were unconvincing, if not disingenuous.

On Social Responsibility

Thirty years of work and belief in the efficacy of social and educational programs to eradicate poverty and/or overcome its effects on children have not produced the profound and enduring results that many believed we would witness. Instead, those hoping to make a permanent difference in the lives of children have found themselves working upstream against the strong pull of the macro-social variables of unemployment, drugs, guns, racism, homelessness, hunger, fractured families and largely decaying urban schools.

On the one hand we might say that well intentioned efforts were constantly being swamped by the macro-social variables of a society structurally designed for unemployment, legally constipated in moving against guns, and seemingly impotent when it comes to controlling the economy of illegally traded drugs. On the other hand, critics of the social programs may well wonder if these explanations are not just self-serving excuses. What if, they can say, intelligence *is* largely determined by genetic inheritance and if those of low intelligence are destined, anyway, in our society, to gravitate to the lower or underside of the social class structure?

Who says that the dispassionate statement in the *Wall Street Journal* has no implications for any particular social policy?—if one believes the statement to be based on valid premises and to be true? But the underlying premises are arguable at best and specious at worst. Indeed, the entire conceptualization of intelligence as an IQ score on a standardized test has been questioned by many who also consider themselves part of mainstream science.

We are on the cusp of the twenty-first century and in the midst of the post-modern period of a technologically driven information/service society. The rewards of jobs with family-sustaining incomes are available to a smaller and smaller segment of the population that has the prerequisite technical skills and knowledge. In a highly efficient economy, there will be no place for surplus labor even as there are humans who want to work at jobs that do not exist and who are the victims of an economy structured to provide them only with jobs that cannot sustain them or their families. Where and how do these macro-social environmental variables affecting the lives of children get factored into understanding the degrees to which we can expect success from micro-psychological early education intervention programs focused on groups of children and their parents and caregivers.

When Head Start began, in an era of environmental optimism, we who cooperated with the effort and who agreed to the use of the IQ as a measure of Head Start's success, did not fully understand how powerful the macro-social variables would prove to be in overwhelming our efforts to provide early social and educational programs to poor children. Undoubtedly, some children and their families benefited a great deal and were helped up out of poverty. Others were not. No one, it would appear, was harmed in any direct way by these programs. But the inherent promise of the Great Society programs—Head Start most especially—that poverty would be eliminated and all children would have equal opportunity for full development was not to be realized.

In the thirty years since Head Start began, we have learned a great deal about the cognitive, emotional and social development of children. We have the ability to apply our knowledge to great effect in helping every child acquire basic skills and an extensive range of information. We know that almost all children, regardless of race and ethnicity, who are fed an adequate diet, who live and grow in stable and emotionally nurturing and economically sufficient environments, free of violence and abuse, and who are given opportunities to learn, will develop normally and will thrive. In the absence of these conditions and opportunities, the level of achievement of many children will be far below their capabilities. It is ironic that in the 1990s the larger social context in which many poor children live can so easily override our greatly enhanced abilities to insure that almost every child born into our society will grow and develop into a productive and contributing adult.

At the end of the twentieth century, the macro-social variables of a technologically driven economy, with fewer and fewer stable family-sustaining jobs, are firmly in control of the course of individual human lives. This is the case at the same time that genetics are said to be in control of individual intelligence by behavioral scientists who do not work at the genetic level but who make inferences about genetic control from distal measures.

The conclusion that intelligence is more influenced by genes than by environment reveals a willingness to ignore the fact that those who actually work at the genetic level offer the picture of a more complex dynamic at work. Specifically, there is considerable evidence that genes and genetic influences are expressed and suppressed and function only as the result of biological and environmental contexts that, themselves, interact. All the evidence of those who work at the genetic and biological levels suggests that genetic influences on complex human behavior are likely to be altered and filtered through biological functions heavily influenced by environmental factors that begin to operate on and interact with the human organism immediately after conception and continue post-natally and across the life span.

Everything points to the fact that those who signed the *Wall Street Journal* statement are speaking from a position of naive hereditarianism that is not very different, in depth of understanding, from those who, in earlier years, spoke from a position of naive environmentalism. The social policy consequences of the naive environmentalism led to great and unrealistic expectations for the efficacy of early education intervention programs, by themselves, to produce large and permanent changes in the developmental outcome of poor children.

What social policy consequences can we expect from naive hereditarianism? Especially when racism is subtly and overtly endemic in our society; especially in the instance of conditions of economic and social stress; especially when there is a growing sense of despair over seemingly intractable social problems that provides a fertile basis for believing assertions that low achieving individuals are genetically inferior. Under such circumstances ideas once thought inimical to a democratic society can begin to take root and produce advocates for exerting social and biological control over the individuals labeled genetically inferior. Such ground can be seen as having been well prepared by a history of seemingly failed social interventions, by declarations that environmentalism is an outmoded belief, and by a lack of concern for the social responsibility inherent in the way in which one frames research questions and the way in which one reports research findings.

The failures of efforts that were based upon naive environmentalism left a society ready to dismiss the efficacy of environmental intervention. It also left a society ready to accept genetic explanations absent the realization that the genetic explanations rest on an equally naive hereditarianism. This naive hereditarianism underestimates the dynamic relationships of genes, biological function and environment. It also simplifies the influence of the macro-social variables of racism, of an economy insufficient to sustain its population and of the consequences for family function in a volatile social context in influencing individual human development.

The full practice of social responsibility required those of us who believed in the efficacy of the micro-psychological educational interventions on children to have taken more seriously the role of the macro-social variables as they affect human development, to have stated our expectations with greater qualification, to have resisted the use of the IQ as a valid outcome measure. We should have promised less and framed our research questions in a more complex form.

Unfortunately, at the end of the twentieth century, behavioral geneticists operating from a position of naive hereditarianism appear not to have learned the lesson that we, as developmental scientists who operated from a position of naive environmentalism, learned. Only now, at the end of the twentieth century, the consequential stakes are very high for the practice or non-practice of social responsibility in expressing ideas about the relative superiority and inferiority of groups of individuals—as they were in the 1930s and 1940s for the well-educated doctors in Nazi Germany.

Notes

1. Quoted from Robert E. Cooke, "Introduction," E. Zigler and J. Valentine, eds., *Project Head Start: A Legacy of the War on Poverty* (New York: The Free Press, 1979), xxv. This volume provides the first comprehensive telling of the story of Head Start as a part of Lyndon B. Johnson's "war on poverty."

2. Arthur Jensen, "How Much Can We Boost IQ and Scholastic Achievement"?, *Harvard Educational Review* 39 (1969):1–23.

3. In Ed Zigler, "Head Start: Not a Program but an Evolving Concept," Ibid., 369.

4. Kenneth Kenniston and the Carnegie Council on Children, *All Our Children: The American Family under Pressure* (New York: Harcourt Brace Jovanovich, 1977), 79. It is interesting to note that one of the Research Associates with the Carnegie Council at the time of this publication was a woman named Hillary Rodham.

5. Richard Herrnstein and Charles Murray, *The Bell Curve: Intelligence and Class Structure in American Life* (New York: The Free Press, 1994).

6. Richard Pintner, *Intelligence Testing* (New York: Henry Holt and Co., 1923), 395.

7. *Wall Street Journal,* December 13, 1994. It is interesting to note that of the 100 individuals approached to be listed assignatories of the statement, only about half agreed to do so.

8

Robert Jay Lifton and Biology:
The Doctor Is In—Knock Twice

Lionel Tiger

In my opinion the most important of Lifton's works is *The Nazi Doctors* because there he comes closest to challenging the congenial zeitgeist of his community which depends on the premise of well-meaning intelligent meliorism. Of course his work on survivors and nuclear bombing is profound and irreplaceable. But it is also within the sentimental comfort zone of our particular period of history. After all, this is a time in which the location of evil within humanity itself is wildly threatening to the ambient general commitment to improvement in all things. This now may conceptually include the human genome, which it is increasingly hoped may be altered or abetted for medical purposes.

This level of physiological realism is at least an improvement over the environmental Lysenkoism which devastated Russian biology and continues to infect North American social science and at least half of contemporary feminist assertion. However we know this genome appears to change as slowly as Death Valley. For example, virtually every important paleoanthropological find extends hominid history further back in time rather than nearer to now. My colleagues Harris and Sileshi at Rutgers have found a tool in Ethiopia over 2.5 million years old which appears to be fully in the hominid line.

Ours is an environmentally skillful and adaptable species able to radiate over the whole planet and robustly occupy an astonishing array of niches. Nevertheless the apparent intransigence of our evolved human material—our conservative gene pool—rarely figures in serious contemporary discussions of behavior. The nature-nurture controversy remains fresh as an argument and a marker of psychosocial positions, even though knowledge about the nature part of the business has expanded mightily, as has our understanding too of what our species finds easy to learn *by nature*, such as Chomskyean language. But the fruitless argument continues to be rekindled by strangely gaseous assertions, recently for example about the biology of intelligence, and race. I.Q. cannot be evaluated by machine-graded tests and anyway has little to do with reproduction, which is what biology is about. Race, however, is an utterly spurious nonbiological category given new life by well-meaning concernocrats earnestly erecting a racist system of social organization in the name of statistically-based equity.

So Lifton has been working in a hazardous intellectual environment in which obedience to the law of parsimony has tended to stop with intermediate sciences such as psychology rather than more molecular ones such as neurophysiology and endocrinology. This had consequence for Lifton's work, and though he is a psychiatrist he had focussed less on the internal secretions in the skull and body which affect behavior than on the external social orders within which people choose their actions.

Nonetheless this is a tribute to a generous life lived with bottomless warmth and an intricate sense of intelligent intrigue. So I want to add to what must be an Upper Broadway showstopper of affectionate praise this small aria of celebration and moderately dyspeptic cavil.

Perhaps it is only diluted neo-Protestantism to conclude that one important measure of a person is the burden they elect to carry. By this standard of personal seriousness, certainly Lifton has chosen to scrutinize some agonizingly huge human tragedies and to do so with frontal courage and a clear unwillingness to explain away such tragedies with a relatively tailored explanation, for example resting on the scapegoat principle. I recall a strenuous conversation at his and BJ's dinner table in which Wiesel was asserting with obvious appropriateness the special nature of German evil during World War Two. Several of us including Robert wanted to retain the option to generalize the existence of the forces which animated such stunning human behavior. Subsequent grisly adventures such as in Rwanda and Bosnia support the unhappy utility of a general not a specific source of explanation for catastrophic human evil. Mark it in your calendar: inhumanity may be panhuman.

And it is only on this point I want to focus briefly. It illustrates a potentially important feature of the emergent science surrounding human aggression and implicitly human evil. A central parsimonious point is that the principal animators and conductors of evil aggression are males. This is consistent with data from the study of other animals and certainly of our fellow higher primates. Therefore the law of parsimony requires we consider the impact of gender and what composes it in the human species. Therefore when we contemplate aggression and violence, this effort should include such gender-linked matters as endocrine secretions, reproductive strategy, impacts of musculature, and the underlying economies of emotional affiliation involved in kinship and mate selection.

Such matters were not primary foci of Lifton's work. There is little reason why they should have been given scientific art at the time and the surely debilitating emotional enormity of what he was confronting. Nonetheless the value of his effort should now be augmented by the addition of what appears to some scientists an irreplaceable array of new data and concepts about human violence and its associated conditions. For example, it is now rather clear that depressed levels of serotonin are linked to enhanced propensity to aggression. While the specific science is not wholly reliable—you can't of course say Joe will run amuck because of neurotransmitter deficits—nonetheless it is plausible to consider that a group of Joes suffering from this might well be more likely than another group to produce violent behavior or at least condone it in its membership. And since we know that depressed serotonin is associated with declines in social status, then broad social factors are intrinsic to the neurophysiology of the matter. Certain kinds of poor people are deprived not just of material things and behavioral options but also of social experience associated with the neurotransmitters of pleasure and satisfaction. And the truncated and harshly hedged reproductive and parental options of contemporary poor males probably have more to do than we suspect with skinhead politics. Marx wrote the political agenda at the beginning of the century but it now seems that Darwin stimulates the central agenda as it ends. There are materialist processes at work in the head and body just as there are outside.

This is not to claim full explanatory power here for such considerations but rather to add them to the list of serious factors to consider in studying this behavior. I presume Lifton would be first to crack the book on the subject, to see what was there. That's his style of intellectual embrace. He really wants to know, however depressing, what animates human tragedy and why people do remarkably bad things. I am personally aware of this because during a period of intellectual and scientific history, particularly in the 70s, when it was not only controversial but even dangerous and emotionally perilous to consider such issues as the biology of gender and aggression, Lifton was not only personally and professionally friendly to what I for one was doing but explicitly open to what the science might reveal. He kept pushing, just as he was unilaterally unwilling to lose at tennis, even to a short guy like me.

It's good that now there's much more to pay attention to which is sturdy and revealing. Shrewder questions, better answers, more reliable tools, a fuller sense of the ingredients of living systems. And in the neighborhood where Lifton patrols, there's treacherously important work left to do. Onward and upward. Onward and inward.

9

Violence, Selfhood, and the Ambiguities of Truth

Lillian Feder

James Ahmed, one of the major characters of V.S. Naipaul's *Guerrillas*,[1] is a fictional version of Michael X, a.k.a. Michael Abdul Malik, a Black Power leader in London and Trinidad during the late 1960s and early 1970s. Once a controversial figure, admired by some, scorned by others, Malik, though now generally forgotten, retains a historical and literary interest as an example of the charismatic con man and as the model who hardly seems to warrant the sympathy his fictive counterpart can evoke.

Malik's brief career can be gleaned from a number of sources, among them newspaper articles that appeared in London and Trinidad, his own ghosted autobiography, *From Michael de Freitas to Michael X*,[2] Derek Humphrey and David Tindall's *False Messiah: The Story of Michael X*,[3] and Naipaul's essay, "Michael X and the Black Power Killings in Trinidad."[4] Together, they cover his years in England and Trinidad, where his activities ranged from dealing in drugs and women to leading a Black Power movement and finally to murder, for which he was sentenced to death. These sources provide the background of the referential action of *Guerrillas*, which depicts individual internalizations of the racial conflict of the 1960s and 1970s. Referential, obviously, not as objective accounts or as bases of absolute legal or moral judgments but as material for the introspective narratives that Michael X and his followers enacted in fact and in fiction. The very divergences of these accounts contribute to our understanding of the violent yet somehow pathetic figure who in Naipaul's fictive characterization finally confronts truths about himself he has long evaded even while driven to betray them as fiction.

The word "truth" occurs frequently throughout Naipaul's writings and interviews, never as some immutable essence, divine or historical. It is rather an ongoing process, an uncharted quest. When he speaks of truth as one's "whole response to the world,"[5] he refers to an individual mind contending with barriers to its authentic interpretations of experience. Many of his characters seek their own forms of truth, impelled and inhibited by their social and personal history. The most unlikely and bizarre of these characters is Jimmy Ahmed.

How does Naipaul educe this measure of dignity from his model, a self-described "hustler," a pimp, drug-pusher, questionable Black activist, would-be writer, and finally murderer? What truths about himself, his society, and the people with whom his life intersects does Jimmy Ahmed, Malik's fictive counterpart, reveal and discover? How are his efforts to define himself and to retreat from self-knowledge central to the action and theme of *Guerrillas*? These issues comprise the subject of my paper.

As an activist in London, Malik was able to attract prominent and wealthy white supporters who donated large sums of money for his various projects. But the Racial Adjustment Action Society (RAAS), Black House, and other institutions he founded received little of these contributions, most of which Malik appropriated. By the end of 1970, facing a criminal indictment for extortion by physical abuse from the manager of an employment agency, he withdrew from the Black Power movement and early in July 1971 fled to Trinidad. There on the strength of his reputation in London, he was able to raise money for a so-called commune in Arima, where he was joined by former associates, among them his old friends, Stanley Abbott and Steve Yeates, and visited by others who had not known him personally but were drawn by his putative accomplishments. Hakim Jamal, a Black American, and Gale Benson, a white Englishwoman, whom Naipaul describes as "an itinerant hustling team,"[6] came seeking refuge. The couple, who had met in England and travelled together to France, Morocco, the United States, and Guyana, performed their own Muslim marriage ceremony. Both psychologically fragile, they provided, however bizarre the means, some measure of stability for each other. Gale announced her symbiotic attachment to Hakim by calling herself Halé Kimga, an anagram of their names. She accepted his designation of himself as God and worshipped him accordingly. He basked in her adoration, encouraged in his projects, comforted in his failures.

Disheartened by the rejection of his various proposals to the government of Guyana and his expulsion from the country, Hakim accepted a passive role in the commune in Trinidad, even surrendering his divinity to Malik. But Gale soon became suspicious of Malik, who concluded that she was a spy. Facing discord among members of his commune, finding it increasingly difficult to raise money, he decided to assert his authority and to reunite his followers through a ritual sacrifice: the scapegoat was Gale Benson. Although Malik instigated the murder and others knew about or were involved in it, it was actually Steve Yeates who on January 2, 1972, struck the final blow. A month later, when Malik's cousin, Joseph Skerritt, became suspicious about Gale Benson's disappearance, Malik himself murdered Skerritt.[7] When the bodies were discovered, Malik was in Guyana, where the police found him hiding in the woods. In August 1972 he was pronounced guilty and sentenced to death for the murder of Skerritt. His appeal was supported by many prominent people, among them William Kunstler, Kate Millett, Dick Gregory, William Burroughs, and John Lennon and Yoko Ono,[8] but to no avail. He was hanged on May 16, 1975.

Malik's autobiography and Naipaul's essay on the Black Power killings provide some insight into the temperament of the man whose life was so bleak and violent, and his metamorphosis into Jimmy Ahmed. The "I" of *From Michael de Freitas to Michael X* is most engaging in its contradictions, resulting chiefly, but not entirely, from his representation of himself as a black man struggling for survival in a white society. Explaining his choice of a white English ghost-writer, whom he names John X, Malik expresses his surprise and delight in their capacity to traverse what had seemed to him impassable avenues of "thought and expression" between the races. But even if the Sunday *Times* (September 24, 1967) had not reported that John X was an officer of the Central Office of Information, obvious disparities between voice and subject would suggest the very barriers that Malik denies. Malik left school at fourteen and for many years was either a seaman or a pimp, yet the language of large parts of the autobiography, especially the sections on social and racial issues, is, with some concessions, that of an educated man. The tone, while sympathetic toward oppressed blacks, is often impersonal. After a passage of reporting and brief analysis of racial conflict, the first-person narrator returns as a surprise. Occasionally, when John X tries to capture the idiom of the shebeen or the marijuana- and alcohol-inspired revels, only a ghostly approximation emerges.

Malik's decisions and projects consistently reveal contradictions between his ambitions and his meager emotional and moral investment in any undertaking. Inspired by one of his lovers, a white Jewish woman, he decided to study "sociology, which was a subject I found increasingly interesting." But, as he explains, he needed money and thus returned to hustling. Finding little or no time left for college, he dropped out after "twenty lessons in all." Yet in the autobiography his ghost presents him as a man of sociological insight, an articulate teacher and lecturer. His personal relations disclose similar separations of act and affect. Having settled down with Desirée, a woman he claims to love, he soon became sexually involved with a prostitute, a relationship he or his ghost calls "a commercial proposition." His use of women for sex and money or both persists throughout the portion of his life recorded in *From Michael de Freitas to Michael X*.

The autobiography repeatedly asserts that communication and trust are impossible between blacks and whites, yet among Malik's friends and supporters were middle- and upper-class whites. The only woman who emerges as a person in her own right is Nancy, a white Jew. "Talking with Nancy," he says, "a slow transformation began in me." He tells of beginning to read seriously and to recognize "how limited my vocabulary and general knowledge were." He refers to the superficiality of his "ideas" and the inadequacy of his "arguments." But, at least from the evidence of his autobiography, his "transformation" was merely into a temporary new guise. Examining himself after he had become a Black Power leader, he feels obliged to admit his hypocrisy: all the while he was lecturing others on the evils of whites and on the degradation of black men in their relations with white women, he had been involved in an affair with a wealthy white woman whom he used as "a source of income" for RAAS. Characteristically, he blames not himself but the inevitable "effects of the ghetto."

Malik's autobiography ends with an assertion and a prophecy. "I have no fear of losing my own identity," he insists as he expresses his objection to interracial marriage and predicts that increasing hostility between blacks and whites in England will end in an "explosion." About himself he was, as usual, deluded. Yet this autobiography tells more about Malik than he was aware of or perhaps wished to reveal. It portrays a man continually adopting pseudo-identities—lover, husband, Black leader, painter, writer, humanitarian—all unearned, authentic only as failed efforts to achieve psychic integration. According to one account, even the name Michael X, which the title suggests is a form of self-definition, was acquired through a misunderstanding during his brief association with Malcolm X, who referred to him as his "brother."[9] As to the "explosion," racial clashes did continue to occur, but certainly not on the scale that Malik predicted.

From Michael de Freitas to Michael X is more interesting for what it suggests than for what it tells, for the clues to what is omitted, which Naipaul followed in his essay and in his novel. In both works he deals chiefly with events following the period covered in the autobiography, but he weaves facts about Malik's earlier life and, especially in *Guerrillas*, feelings unexpressed but intimated into the violent outcome of Malik's return to Trinidad. Throughout "Michael X and the Black Power Killings in Trinidad" he views Malik as "shallow and unoriginal, . . . an entertainer." Of the autobiography he says: "It is not the story of a life or the development of a personality." Malik "is without a personality; he is only a haphazard succession of roles." Still, when he briefly explores the etiology of Malik's instability, his shifting "personalities," it is with compassion for a figure whose conduct hardly elicits it.

Naipaul's leading clue is Malik's relationship with his mother, who, as portrayed in *From Michael de Freitas to Michael X*, "is as puzzling as Malik." His summary of this puzzle includes Malik's mixed parentage—his mother was black, his father a Portuguese shopkeeper, de Freitas, who deserted her and their son—and the contradictory behavior of the mother, as Malik describes her, a racist snob, "forever preaching the beauty of whiteness," which she equated with propriety, but herself a drunkard, a hustler, and a brothel keeper. "Certain facts about his mother are too important to the narrator for him to leave out," says Naipaul. "But the facts have been scattered about the picaresque narrative: a pain greater than the one stated is being concealed." What Naipaul surmises is that the mother, who came from Barbados and was a stranger in Trinidad, now married to a black man, "was disgraced by her red bastard" son, as he "was disgraced" by her bizarre conduct. "She was uneducated, drunken, vicious."

Naipaul considers a letter that Malik sent to his mother from London, defining himself as a "negro" and recalling how she had repeatedly humiliated him, "the truest thing Malik ever wrote, and the most moving. It explains the change of names from de Freitas to X, the assumption of so many personalities, the anxiety to please. A real torment was buried in the clowning of the racial entertainer. Black power gave order and logic to the life; it provided Malik with a complete system." As the autobiography and Naipaul's further comments on Malik's exploits suggest, the Black Power movement was but one of several avenues in Malik's quest for self-definition. In fact, each time Naipaul touches on this central unfulfilled need, the harshness of his portrayal of Malik in the essay is mitigated by his apprehension of Malik's "torment."

The autobiography confirms Naipaul's view that Malik regarded the educated, professional black as "not quite a Negro," that the "real Negro" who "lived in a place called the 'ghetto' . . . was a ponce or a drug peddler; he begged and stole; he was that attractive Negro thing, a 'hustler.' " But Naipaul's conclusion that to Malik the "real Negro" was "someone like" himself speaks for only one of the self-images Malik enacted. The other, the would-be writer, teacher, lecturer, who had white friends and lovers, comes all too close to being "not quite a Negro."

If the first image was, as Naipaul says, "a construct for a provincial market," it was fundamentally, I believe, a retaliation against the mother who denied his blackness and thus his elemental connection with herself. The second, which conformed, however meretriciously, to his mother's demands, was yet to be used in the service of the first. Hence, while defying the mother he rejected, he never quite relinquished his desire to be the son she would accept. This conflict, at the heart of Malik's anguish, remained unresolved; he enacted it throughout his life.

"Michael X and the Black Power Killings in Trinidad" contains examples of Malik's writings, even with their errors in spelling and grammar and their "borrowed words," straining for an ideal of himself that would integrate these two roles. As author, narrator, or character, Malik is "famous" and handsome, his "beautiful golden brown skin" uniting his African and Portuguese heritage. In notes he took while still in England for a planned but unwritten sequel to his autobiography, he refers to his "Hero Image," which is "greater overseas." But, as Naipaul's quotations from the novel Malik was writing in Trinidad suggest, this exalted image was only part of his psychic and fictive narrative. In fragments of this novel Naipaul sees evidence of a "resentment, soon settling into hatred . . . of the English middle class [Malik] had got to know." Malik, who appears in the novel under his own name, is at first a figure who inspires admiration and even awe among the powerful English characters, but they soon grow to fear him. In Guyana, where the novel is set, he is regarded as a "hero," and, in Naipaul's paraphrase, "there are people in the streets who shout for him to be king." The narrators shift from Lena Boyd-Richardson, a young Englishwoman, to third person, to Sir Harold, a friend of Lena's father. As narrator, Lena is contemptuous of the "natives" but clearly has mixed feelings about Mike (Malik), whom she describes as "like some statue on a Pedestal, some god," worshipped by his followers. Since he appears to be well-read, she is astonished when he addresses her alternately in pidgin and in Cockney, and she is troubled by evidence of his "weird double Life." She then admits to being "scared . . . mortally afraid of this man of this Mike the grinning ape," whom she can't help liking. An episode Lena recounts suggests that she has good reason for fearing his apparently motiveless rage with its threat of violence. These fragments, says Naipaul, "survived the events they seem so curiously to foreshadow."

If Malik, writing this novel in his commune in Trinidad, was "arriving," as Naipaul says, "at some new definition of himself," it consisted of more grandiose versions of his earlier conflicting images: of the canny black hustler who could best the white middle class and the cultured black leader apotheosized. But nothing that Malik could achieve in Trinidad—neither his agricultural commune nor his comfortable house in Arima nor the aid of supporters in England and the United States—could match his own fictive imaginings. No Sir Harold would ever shout: "We go crown him king." Finally, he enacted the alienation and rage that motivated these fantasies of omnipotence in murder.

After quoting fragments of Malik's novel, Naipaul comments: "An autobiography can distort; facts can be aligned. But fiction never lies: it reveals the writer totally." He is here comparing Malik's ghosted autobiography with his fiction, but the statement has broader implications. Throughout Naipaul's work the development of selfhood is continuous exploration, inner narratives expressed in action, dialogue, and often in writing, all of which reveal individuals' drive to create themselves within the context, and often against the constraints, of their society and history. Thus, the self is the conveyor of "the truth of [one's] responses,"[10] especially in the act of writing. When his characters write, their words obliquely disclose desires and motives they have not previously acknowledged, even to themselves. In *Guerrillas*, James Ahmed (Jimmy), Malik's fictive counterpart, emerges as a more vivid figure than his model; he elucidates Malik's aspirations, his struggle for autonomy, his pain, and his violence. Jimmy's fiction is part of this revelation as are his relations with other characters in the novel.

Guerrillas portrays the elaborate political and psychic stratagems devised to avoid the truth of experience during a period of racial conflict on an unidentified Caribbean island which bears a strong resemblance to Trinidad. Jimmy, the son of a black mother and a Chinese father, is but one of three leading characters. Like Malik, he has fled from the law in London, but unlike Malik, who was accompanied by his wife and children, Jimmy arrives alone. His deepest erotic attraction is to one of the members of his commune, Bryant, a poor uneducated young man who can only "grieve for what was denied him": the opportunity to become what he truly was, "a man as loved and as happy as Sidney Poitier in the film *For Love of Ivy.*

The other major characters are Peter Roche, a white South African, who seems culturally and psychologically related to Malik's British supporters, and Jane (she is given no surname), his English lover, who bears some resemblance to Naipaul's depiction of Gale Benson in his essay.

Roche, who was tortured in his homeland for engaging in protests against apartheid, now works in public relations for Sablich's, a firm eager to atone for its unsavory history as slave-traders by sponsoring Jimmy's so-called agricultural commune. His dubious role on the island exacts his admission that "every decision he had made had been made after he had disregarded some element of the truth." Jane has come from England to join Roche, hoping to identify herself with a man and a cause. Chief among the other characters who enact the narrator's multifaceted conception of truth are Meredith Herbert, a black journalist, solicitor, and politician whose wish "just to be oneself" articulates a goal he knows he cannot achieve or abandon; and Harry de Tunja, a type of wandering Jew whom Meredith describes as "never blind . . . The one man in the country."

The novel opens soon after Jane's arrival as she and Roche are on their way to visit Jimmy at his commune, Thrushcross Grange. As they drive, the windows of these outsiders' car frame politics, commerce, and nature reacting on each other: political slogans, a sea smelling of "swamp," "bauxite dust," a dump, a new housing development already decaying, hills, suburbs, and factories. The approach to the commune is indicated by signs announcing *For the Land and the Revolution,* donated by American and local firms protecting their investments by cynical accommodation to Jimmy's demands. Roche's and Jane's disillusion with each other is intensified by the atmosphere of waste, rot, exploitation. Soon after Jane is introduced to Jimmy, the three are bound together in their despair of finding satisfaction in who they are or what they do, as each recognizes the others' efforts to buttress a fragile sense of self by embracing the struggle against racial discrimination.

After their first meeting Jimmy uses Jane as a fictive projection of his fantasies of omnipotence—a blend of hate and longing for esteem. Disturbed by his reaction to Jane's and Roche's visit, he seeks relief from feelings of depersonalization, from "a vision of darkness," in a narrative written from her first-person point of view, harsh toward the island with its "good-for-nothing natives" and adoring toward him. Having perceived the beginnings of Jane's disillusionment with Roche, he attributes to her surrogate his own contempt for Peter's motives as Sablich's representative at the commune: he is merely using the "natives," including Jimmy himself, to enhance his own reputation as a leader who endured torture for the black people of South Africa.

Jimmy, on the other hand, who "was like a celebrity in London," is a "savior" who "understands and loves the common man" and inspires fear in "the rich white firms." She responds to his color, "not black, but golden, like some bronze god." Roche, she says, is becoming "jealous" of him and has become physically "repugnant" to her. Only at the end of this outpouring of self-adulation does Jimmy, writing with mounting excitement, grant his smitten narrator the insight he has gleaned in the act of writing as he fuses a memory of his brief triumph in London with his present fantasy, which is a clue to his future. After his fictive Jane acknowledges that Jimmy "must hate people like me," since she is "middle-class born and bred," she echoes a description of him by a woman quoted in an English newspaper: "I have only to look in his eyes to understand the meaning of hate." The reader learns that it is a quotation only later in the novel when Meredith mockingly asks Jane, "Did you look into his eyes and understand the meaning of hate?" and then goes on to reveal its source. Through Meredith's prescience Naipaul unites fact with several levels of fiction: Malik's calculating approach to the women he lured in London and his reputation as a dangerous ladies' man become part of Jimmy's past—the background of his present conduct and of his fiction which, like Malik's, "never lies." Meredith's question also presages the danger that Jane is to court in her flirtation with Jimmy.

The distortions of Jimmy's narrative, like those of a dream, disclose the processes of their creation: his self-hatred projected on the "natives" and transformed into its opposite in his grandiose image of goodness and power. The world he has fashioned Jane to represent, which he envies and wishes to possess and to destroy, is condensed in her adoration, her desire to take him in and to be possessed. But recognition of the generation of his desire in hatred leaves Jimmy spent. Only the source of his narrative remains: "Melancholy, . . . like fatigue, like rage, like a sense of doom." When he tries to resume writing, the words are "false." A short time later, he begins a letter to an English friend named Roy to whom he is more direct in expressing his despair, which combines pity and rage at the condition to which those for whom "the world is made" have reduced the underprivileged, particularly the boys at his commune, deprived even of hope. His only recourse, he says, is to "destroy the world" which has betrayed him and them. But this "destructive urge" passes, replaced by an admission that all he can actually do is exploit "liberals" like Roche, whom he despises: "I play along, what can you do—" Like Bryant, Jimmy sees himself as "lost" and, turning to him, he seeks comfort in embracing his most forlorn image of himself.

This episode foreshadows the two "sexual scenes" on which Naipaul has said the novel "hangs."[11] These, which involve Jimmy and Jane, with Roche and Bryant as accessories, have nothing to do with affection or

even physical attraction. Parodies of lovemaking, they are desperate forays into a fantasy domain of selfhood by people who lack the psychological and moral integrity to withstand or counter the political cynicism
and cultural instability of their society. These scenes are focal because
they enact the most extreme effects of alienation on society's most vulnerable individuals, whatever their race or class.

Jane had been drawn to Roche in London after reading his recently
published book on his imprisonment and torture in South Africa. Aim-
less, emotionally empty, regarding herself as a victim, she had chosen
him as her guide to "real events and real action," her rescuer from the
decay she perceived in the middle-class environment into which she was
born and which she blamed for the blight on her early marriage, on her
love affairs, on her very hopes for personal fulfillment. Imagining Roche
as the "doer" who had chosen to leave London for "some new and as
yet unsuspected center of world disturbance," she had joined him on
the island, only to discover that once again her homemade hero was no
longer of use to her and, like all her earlier products, disposable. It is an
old story in life and in art, but Naipaul invests it with a new psychological
complexity that reveals how intimately individual conduct is linked to
the political and social consequences of colonialism.

Having realized that Roche, the seeming enemy of imperialism, is actually its offspring and has become its appeaser, a "half-colonial" himself, Jane plans to return to London. She has given up not only on Roche
but on life on the Ridge, a suburb inhabited by transient bureaucrats
and expatriots intimidated by newspaper reports of guerrillas threatening what little stability the island had offered them. But she puts off her
departure. Four months after her arrival, she is ripe for still another
victimization—this time by Jimmy.

The prelude to the first "sexual scene" repeats the pattern of Jimmy's
reaction to Jane's and Roche's visit with which the novel begins: Jimmy
writing, his uneasiness at his own disclosures, his reaching out to Bryant
for physical and emotional comfort. This time, however, he will attempt
to enact his written narrative with Jane, who remains the narrator of his
novel, now named Clarissa.

Jimmy has been writing about a meeting with Clarissa, who once again
expresses her conviction that only "a woman of [her] class" can appreciate his intrinsic nobility, and foresees the day when the "shiftless" blacks
will present him with a crown. Longing for Jimmy, Clarissa confesses
that she phoned him but was so overcome by her feelings that she was
unable to speak when he answered. "I put the phone down," says the
narrator. Soon after writing this passage Jimmy phones Jane twice to

arrange for a meeting. The first time, hearing her maid's voice, he "put the telephone down." Jimmy returns to Clarissa who, seeking knowledge of her hero in the newspaper, discovers that he is to address the Lions at the Prince Albert Hotel, where she encounters him after his speech.

Again Jimmy's narrative method becomes that of a dream, merging past with present as Jane/Clarissa is abruptly metamorphosed into a figure out of Jimmy's boyhood. He knew only her story, told by his classmates, "but it had become like a memory." A white girl who had been raped by a gang on a beach had screamed, then fainted, and one of the rapists had brought her water from a creek nearby. This story of an abused, bleeding girl responding with "grateful eyes, remembering terror" to the "cupped hands offering water" had become Jimmy's prototype of romance. Identifying himself with both victim and aggressor, he has fantasized himself involved in a conquest in which he asserts power through sexual cruelty and humiliation, thus incorporating what he hates and envies. In his adaptation of this fantasy to fiction, Jane/Clarissa becomes the raped girl, assuming her "terror" and anticipating the moment when her hero "will bring water in his own cupped hands and I will drink water from his tender hands and I will not be afraid of him anymore."

Writing this passage, Jimmy has become sexually aroused but, as the fantasy fades, he grows uneasy, aware of the "emptiness" of the present. He cannot continue writing. Having long since internalized the raped girl, he conceives of himself as a victim: "He could have screamed like the girl on the Ford fender." After turning to Bryant for comfort, he abruptly leaves him to again phone Jane, asking her to meet him at the Prince Albert the next day, pretending that he has an appointment there with some business executives.

Naipaul, it will be recalled, described Malik in "Michael X and the Black Power Killings in Trinidad" as "only a succession of roles." In *Guerrillas*, depicting Jimmy, like Malik, merging with various figures he knows or invents—Bryant, the raped girl, and now Jane, he portrays this process manifested in Jimmy's fiction and then in the devious turns of the narrative enacted with a partner whose responses are, to a large extent, beyond his control.

When Jane and Jimmy meet at the Prince Albert it is clear that he is hardly motivated by sexual attraction. As Jane approaches the lobby, Jimmy notes her "clumsy" walk, her "characterless" face, her mouth intimating weakness and "cruelty." Jane asks about his so-called meeting, but Jimmy has momentarily forgotten his pretense: "As in a dream he saw confused swift events: a drive to his house, her reading of his writings, exposure." On some level Jimmy perceives the connection between the sado-masochistic fantasies of his novel and his interest in Jane. When she refers to his speech to the business men, he asks, "The Lions?" an allusion to his fiction, now fused with the telephone invitation in which he had mentioned only executives. Jane's immediate association is Roche. "Peter is a Lion," she says. "Was he there?" Jimmy's response is a bitter attack on Sablich's, founded by slave traders, hated for its past corruption and present efforts at respectability. "Massa's firm," he calls it. To Jane's insistence, "But not mine," Jimmy replies ambiguously, "Look. I don't want us to be friends." Suppressing her initial uneasiness, Jane interprets the comment as an avowal of sexual interest, evading the implications of his refusal to accept her dissociation from Roche's guilt.

On the way to Jimmy's house a moving car is once more a literal and figurative vehicle of perception as Jane, looking out the window, observes details of the city she had hitherto ignored. Focusing on an old female vendor, beggars, dying dogs, slums infesting natural beauty, she projects on the city her own emotional slumming, fearing yet seeking psychic dissolution. But when they arrive, the excitement she has induced is gone. His home, Jimmy himself, have become all too mundane, and she turns to the business of the afternoon, sex, with aggressive detachment.

From the beginning their efforts at lovemaking are frustrating, Jane's demands and Jimmy's fantasies unfulfilled. Soon they are interrupted by a phone call from Roche, followed by Bryant's footsteps "somewhere in the house," both foreshadowing political turmoil and personal disaster. The fruitless exertions to which they return—her contrivances, his rage emerging in an attempt at sodomy, and finally her effort to evoke some feeling with the ritualistic formula "Love, love"—end in impotence and hatred. Three times Naipaul refers to Jimmy's disappointment in "losing the moment" he had wished to "witness," the moment of his conquest of the rich white adversary reduced to his adoring slave. But Jane has refused the role of Clarissa or the raped girl. As she leaves him, Jimmy associates her with a "prostitute," emerging "triumphant" after "defeat and degradation." In pain and despair, he longs for "Bryant's warm firm flesh and his relieving mouth and tongue."

Typically, Jimmy's image of Jane as "triumphant" is a reaction to his spoiled narrative. It has nothing to do with the actual woman whom he has no desire to understand. On the way home in a hired car, Jane feels only the "distress" of repeated frustration as an inner voice reviews her own past and present conduct: "I've looked *everywhere*. I've looked and looked." Shifting from his character's narrative to his own, Naipaul uses the word "looked" three times, as she does, conveying empathy in the repetition: "She looked at the driver's mirror," feeling judged as she met his stare. In an effort to escape him, she "looked" out the window, but she was drawn back to the mirror, "and whenever she looked . . . she saw his red assessing eyes." There is empathy also in the contrast between the two ways of looking: Jane's looking "everywhere" has been an evasion of herself, a search for a projected savior, which has led her to the present reality that she feels compelled to confront in the driver's eyes. Now the warning, "I've been playing with fire," comes to her "like an intimation of the truth." For readers acquainted with Naipaul's essay it is as if the narrator who has modeled her neediness and vulnerability on Gale Benson's would save both of them from themselves. But, given his "truth" to the events that compel him and the character of Jane, he cannot.

That night Jane turns to Roche for comfort, asking to share his bed. Meanwhile Jimmy, impatiently awaiting Bryant's return, continues his letter to Roy, in which he depicts himself as the despairing leader who can no longer "control the revolution." He mentions Stephens, a young gang leader who has left the Grange and whom he now considers a rival and a threat. It is here that he enlarges on his earlier contemptuous assessment of Stephens, "Everybody wants to be a leader," with the statement that Naipaul uses as his epigraph: "When everybody wants to fight, there's nothing to fight for. Everybody wants to fight his own little war, everybody is a guerrilla."

Bryant appears, obviously enraged by Jane's visit, but nonetheless the representative of lost, subservient youth dependent on the master, a presence comforting enough to lift Jimmy's despair and restore his sense of control. When he continues writing, he takes up his novel and the voice of Clarissa, who is obviously being punished for Jane's rejection of her assigned role. This section of Jimmy's novel begins where the last one left off, repeating the same motifs; only here his hatred and fear are intensified by his failure to subjugate his oppressors personified in Jane. When Clarissa warns the hero that they intend to "destroy the leaders," he accuses her of belonging to "the establishment." Hatred of the vestiges of colonialism in his society and in himself are expressed in sexual terms throughout this passage: Jimmy tells Clarissa that she is "rotten meat," and she senses his judgment in the eyes of waiters and taxi drivers, in "every face I see." The seemingly innocuous phrase "Of course" takes on sinister implications as it introduces her confession (and through her, Jimmy's own) of hatred for the "shiftless" people and the acknowledgment that "this hate and scorn . . . is bringing retribution." Finally, she is chased by boys who look like Bryant and she becomes the raped girl. At this point Bryant, who has been sitting in the room, screams, "Jimmy I see the white rat today." Jimmy's response is a promise to "give her to" him.

By the end of the first third of *Guerrillas* Jimmy has plotted his narrative for the next sexual scene, which is to take place a few pages before the book's conclusion. Between these two episodes rebellion against the government intensifies, indicating that however megalomaniacal Jimmy's fictive self-image and however melodramatic his view of the inevitable "revolution," he is a shrewd observer of the political scene and of the individuals involved as participants or victims. More acute than Malik, he is as incapable as his model of action immune from his self-destructive impulses.

At a gathering at the beach house of Harry de Tunja, whose surname is one of several his family had come by as people identified them by "the last place" they had fled, he tells his guests of an old black man he encountered on the street recently who pointed at him and said, "You! You is a Jew!" For Harry the episode is but one of many signs that he does not belong on the island, that it is again time to flee. To the consternation of Jane, Roche, and other middle-class Caucasians, the De Tunjas have been planning to emigrate to Canada. Equally unsettling is the news that Harry's wife has left him. The couple, whom they had chosen to represent harmonious family life, has become another example of the instability threatening them all.

With the arrival of Meredith Herbert at the beach house the tension increases as precarious political and social affiliations merge to arouse suspicion in relations that had once seemed secure. Roche had admired Meredith's integrity, his pleasure in his work as solicitor and radio interviewer as well as in his family, but gradually, influenced by Jane, he had begun to mistrust "the personality that had attracted him and seemed so restful," regarding it as a mere "creation." Harry, the most open and direct of men, suspects Meredith of "getting a little closer to the powers that be." Both assessments have some validity, but both fall short of the complex figure Naipaul has portrayed as simultaneously bound to and reacting against historical forces. For Meredith self-creation is not the disguise that Roche assumes it is. The "hysteria, . . . the deprivations, and unappeased ambition" that Roche senses behind Meredith's domesticity are no more definitive than is his image of personal wholeness in a fragmented society. Implicit in Meredith's expression of the wish to be himself totally is a lifetime's struggle against the oppression his race and class have endured. The very intelligence and talent that have made it possible for him to achieve a leading role in his society have rendered whatever compromises he made on the way violations of the self-image he retains against all odds.

Meredith seems compelled to speak of Jimmy, whom he had known as a child and was to encounter later in London where he had become "this great Negro leader." Jimmy's "English glamour," he says, is "dangerous," a cover for his inner emptiness: "he's nothing at all" and thus can be used to "create chaos." Roche, as usual, temporizes, refusing to heed the warning. This exchange occurs as riots break out in reaction to the killing of Stephens by the police that very morning. In the state of emergency declared by the government amid fires and explosions, the rebellion seems to have no center, no program or established leaders. Harry de Tunja, on hearing that the police are abandoning their posts, confirms Jimmy's earlier observations: "I don't see how you can blame the police. They don't know who they are fighting or who they are fighting for. Everybody down there is a leader now."

Isolated on the Ridge, Jane and Roche rely on Harry for whatever information he can obtain. His levelheadedness in this crisis contrasts with their confusion, his kindness to them with their open hatred for each other. Feeling themselves trapped on the island, their customary defenses useless, each faces the situation alone.

Down in the city, Jimmy, leading the rioters bearing Stephens' body through the streets, and Meredith, representing a government he mistrusts, are alike in denying what they know. Both pay for their compromises. Jimmy is soon dropped by the rioters, replaced by others who declare themselves leaders. Meredith is stripped and assailed by the mob. As Harry says, "A child could have told Meredith that they were calling him back to the government just to throw him to the crowd."

With the arrival of American helicopters, the rebellion comes to an end. "The Americans are not going to let anybody here stop them lifting the bauxite," says Harry, yet he has scoffed at the radio news report that "the disturbances were sparked off by radical youth groups protesting against unemployment and what they see as continued foreign domination of the economy." It is true that the young gang leaders' slogans reveal no consciousness of the bases of their dissatisfactions, only messianic visions of undefined black power. In "Michael X and the Black Power Killings in Trinidad," Naipaul regards race as an "irrelevance" in Trinidad, "but the situation" as "well suited to the hysteria and evasions of racial politics." The situation he describes is one in which "agriculture . . . declines," and "industry, where it exists, is rudimentary, protected and inflationary." Poverty and unemployment are widespread. There is "the sense of a land being pillaged rather than built up." Still, in his portraits of Malik in that essay and, in *Guerrillas* of Jimmy and of Meredith, so different from both except in this one respect, race is not irrelevant. The past of colonialism and slavery and continues to exert its hold on the present in the economic, cultural and psychic deprivations recurrent in Jimmy's and Meredith's memories and are the heritage of the black gang leaders. The outcome of the contest between the gangs and the American helicopters was never in question. Acceding, however ambivalently, to Sablich's paternalism, to foreign exploitation of the island's natural resources, Roche thinks it "odd" that people on the island speak of "their childhoods as of a period only just discovered and understood." Ever an outsider, he cannot comprehend that a measure of political independence so recently acquired exposes the infirmities of the self formed in servitude. Disorganized and ultimately ineffectual, the rioters nonetheless communicate a desire for self-determination. Malik's and Jimmy's final cruelty and violence enact the most disastrous effects of what Naipaul considers the essential "problems" of their society: "dignity and identity."[12]

As the city returns to normal, Meredith uses a radio interview with Roche to strengthen his restored position as minister in the surviving government. In a dusty, stifling room, the air-conditioner intentionally turned off, Roche is again a victim, this time submitting to intellectual bullying reinforced with physical discomfort, a milder version of his treatment in South Africa. Too passive to protest, he is gradually manipulated into mentioning Jimmy, opening the way for Meredith's denunciation of him as a dangerous fraud. Questions about Roche's book and thus about his admittedly fruitless guerrilla activities in South Africa lead to the issue of Thrushcross Grange as a "cover for the guerrillas." Later, discussing the interview with Jane, Roche can only assent to her judgment: "You've left Jimmy out there for Meredith and those other people to kill." For Roche the interview had been a public confession of the failure of his work with Jimmy and the so-called commune, of the shallowness of his commitment to the cause of racial equality, of a life without focus, personal or political. Now, prolonging his humiliation, he confesses to Jane that he left England not out of conviction but out of fear, which she interprets as a personal affront, an exposure of the last traces of her spoiled fantasy. She retaliates by announcing that Jimmy has been her lover, their one frustrated attempt at loveless coupling her only defense against nothingness. To this she returns.

Once again before Jane's visit, Jimmy is writing, this time a letter to

Marjorie, a woman with whom he had an affair in London, telling her that her prophecy is "coming true. I am dying alone and unloved and I will die in anger." Part self-analysis, part apologia, the letter conveys the convergence of impulses to be enacted in the rape and murder of Jane. To Marjorie, the woman who first revealed his "manhood" to him and who, like everyone else, has betrayed him, Jimmy writes in his own person of the hate that his fictive persona Clarissa had seen in his eyes. His portrayal of Marjorie, his "maker" and destroyer, is an indictment of all women. With her he could "know the joy" of being himself, but the consequences of such knowledge were renunciation of the disguises he had first assumed in childhood and the admission that he was indeed "that child in the backroom" of his Chinese father's shop. Inveighing against women who "have no shame and thought for the children who come after them who have to endure all they did," he is no doubt thinking of his mother, described by Meredith as one of "our women [who] went to live with Chinese shopkeepers" for the economic security they offered. Like Malik, he is bitter about his anomalous heritage, especially about the mother who deprived him of his black identity, his source of an authentic self. Like Malik too, he is finally unable to displace his personal alienation in social programs and revolutionary schemes, however spurious. Only his earliest rage and shame remain. Rejected by his former adherents in London, he was sent back to the island "to be nothing," the very word Meredith had used to describe him. Rejected there as a leader by the people he claimed to represent, he is, he admits, "a lost man," lost since childhood.

In the past, writing had aroused him sexually as he concocted sadistic fantasies embellished by his role as savior. Now, having identified himself in the last sentence of his letter with "dead men [who] come once," he exerts the only control left him in the anal rape and murder of Jane, his vengeance on all those he perceives as having used him and finally abandoned him to his enemies. Helpless against the government, Meredith, and Roche, he passes sentence on Jane, the last object of his skewed fantasy of power and romance. Calling her "rotten meat," he then demands recognition: "You know what you are now." This last remark is a slightly revised version of Naipaul's interpretation of Gale Benson's struggle against her murderers. Voiced by Jimmy, its falsity ironically emphasizes the pathos of Jane, who knows so little about herself emotionally and sexually. To the end she does not understand what is happening to her. After the rape she says she will phone for a taxi, but she allows Jimmy to dissuade her. Nor does she struggle when she is cut by Bryant and finally strangled by Jimmy. Having defined herself as a victim for most of her life, she goes to her final victimization passively, as if she could experience herself in no other way.

After he murders Jane, Jimmy feels "nothing except desolation." His devious fantasies, which in the past had offered relief from pain and rage, now confront him with the violence that was their ultimate aim. Jane's dead eyes, on which he can project "nothing," dismiss the girl raped on the beach who had offered him love. He is lost in "a void."

At the end of the novel, Jimmy, aware that Roche knows he has murdered Jane, nonetheless phones him asking for help. Roche's subterfuge, which he assumes Jimmy will comprehend, is that Jane and he are returning to England. Only indirectly does he threaten Jimmy: "I'm leaving you alone," he says. "That's the way it's going to be." Abandoned to be killed, Jimmy replies in the last word of the novel: "Massa." All that is left him is this double-edged epithet, his final self-mockery hurled at the oppressor who came in the name of benefactor.

Roche cannot know that by now Jimmy has accepted the defeat of his long efforts to avoid extinction. Bizarre as his writings are, they constitute his defense against the threat of depersonalization, failed attempts literally to make something of himself. His fiction and letters are a record of pain and rage against injustice distorted into megalomania, cruelty, and even—as in Clarissa in the role of the raped girl—a warped compassion. They are revelations of the inner emptiness he has tried to fill with visions of leadership and power. His final revelations to Marjorie, "I knew I was fooling myself," and to himself, after Jane's murder, "I didn't know who or what I was," obviously do not justify or even fully explain his terrible deeds, but they are his testament to a lifetime's conflict between a need to evade and a compulsion to face truths about himself so damaging as to finally destroy him.

Notes

1. *Guerrillas* (New York: Vintage, 1980 [1975 rpt.]).

2. Michael Abdul Malik, *From Michael de Freitas to Michael X* (London: André Deutsch, 1968).

3. *False Messiah: The Story of Michael X* (London: Hart-Davis, Mac Gibbon, 1977).

4. *The Return of Eva Perón with The Killings in Trinidad* (1980; rpt. New York: Vintage, 1981): 3–97.

5. "V. S. Naipaul," an interview with Adrian Rowe-Evans, *Transition* 40 (1971): 58.

6. "Michael X and the Black Power Killings in Trinidad," 59. A more sympa-

thetic view of the pair, especially of Jamal, can be found in Diana Athill, *Make Believe* (London: Sinclair-Stevenson, 1993).

7. See *False Messiah*, 160–63. Naipaul suggests that "Skerritt had become uneasy with Malik; he began to hide from him," "Michael X and the Black Power Killings in Trinidad," 20.

8. See *False Messiah*, 206–208.

9. Ibid., 48.

10. Rowe-Evans, interview, 56.

11. Bharati Mukherjee and Robert Boyers, "A Conversation with V. S. Naipaul," [May 1979] *Salmagundi* 54 (Fall 1981): 16.

12. "Power," *The Overcrowded Barracoon* (New York: Knopf, 1973): 250.

10

Socialism and Human Nature, Once Again

Norman Birnbaum

The apologist for Nazism, Ernst Nolte, recently observed that in modern Europe, if appeals for the revolutionary transformation of society had only fragmentary resonance, large majorities were ready to join anti-Semitic campaigns. Morally repellent as the assertion is, it has an historical basis: anti-Semitism (and the authoritarian, chauvinist and xenophobic movements of which it was so essential an element) were mass phenomena which precluded for much of this century the attainment of the politically democratic and culturally progressive ends of socialism, ends which attested its character as a direct descendant of the Enlightenment. It is true that liberalism and Christian democracy were, equally, attacked and blocked by the authoritarian right, but the socialist defeat was especially troubling. For one thing, the movements of the right frequently espoused some of the socialists' economic and social goals. The Nazi Party was, not incidentally, termed the National Socialist German Workers Party. Some of the social Christian movements embraced ideas of the subordination of market to community. Indeed, as the case of Mussolini showed, many who began as socialists ended as tribunes of the authoritarian right. Moreover, not the least of the devastating results of Stalinism is the realisation that a revolution proclaiming initial fidelity to the legacy of the French Revolution was with astonishing rapidity transformed into a chauvinist, hierarchical, patriarchal and repressive system, which caricatured by accentuating the features of the Tsarism it had replaced. Finally, as we look at the post-war social contracts in the democracies (the welfare states in western Europe and their American equivalent, which lasted from Truman through Nixon) we have to ask if they did not so emphasize material ends, minimal redistribution and social protection, made possible by managing a constant rise in living standards, that they ignored the spiritual transformation which was the

119

original socialist purpose. Prosperity now threatened, brutal inequality returning, some very old demons have re-emerged on both sides of the Atlantic. True, it is not only the socialist legacy but the entire democratic project of civic education which is threatened—but the socialist failure seems especially pathetic.

Liberalism and the democratic varieties of social Christianity, after all, were (if for very different reasons) either restrained or silent about human transformation. Liberal restraint consisted in eschewing the aim entirely: it was held that by allowing humans to decide autonomously and freely, such good as there was in human nature would at least hold its own. The Christians had the inestimable advantage of assuming that humans were sinful: anything beyond a descent into utter moral degredation was, therefore, a triumph. The socialists, however, were neither modest nor restrained. Let us take Marx as their spokesman: he held that humans could end alienation. In a new realm of freedom to be achieved by mastering the realm of necessity, they would realize Schiller's aesthetic, which argued that humans were never so much themselves as when at play. There are even in Marx (in the passage in his *Grundrisse* on the permanent appeal of Greek art) anticipations of Freud's observation that a happy civilisation—unlike ours—would recapture something of the spontaneity and wonder of the child. The psychological paradox in Marx was that to liberate themselves, outwardly and inwardly, from the several forms of servitude imposed by capitalism, humans would have to possess just those characteristics (the capacity for autonomy, reason, and solidarity) that socialism was supposed to develop. It is true that Marx implied that the very process of revolution was to be a form of self-transformation. It is equally true that much of his psychological thought was implicit or schematic. Nonetheless, Marx held that a post-revolutionary humanity would be one in full possession of its potential, a humanity reconciled with itself.

The record, of course, has brought only fragmentary and halting confirmation of these hopes. Within the socialist tradition, and in creative antagonism with it, there have developed different and far more differentiated psychologies—not least with the intention of explaining the vast disappointment that socialism has been, and sometimes with the hope of eventually curing that in a newer and more profound socialist project.

Freud himself, of course, matured in a society with a large socialist movement—as well as an active anti-Semitic one. There are many reasons for not reading Freud as a conservative. His reference to psychoanalysis as a movement, his reiterated belief that perhaps its major contribution would be to the self-understanding of culture, his not entirely implicit anticipation of radical psychoanalytic revisions of moral pedagogy in the society as a whole, bespeak his adherence to the project of the Enlightenment. Schorske's superb analysis of what he termed the dream of revolution reminds us of how little Freud was inclined to bow to authority. Of course, *Civilization and Its Discontents* was profoundly critical of socialism (and of western culture as a whole) but it did entail a desperate conviction that reason could apprehend the human predicament, and eventually transform it. Of the attempts to confront and conjoin Marxism and psychoanalysis, consider two. Reich began with a very major contribution to the theory of the ego and then broadened his scope to examine the political consequences of patriarchal authoritarianism and sexual repression. He argued that a working class which had so internalized authority that it reproduced in its familial setting the oppressiveness of society could hardly be expected to generate revolutionary *élan*. Sexual liberation would have to precede social transformation. The Frankfurt Institute of Social Research initiated its studies of authority and the family when there still was a possibility that the socialist movement in Germany, even if divided by Stalinism, would succeed in resisting a total regression of German society to a pre-Enlightenment condition. Resistance, by militants, occurred—but the majority of those who had been Communists or Socialists did not resist. Whatever they may have thought of Goebbels' cry on 31 January 1933 ("Now we have finished definitely with 1789") their behavior made it true. The subsequent inquiries by the Frankfurt group led after the war to the publication in the United States of *The Authoritarian Personality*, which placed the psychological roots of fascism in a definite personality type, but which did not dwell overmuch on the question which had initially concerned the Frankfurt scholars—what historical conditions combine to produce that type?

The original effort to connect the analysis of the psyche to larger historical processes was continued in the work of Marcuse, especially his *Eros and Civilization*. Marcuse took a radically historical view of the depiction of psychic process and structure by Freud. Classical psychoanalysis constituted in his view a true image of the psyche in the epoch of high capitalism—but now that the system had changed, it had to be drastically revised. There was no universal developmental requirement for the quantity and quality of repression in the phase of Western culture caught by Freud in *Civilization and Its Discontents*. Now that productivity had increased, the objective possibility of creating a realm of freedom—especially instinctual freedom—was given. Capitalism had extracted surplus economic value, it was time to see that it was demanding surplus repression as well. The reappropriation of lost or, more precisely, alienated instinctual pleasure could be understood as a modern equivalent of revolutionary activity. Marcuse developed this programmatic politics in *One Dimensional Man*—a work which articulated some of the major themes of the protest movements of the 1960s. Meanwhile, Juliet Mitchell, in *Psychoanalysis and Feminism* situated Freud's theory of gender difference historically: in a patriarchal society, a patriarchal psychology was true.

The excitements and hopes of the sixties are behind us and in the current confusion, it is quite impossible to say that the rest of the nineties will offer chances of change for the better. The veterans of the sixties are, some of them, still active in politics as secularized radicals. A nineteenth century aphorism on religion declared: "We expected the kingdom of heaven, and got the Roman Catholic Church instead." The socialist movement can declare that it wanted a total transformation of existence, but has settled in the nations of welfare capitalism for six weeks of paid vacation and a good many other social benefits (missing under our backward American conditions.) The sixties veterans who have joined the socialist movements, or fashioned post-socialist groups like the German Greens, espouse a considerable variety of causes and issues, the resolution of any number of which would make our societies appreciably more humane and rational. They do not have an integrated project of social transformation and their therapeutic concerns are modestly ameliorative, seeking to enlarge the solidarity of which we are now capable. The millenial (or messianic) undertone in early socialism (in which humans were to become as Gods) has gone. Without this metahistorical substratum, however, a good deal of moral energy has also been lost.

Taking human nature as it is attests a large degree of realism, taken by some as a sign of maturity but perhaps more accurately characterized as resignation. It does mean accepting as likely to continue for the indefinite future brutality, exploitativeness, hatred and selfishness—used by those not especially proud of these characteristics as excuses for their own limited expectations of themselves.

Of the acuity—no, profundity—of the work of Marcuse and Mitchell there can be no doubt. They have given a radical critique of society new depth by taking psychoanalytic theory to its limits—and beyond. They have also increased our knowledge of some contemporary social movements. Marcuse's account of surplus repression explains in part the predominance of what have been termed post-materialist themes in the movements that drew so much attention in the sixties, but which were there far before. Mitchell's account of patriarchy makes more comprehensible the women's movement in all of its dimensions. I write this as the Population Council is diffusing a report, "Families In Focus" which substantiates the view that deep and permanent changes in the family, and in women's role, are evident everywhere in the world. The complaint by some cultural critics, then, that feminism is largely a product of the careerist drives of educated American women in our urban areas is evidence only for the critics' sovereign provincialism. What Marcuse and Mitchell do not do is to deepen our understanding of why these movements have incurred so much resistance—and why our present historical situation, worldwide, has generated so much regression and repression. The practise of emancipation of course will provoke its adversaries, but if emancipation is inscribed on the agenda of history, it is unclear why it has remained so incomplete, has not produced a coherent challenge to the institutions of economic and social power.

It is true that Marcuse also described "repressive desublimation"—an idea which would explain why those who enjoy some instinctual liberation remain in their politics cretinous and servile. We require other ideas. I turn to two other thinkers in the psychoanalytic tradition. Erikson was initially part of the German youth movement, whose attack on bourgeois routine and sensibility had ambiguous consequences for the nation. He worked in Vienna, with its socialist atmosphere, and in the United States clearly situated himself amongst the American exponents of a critical tradition. (Witness his refusal to sign the loyalty oath required of teachers at the University of California, with the engaging explanation that he was employed by the people of California to analyze obsessive rituals, not participate in them.) No doubt, his work on identity drew on the work in ego psychology of the second psychoanalytic generation. It also attempted a synthesis of ego analysis, and the psychology of development, with cultural and historical inquiry. Erikson was a progressive (he at one point considered a study of the young Marx), but his view of history was undogmatically free of dependence upon a happy historical sequence. Erikson was drawn to ideas of the historicity of ethical and philosophical perspectives, of the relativization of thought in the modern age, but was quite aware that this rendered much of humanity uncomfortable, no, furious. Recall the essay on Hitler in which he drew upon his own experience as a German. In the face of historical destructiveness and rage, Erikson did adopt a rather contemplative, but not detached, attitude. In his constant return to the theme of history's offspring seeking identities as ways of meeting, if not mastering, anguish

and deprivation he may have been re-enacting in his work his early attachment to the youth movement. There followed his experiment as an
artist, that is, a career far from bourgeois routine. Erikson knew Freud.
Schorske holds that instead of using Freud's Oedipus complex to explain revolutionary or anti-authoritarian politics, we might understand
Freud's development of the idea as a sublimation of his own frustrated
revolutionary ambitions. In default of a larger social project for the alter-
ation of a very unsatisfactory world, Erikson's subjects are forever taking
the detritus of their own personal histories and using these to recon-
struct themselves. There is a large political implication to his work.
When *Childhood and Society* was published in 1951, *Commentary* gave this
book by an established psychoanalyst unknown to the general public to
review to an utterly unestablished and unknown graduate student in
sociology at Harvard. The editors were, one gathered, sceptical that the
book was important enough to merit reviewing at all. The reviewer
found much to praise in the book, especially its effort to raise psychoan-
alytical theory again from a clinical plane to a canon of historical inquiry. That caused the editor of *Commentary*, Elliot Cohen, to refuse the
review—because the reviewer, or the author, or both were in their insistence on the social dimensions of the psyche's formation and function
ipso facto "Stalinoid." Cohen, of course, was not impossibly remote, at
one time, from the American Communist Party: enough said.

It is striking that the term "identity" has now entered common discourse in all kinds of ways. Just the other day I heard the Japanese Am-
bassador to the United States, a senior professional, discuss Japan's
search for a modern identity. I did once ask Erikson if perhaps the difficulty of most persons was not that they were searching for identities, but
that they were painfully aware that they had identities they wished to
discard—usually, with reason. Erikson noted the similarity to the Marxist
theme of alienation, but we never pursued the discussion. Perhaps that
was a way of acknowledging that his use of the term was part of an incomplete personal search for a political identity.

Politics, in the larger sense of the search for a more humane and just
community, has been much more an explicit part of the work of Robert
Lifton. Consider three of his major themes. One is the view that a response to death (a response which is far broader and more varied than
fear) is a rather more pervasive force in the psyche than libido. One
human defense against death, in the metaphorical realm of the spirit, is
memory—yet another of Lifton's themes. The cultivation of memory
makes possible inner regeneration after trauma, makes culture possible
in the sense of inter-generational connection, and constitutes education

in the larger sense of the communication of moral experience. Finally, Lifton's description of the protean self as a creative adaptation to destructive disruptions of historical discontinuity is an affirmation of human and social possibility: change, and change for the better, is possible.

It is true that these processes are located in a psycho-cultural borderland, between the social biology of the psyche and our integration in culture. That integration, however, is never complete and total: persons become persons precisely in struggling against as well as in a milieu, and in both cases, alter it. Movement between milieux is, or rather can be, a protean education. Lifton certainly does not underestimate what can go wrong, and has gone wrong, in our own history. A defense against death can assume the pathological form of siding with death, temporarily, by dispensing it. Memory can be distorted, falsified and rigidified. Proteanism can allow, or rather produce, large moral renewals in persons. It can also allow mergers of weak selves with sinister strong ones.

Lifton has his own universe of discourse, but three elements are not quite hidden in it. Psychoanalysis, especially ego theory and to some extent the theory of object relations, is subsumed—not taken for granted, but critically deployed. Erikson's work on culture and identity, given particular and specific form by Erikson in his historical ventures, reappears in Lifton's writing as a generic history of the self. Finally, Lifton's attention to torment (Hiroshima and Auschwitz) has more than a reminiscence of the Old Testament about it. There is no truly human self, Lifton insists, without moral conflict and no resolution of conflict apart from the demands of a very imperfect world.

How are we helped to understand the failure of socialism, and the related crisis of the Enlightenment project in its entirety? That failure, and the crisis, are not without historical nuances, differences of density in different settings. Erikson and Lifton, if in ways specific to each, give us explanatory models which do take account of history in a way which is not quite linear. Freud (and Marcuse and Mitchell) was appreciably closer to Marx: there was one human history and we were at its apex. Lifton, like Erikson, is rather less convinced that he stands at the apex, indeed, intimates that the notion of apex requires reconsideration. He reminds us of Geertz and Levi-Straus, rather than (let us say) of Sartre. In a way, that can reconcile us with socialism's very partial successes—or with such resistance as we have been able to mount against barbarism's insistent reliance on inauthentic order to counter genuine chaos.

Still, those of us in the socialist tradition seek more than reconciliation. We seek a new political pedagogy, which would take account of what we have learned of the psychic sources of morality to answer the question: what would constitute plausible and promising first steps toward a different sort of politics? One clue comes from the anarchists, the utopians, so derided in their lifetimes by Engels and Marx. A contemporary thinker put matters in the phrase, the future is now. A certain emphasis on immediate clarity of motive, on the exemplary value of small steps, is a necessary antithesis to that historical schematism which in the past has allowed any compromise (and sometimes worse) in the pursuit of a grand design. We come immediately to our entrapment in a circular position: how can moral energies be mobilized in a society which more often than not finds little use for these, and frequently actively disparages them?

Perhaps the answer is to be found in what was once the sublime by-product of participation in a larger movement, the sense of solidarity and of self-transcendence which comes from serving a good cause. The counter-argument is obvious: bad causes often legitimate themselves by the good motives of unreflective supporters. To that the answer is that group solidarity purchased at the price of the outward deflection of hate is bound to disintegrate, and in any event is hardly evidence for a higher political culture.

In any event, the disintegration of the inter-generational continuity of families in the working class is part of the end of the relatively fixed and intact culture which once gave rise to movements of solidarity. There is no point to retroactive idealization: closed communities often harbour and transmit primitive views of the world. The historical falsifications of a quasi-literate crank (*Mein Kampf*) had their sources not only in his reading but in the common sense of those largely excluded from the capacity to acquire or reflect on knowledge. Once-closed communities are now open—to the continuous bombardment of omnipresent media, which trivialize and vulgarize the world as well as distort it. Counter-cultures from below are as likely to resemble the European xenophobes and our militia as anything else, perhaps more likely to do so. The attraction of a higher culture for those denied access to it or use for it is distinctly limited. The bearers of culture, meanwhile, are not well placed to function as a new political vanguard. The mobilisation against them of every sort of plebian *ressentiment* is not difficult.

The external conditions for the return of an ethicized socialism in modern form are, then, exceedingly unfavorable. To make matters more complex and difficult, we do not know except in very general terms what will encourage the development of autonomous, critical persons capable of the persistent exercise of solidarity. Clearly, miserable material conditions will not help—but disorder in the psyche does not decrease as we climb the scale of education, income and power. An empathic capacity is supposed to be the result of education, but where the educated themselves are struggling to maintain their social positions, it often functions as a very expensive luxury—or, again, the unintended result of very unusual developmental circumstances: a good family. In any event, the capacity to imagine exceedingly different social arrangements is increasingly rare—even amongst artists, cineasts and novelists.

Their devastating pictures of our world are not usually accompanied by suggestions for repair. Where some sorts of socialist traditions are still intact, that appears to be a consequence of the fortunate confluence in national histories of several traditions: an alliance, as in France, Germany and Italy, of socialism with social Christianity. Even where tradition is strong, the social historical drift toward the fragmentation and individuation of society converts ideas of solidarity into demands for the defense of acquired interests.

Joining those demands to a somewhat larger social project, a design for minimal solidarity, is difficult enough (as recent American experience shows: who now recalls that Franklin Roosevelt in 1944 proposed an economic Bill of Rights?) Why not accept that, and with it what I have termed a secularized socialism—devoid of the consolation and illusion of its metahistorical belief in human transformation—and turn to the tasks of the day? Why not, indeed, especially as we are at a very large loss when challenged to say how new political or social projects could render humans more whole. Our knowledge, moreover, of the conditions under which persons are ready and willing to join in projects of empathy and solidarity is at best fragmentary,

There are, perhaps, reasons for larger spiritual ambitions. Given the acuity and depth of our historical crisis, only the pursuit of larger visions—in thought and practise—may give us the resources to save a human meaning. We may be modest, those who combine brutality, hatred and ignorance with an inexpungable drive for power are not. The example of our teachers (like Lifton) does suggest, finally, that the constant struggle to examine moral vision against the vicissitudes of history is creativity itself.

Part III
Self and Transformation

Self and Soul

Erik Erikson and Robert Lifton: The Pattern of a Relationship, *Lawrence J. Friedman*
Mélusine as Feminist: Shape-Shifting in Surrealism, *Mary Ann Caws*
The Protean Woman: Anxiety and Opportunity, *Cynthia Fuchs Epstein*
A Quest of Eternal Life, *John S. Dunne*

Group Psychology

The Second Scar, *Richard Sennett*
The Japanese Psyche: Myth and Realty, *Takeo Doi*
Symbolic Immortality in Modern Japanese Literature, *David G. Goodman*
Reflections on the Self of Homo Hippocraticus and the Quest for Symbolic Immortality, *Phyllis Palgi (with Joshua Dorban)*

Narratives

Illicit Stories, *Peter Brooks*
Life in Death, *Noel Walsh*

Qualms and Questions

"How Pliant Is Science," *Gerald Holton*
Confidentiality: In the College Presidential Search Process and Beyond, *David Riesman*
Shame and Public Life, *Jean Bethke Elshtain*

11

Erik Erikson and Robert Lifton: The Pattern of a Relationship

---

Lawrence J. Friedman

Erik Erikson never described himself as Robert Lifton's mentor despite his eminence and his twenty-four-year seniority. Instead, he characterized himself as "some kind of an ancestor" and a sometimes "unreliable friend." In "a sense," he once noted, Lifton was "my student," though Lifton was always very independent and sometimes "proceeded rather dictatorially" at making arrangements for the annual Wellfleet meetings on psychohistory. In contrast, Lifton described Erikson as his "mentor" in a very special sense. Erikson "did not cultivate disciples but was bent upon extending and consolidating his ideas," and this often meant that he blended Lifton's research into his own. Yet as their relationship evolved and as he mastered Erikson's writings, Lifton recalled, he felt increasingly free to strike out on his own and "to explore directions" that interested him quite independently. Erikson's unconventional quasi-mentorship was "quickly transformed into full dialogue" so that he could engage in "receptive confrontation and imaginative re-creation" of Erikson's "legacy."[1]

I

Contact between the two began in 1956 after Robert Lifton had completed a psychiatric residency in New York City and had launched research on his first book concerning Maoist "brainwashing" in China. The project was not going well, for he could not determine why "brainwashing" techniques caused some people to change dramatically and others not at all. Then he read Erikson's recent article "The Problem of Ego Identity" in the *Journal of the American Psychoanalytic Association.*

131

"That's my answer," he proclaimed. Lifton concluded that Maoist "brainwashing" was really an attempt "to bring about a change in identity in the participant. . . ." It was "a coercive form of psychotherapy" designed to obliterate one's old identity and to establish a new one. At the suggestion of his friend, Yale psychiatrist Fritz Redlich, he wrote to Erikson explaining his project and requesting an appointment.[2]

They met at Erikson's home in Stockbridge, Massachusetts, in 1957 and walked all over town in European fashion talking about their respective research projects. Erikson was taken by how his concept of identity clarified Maoist "thought reform." He was writing *Young Man Luther* and was also struck by the connection between Maoist "brainwashing" and totalistic forces in Luther's childrearing and early religious training. For Lifton, this was "the beginning of an extraordinary friendship and a profound education."[3]

During the walk through Stockbridge, Erikson mentioned that when he had trained under Anna Freud in Vienna half a century earlier, there was an element of "thought reform" not unlike Maoist "totalism" within the psychoanalytic community. Lifton had just begun an unhappy training program at the Boston Psychoanalytic Institute, and as he listened to Erikson, he began to connect that training to his Maoist project. He thought about it for the next two-and-a-half years and concluded *Thought Reform and the Psychology of Totalism* with several pages linking the process of Chinese thought control with psychoanalytic training. Both sought to break down a person's old identity and establish a new one. Lifton had completed his analysis when his book came out but had yet to take on analytic control cases. He never assumed those cases and dropped out of his training. The decision to quit analytic training and the discussion in his book connecting such training with Maoist "brainwashing" represented his way of departing from the psychoanalytic movement. That decision disturbed Erikson, whose only formal credential was from the Vienna Psychoanalytic Institute and whose professional identity had long been grounded in the psychoanalytic movement. But while David Rappaport, who appreciated Lifton's intellectual promise, had tried to dissuade him from the break, Erikson had not. He felt that Lifton had secured training in unconscious processes while remaining keenly aware of world affairs, and that was sufficient. If Lifton was no obedient young student, Erikson was not the traditional mentor who demanded that the student's training replicate his own.[4]

The formative stage of the relationship during the late 1950s had involved the completion of two books, both psychological inquiries into historical events, and both focused on how the sense of self emerged and contracted in conjunction with social-political circumstances. Yet *Thought Reform and the Psychology of Totalism* differed from *Young Man Luther* in its unit of study. Whereas Erikson's focus had been biographical, describing how changes in Luther resonated with the larger society, Lifton's focus was on collective behavior. Maoist thought reform had concerned many actors involved in a broad social process. Yet at this point in their relationship, neither Erikson nor Lifton criticized the focus of the other. The differences were respectful and mutually engaging.

There was a family dimension to the relationship. Erikson became especially close to Betty Jean Lifton, Robert's wife and a pioneer in the movement for the rights of adoptee children. B. J. had struggled for years to find her real mother, and Erikson had long sought to discover who had fathered him. She succeeded whereas he had not, but they talked frequently about adoption and missing parents.[5]

Lifton also became quite close to Kai Theodor Erikson, the eldest of Erik's three children. He had completed a doctorate in sociology and concentrated his research on the social and psychological ways in which the self can be maintained and obliterated. *Wayward Puritans*, his first book, showed, for example, how seventeenth-century New England Puritans sought to shore up their ebbing senses of identity by castigating community deviants. Close in age to Kai, Lifton liked the way he developed the identity theme through collective social psychology and in the course of the 1960s they became good friends. Kai Erikson's second book on the Buffalo Creek, West Virginia, flood of 1972 drew as heavily on Lifton's work on collective death anxiety as it relied on Erik's view of the resiliency and decline of viable selfhood. Kai and his wife Joanne became very close to the Liftons.[6]

The personal and intellectual dimensions of the relationship between Erik Erikson and Robert Lifton and their families was augmented by the Wellfleet (lower Cape Cod) psychohistorical meetings each summer in Lifton's beach cottage. In large measure, Lifton and Yale colleague Kenneth Kenniston had established the "Group for the Study of Psychohistorical Process" in 1966 as a forum for Erikson's ideas and writings. Intellectual associates with whom Erikson felt comfortable were invited to attend and to bring their families for several days on the Cape every summer. Erikson's report on work in progress, such as his study of Gandhi, was to be a point of departure for other presentations which were to extend the domain of his conceptualizations.[7]

If Wellfleet was to provide the institutional structure for an Eriksonian movement, not even the kernel of such an agency was discernable at the initial August 1966 gathering or at those that followed. With tough-minded critical thinkers like Philip Rieff, Bruce Mazlish, H. Stuart Hughes, plus Lifton and Kenniston attending from the start, Erikson was regarded as a very distinguished and creative senior scholar but not as the leader of a movement or school. Although his presentations on Gandhi were appreciated, they rarely dominated more than half a day of discussion. He did not treat other participants as followers or successors. Lifton presided over the meetings, and without his prodding Erikson would not have presented his work in progress or even offered comments when others presented. Those whose thinking most closely approximated Erikson's—Kenniston, Lifton, and Robert Coles—rarely underscored or elaborated his ideas. Indeed, at no point in its twenty-nine-year history could Wellfleet be regarded as an Eriksonian forum.[8]

By March of 1973, when the New Yorker Robert Lifton visited Erik Erikson in his Marin County, California, retirement home, the relationship between them had become exceedingly close. Lifton received widespread acclaim for his second book, *Death in Life* (1967), on the survivors of Hiroshima, was a Foundations' Fund for Research Professor of Psychiatry at Yale, and was sought out as a public lecturer. For his part, Erikson was probably at the height of his popularity. His photograph had appeared on the cover of national news magazines, and he was preparing to deliver the prestigeous Jefferson Lectures sponsored by the National Endowment for the Humanities. Alone by themselves, the two ate and drank and talked for hours. After the visit, Lifton wrote up a very revealing document on their time together.

Erikson's Belvedere home overlooked the splendor of San Francisco Bay and he answered the door: "We embrace when we meet," Lifton noted, "he looks magnificent—I had forgotten how much I love the man, with that magnificent white mane—and there flashes across my mind an amorphous but powerful image of how much he has taught me, how much he has meant to me. . . ." Joan Erikson was away, Erik explained, to help a friend with a schizophrenic son who had helped her thirty years earlier during her own family crisis. "Then, rapid-fire, Erik tells me something I had never heard before," Lifton recounted, and it concerned the major crisis in his long marriage to Joan. She had given birth to a Downs Syndrome child in the mid-1940s. The child was hospitalized for a long while, but the Eriksons had told their three normal children that he had died. (He lived for twenty-one years, spending most of the time in a special northern California facility.) The episode tore the family in diverse emotional directions but was a well-kept secret. Before he told the matter to Lifton, Erikson had apparently recounted it to only one other colleague—Margaret Mead. It was not a topic that a mentor revealed to a student.[9]

At this point, Lifton inquired about the state of Erikson's NEH sponsored lectures that were to be delivered in Washington, D.C., in little more than a month. They were to be on Thomas Jefferson and American identity, and Erikson reported that he was drawing upon Lifton's "Protean Man" article that was initially published in 1968 and came out in revised form in 1971. The protean personality, as Lifton developed it, had no fixed character or personality but was characterized by a constant remaking of the self in response to change and flux all about. Lifton feared that Erikson "will absorb the concept in his own way, use it for his purposes," and leave Lifton unacknowledged. After all, Erikson had absorbed other people's concepts without attribution. Lifton's apprehension over this aspect of Erikson's scholarship represented no inconsiderable strain on their relationship.[10]

They cooked dinner together and had their familiar debate about how to prepare steak. Lifton chided Erikson for being a European who did not drink wine with his food and Erikson retorted that it was because he was a Dane. Talk continued in the evening on psychoanalysis, politics, R. D. Laing, and other topics—all ultimately returning to Erikson's preoccupation with his lectures on Jefferson. As they went to bed, Lifton felt Erikson had turned to him as Freud had sought Fliess—to meet "his need for an 'audience.' " That is, Erikson needed Lifton to present outwardly what he was wrestling with inwardly.[11]

The next morning they swam in Erikson's pool and ate his soft-boiled eggs mixed with catsup and toast bits. Erikson had long experienced a troubled relationship with Anna Freud, his analyst and formally his mentor, and he told Lifton of his trepidation of meeting her on a panel of the Philadelphia Psychoanalytic Association only a few days before his NEH lectures. He had wanted to avoid what he was sure would be a confrontational occasion, but Ms. Freud had asked him to attend so that they could have "fun" together on the panel. "We laughed together at what Anna Freud considered 'fun,' " Lifton recounted. Erikson had informed him of his own problematic mentor-student relationship and Lifton was relieved that his own relationship with Erikson did not replicate its formal, hierarchic, uncomfortable qualities.[12]

Nearing the time the limousine was due to take Lifton to San Francisco Airport, Erikson returned to Jefferson—to the Virginian's fascination with Jesus' sense of "I." Erikson was beginning to travel the intellectual road from Jefferson to the sense of "I" in Jesus' Galilean sayings—the last major scholarly project of his life. He then seemed to switch topics abruptly, bringing up death and Lifton's work on the sense of "mortality." "Things were now moving fast, just slightly beyond co-herence," Lifton recalled, and as the limousine appeared, "Erik half-apologized for talking so much, saying that I must understand he has not talked to anybody about any of these things for a very long time." They embraced and Lifton left, reflecting on the way to the airport about the nature of their relationship. It was not one of mentor and student, for although Erikson had done most of the talking and had ruminated on his major intellectual preoccupations, he had not simply listened to Erik's thoughts. He had provided terms and concepts that Erikson had wrestled with and embraced in his own writing. Although Erikson had hosted Lifton, Lifton had spent much of their time together promoting Erikson's intellectual development.[13]

II

Historical perspective was central to all dialogues between Erikson and Lifton. As early as his 1923–24 *Wanderschaft* journal written while he walked through the south of Europe toward Florence, Erikson was pro-foundly interested in the dynamics of historical change. Beginning with this journal, he focused on the way emotional needs within the leader resonated with the needs of the society about him. Erikson explored this process in the 1940s to account for Hitler's appeal to German youth. In the 1950s he showed how young Luther resonated with the need of his German compatriots for psychological and religious change. During the 1960s he wrote of Gandhi's deployment of the politics of nonviolence to free India of British rule. He described Jefferson's national leadership and spirituality in the early 1970s, and then sought to explore the his-toric consequences of Jesus' Galilean ministry. Although Erikson's abid-ing historical interests much enhanced Lifton's commitment to psycho-logically oriented historical inquiry, *Thought Reform and the Psychology of Totalism* drew him away from psychobiography and toward exploration of broader collective historical experiences. The widespread recognition of *Death in Life: Survivors of Hiroshima* deepened Lifton's commitment not only to understanding the common psychological experiences of specific historic collectivities. Unlike Erikson, who focused on the role of the great man in history, he always felt compelled to explore "shared themes" in the lives of non-elite peoples.

Within these contrasting units for historical study, Erikson and Lifton had different controlling images and paradigms of how humans functioned. Both took off from Freud's image of instinct (mostly sexual) and defense (mostly repression of instinct). For Freud, demonic instincts or drives battled against a fragile superstructure of civilized reason in humans. Erikson incorporated this idea of instinct and defense into his theory of identity and the search for a sense of coherence and sameness in the course of the human life cycle. This struggle within each individual had its own particular pattern or "configuration." The configuration was the pattern or shape of the convergence between a person's inner emotional concerns and the issues within the society and culture about him. In a sense, Erikson's imagery of a configuration liberated Freud's imagery from its mechanistic clash between drives and defenses and its preoccupation with the inner psyche.

Lifton's formative theory, on the other hand, completely abandoned Freud's drive theory. Using Freud's concept of a life instinct at war with a death instinct only as his launching point, Lifton argued for a controlling image (not instinct) of death and the continuity of life. In individual but especially in group experience, Lifton focused on the shapes or forms that human symbolization took as people struggled to maintain and extend life in the face of death (i.e., a struggle between the continuity and discontinuity of life). This struggle preoccupied all humans with symbolic mortality; they needed to create symbolizations of continuity over time and space in their children, a spirituality that transcended death, and a sense of psychic transcendence that made time and death disappear. At base, the human struggled to evoke and preserve images of a self that was alive individually and collectively, and avoided images of the self as dead.[14]

Lifton characterized his imagery of what he has called "psychoformations" as an advance on Erikson's theory in the sense that it moved fully beyond Freudian drive theory and embraced common collective experience more fully. Most important, it "carries Erikson's principle of configuration still further. I interpret individual feelings and actions on the basis of immediate struggles to harmonize and recast the forms and images that have been evolving over the course of the life cycle." Erikson, however, never described Lifton's "psychoformative" imagery as an advance on his own or behind his own; it was simply different. Yet he felt free to borrow from it freely in addressing historical issues owing to its emphasis on both psychobiology and culture, its concern with the life cycle, and its emphasis on the form or shape of psychic experience. This contrast in the way the two men saw each others imagery suggests that Lifton viewed their relationship more from a mentor-student perspective than Erikson did. Lifton, the student, felt that he had enlarged and extended the perspective of the mentor. For Erikson, both he and his young friend were doing interesting work from which they both shared and borrowed. Neither advanced beyond Freud or beyond one another.[15]

III

During the 1960s Erikson and Lifton both struggled to complete perhaps their major psychohistorical undertakings. Erikson's *Gandhi's Truth: On the Origins of Militant Nonviolence* and Lifton's *Death in Life: Survivors of Hiroshima* were both published at the end of that tumultuous decade. Erikson won a Pulitzer Prize and Lifton a National Book Award in Science. Perhaps better than any other undertakings, the support and encouragement each gave to the other's project, despite differences over biography versus group experience ("shared themes"), drive theory, and images of the life cycle, revealed that one did not advance beyond the other. Indeed, these very differences tended to blur or at least ebb in their significance.

At the very first Wellfleet psychohistorical meeting in August of 1966, Erikson presented on his Gandhi project and Lifton talked of the *hibakusha* who had experienced the atomic bombing of Hiroshima. They did so again until each had brought his book to completion and they talked on many other occasions about their work. They dialogued within the context of an escalating American military presence in Vietnam, which both opposed, and the danger of a Soviet-American nuclear missle exchange that might have resulted in global nuclear destruction. Interviews of the *hibakusha* victims of America's earlier Asian military venture—the 1945 bombing of Hiroshima—intensified Lifton's growing distress with the immorality of his country in Vietnam. Yet he was impressed with how some of the *hibakusha* gained mastery over their "indelibly imprinted death immersion" through affirming images of hope and survival as "death immersion" turned others toward incapacitating despair and psychic numbing. If his Hiroshima research at the time of the Vietnam War and Cold War nuclearism brought Lifton to sense the emergence of a new historic level of danger for humankind, he felt that Erikson's work on Gandhi's nonviolent opposition to the British articulated a new and effective level of pacific counterpoising against that danger. Indeed, Lifton felt that Erikson understood how his life had come to center on the trauma caused by the Hiroshima bombing of the *hibakusha*. By familiarizing Lifton with Gandhi's pacific principles and practices, Erikson appeared to be giving his friend hope and "grounding" to help him to deal with that trauma.[16]

In turn, Lifton's Hiroshima project decidedly influenced the final shape of *Gandhi's Truth*. Erikson felt that his attempt to give Lifton hope by acquainting him with Gandhi's *satyagraha*, or pacific strategies, was an intergenerational act of generativity—an older person giving to and supporting a younger person. This deepened and reinforced Erikson's understanding of a central element in *Gandhi's Truth*—how Gandhi's *satyagraha* was itself a generative act to all humankind. The concept of generativity (long the seventh stage of Erikson's life-cycle model and the central psychological task of adult life) was fleshed out and deepened as Erikson never had been able to before as he explained Gandhi's *satyagraha*. This explanation gave Lifton better balance and perspective in dealing with the traumatized *hibakusha* and made Erikson all the more determined to tie generativity to *satyagraha*. With the publication of *Gandhi's Truth*, generativity became as important in Erikson's life cycle as the identity stage, and the generative act of a man in his late sixties giving and supporting a friend in his early forties contributed significantly to this result.

Lifton's Hiroshima research also contributed significantly to Erikson's appraisal of American history and culture. Beginning with his exploration in the late 1930s and early 1940s of the Nazi movement in Germany, Erikson had been suspicious of what Lifton called "technicism"—the assumption that the expansion of technical knowledge was inherently virtuous. But before he befriended Lifton, he had never characterized the United States as a "technicist" power. It was the welcoming nation he had come to in the fall of 1933 with President Roosevelt radiating hope and immigrants from the world's trouble spots finding in America a new lease on life. To be sure, there was a short, cautionary note in *Childhood and Society* (1950) on how American physicists had "striven in shortest order" to perfect the atomic bomb without adequate reflection of its harmful consequences. But as Lifton shared with him the traumas of the Hiroshima *hibakusha* rendered by America's atomic bomb, and coupled it with intense discussion of American technical weaponry against the Vietnamese, Erikson came increasingly to share Lifton's feeling that America had become a "technicist" power. By 1970 he spoke publicly in *Newsweek* of America's romance with machines—"that way of life has led to Hiroshima." In his 1972 Godkin Lectures at Harvard, Erikson equated American "technicism" with "the American Way of Death, which means the passionless use of overkill against other species, [which] has reached its climax in Hiroshima." By then he had come to regard *Childhood and Society* as a volume reflecting the spirit of an earlier, more innocent point in history before Nazi genocide and American use of the atomic bomb. *Gandhi's Truth* reflected this evolution in Erikson's thought away from his 1933 vision of America as a hopeful and humane nation of immigrants. Gandhi and India had produced *satyagraha* as a pacific and enobling alternative to the American "technicist" presence in Hiroshima and Vietnam. He acknowledged Lifton and his Wellfleet meeting in "hosting the development of his chapters and dedicated the book "to the memory of Martin Luther King"—practicioner of *satyagraha* and opponent of American military ventures in Asia.[17]

At the 1974 Wellfleet gathering, several years after *Death in Life* and *Gandhi's Truth* were published, Erikson continued to voice his distaste for America's role in Vietnam and coupled it with distress over the American Watergate scandals. Yet he promoted the remedies of Freud ("Eros"), of Lifton ("survival, immortality"), and of his own thinking over the past decade ("One Species"). Freud had pressed for eros over thanatos, which Erikson advocated. Lifton had advanced the survivor's mastery over death imagery through symbolic immortality—a sense of the continuity of life through time and space—and this was also beneficial. In the course of preparing *Gandhi's Truth* and essentially committing himself to *satyagraha*, Erikson had embraced the premise that all of humanity was of "one species." When differences were advanced based on race, nationality, and similar exclusionary categories to justify violent indignities toward others ("pseudospeciation"), these had to be overcome by enhancing man's sense of "universal speciehood." All in all, Erikson was suggesting that Freud's thinking, Lifton's, Gandhi's, and his own seemed to overlap decidedly in their humanism and hope while retaining their own terms and emphases. He refused to place them in a hierarchical order, with one representing an advancement beyond the other. Freud was no more his mentor than he was Lifton's. Dialogues, mutually enriching but not linear or necessarily progressing, would continue among thinkers with proposals that were important to humanity's survival.[18]

IV

In 1993 Lifton published *The Protean Self: Human Resilience in an Age of Fragmentation*. It represented an enlargement of his important 1968 and 1971 articles on "Protean Man." The protean self departed from the Freudian concept of a fixed, contained personality. It was a personality style "characterzed by interminable exploration and flux, by a self-process capable of relatively easy shifts in belief and identification—a life style that is postmodern and in some ways post-Freudian." This evershifting, changing personality of our time had an identity that was flexible, tentative, and impermanent. It lacked location or direction. As such, the "protean self" represented an overturning of the relatively firm and stable criteria for symbolizing the human condition that had emerged from the Renaissance and the Enlightenment. Modern images of extinction represented by phenomena like nuclear war and global warming had done much to shatter any fixed sense of selfhood and to promote a sense of tentativeness and fluidity in the face of dire potentialities. So had the mass media, which had developed a capacity to present any image from any point in space and time, thereby presenting the self with endless alternatives in every sphere of life. Rather than bemoan the emergence of the protean self or depict it as pathological, Lifton characterized it as a new historical style of self-process. It allowed people to immerse themselves in fresh new ventures and to display a new openness to all sorts of potential changes.[19]

Lifton asserted that he first observed proteanism as he watched how Chinese youth responded to Maoist brainwashing and how postwar Japanese youth behaved under the shadow of Hiroshima and military defeat. Beginning with his 1968 and 1971 "Protean Man" articles, Lifton insisted that the protean self was not explained by Erikson's work on identity formation because Erikson has tied identity too closely to Freud's concept of a fixed self and had premised identity on an inner sameness of experience. For Lifton, identity formation was not universal but represented a specific social value of middle class culture at a particular point in time and was in the process of becoming obsolete by the late twentieth century. If his protean self concept was not necessarily deeper or more profound than Erikson's identity concept, Lifton held that it better explained the nature of personality development in the contemporary world.[20]

Essentially, then, Lifton claimed that his formulation on proteanism bypassed Erikson's on identity. Based upon extensive marginal comments that Erikson wrote on the 1971 published version of Lifton's "Protean Man" paper, he disliked what he read. When Lifton had described the protean self engaged constantly in "self-process" and "role-process" rather than being a fixed entity, Erikson wrote: "That's what I meant; and identity [is] still necessary as [a] concept to see what held them *together*." Identity was the vessel that held or contained the constant shifts of the self. Where Lifton described the protean person as

constantly changing and being indisposed "to commit himself to a single form, the form most his own," Erikson wrote "Identity vs. Identity
Confusion." Erikson also described Lifton's use of examples to illustrate
the protean self as "all too glib and terribly superficial." Where Lifton
had maintained that the protean self lacked a "classic superego" that
had internalized clear criteria of right and wrong, Erikson noted that
Lifton personally exemplified just that "classic superego" ("See Lifton
himself."). Finally, at the end of the article, Erikson suggested that Lifton was really describing his own personality: "He himself: same old
Jewish Messianic super-ego in a number or roles: revolutionary
doctor."[21]

If Erikson did not view identity formation by the early 1970s as a fixed
or contained entity that was incompatible with proteanism, this had not
always been the case. In the first edition of *Childhood and Society* (1950),
Erikson dismissed explicitly as a "misconception" the view that a person
achieved a sense of identity "through his indefinite adaptation to the
demands of social change. This, of course, would mean a fixation on an
adolescent solution." But in the course of the 1960s as he and Lifton
deepened their exchange of ideas, both became taken increasingly by
the proliferation of protean qualities in modern life. At a Bellagio conference in 1968, just before the first of Lifton's "Protean Man" articles
was published, for example, Erikson underscored the difficulty for modern youth to say "here I stand" as young Luther had done: "For where
change was once a transitional stage to a regained equilibrium in line
with ancient tradition, change is now self-sustaining, and no generation
can predict what the world will look like to the next." Unlike young
Luther's generation, Erikson cautioned, a modern youth "feels in need
of an ethical flexibility, a capacity for 'being with it' ". Between Luther's
day and the last half of the twentieth century, the very nature of identity
had changed; it had assumed qualities like those Lifton characterized as
protean.[22]

Consequently, despite Erikson's distaste for and criticisms of Lifton's
1971 "Protean Man" article, his very contrast of an earlier fixed historical identity with a modern sense of identity involving constant process
and adaptation indicated that Erikson and Lifton were not very far
apart. Erikson's 1973 Jefferson lectures for the National Endowment for
the Humanities attested to this. He characterized Thomas Jefferson as
an early version of the protean American personality. This was evident
in Jefferson's many and shifting occupations as farmer and architect,
statesman and scholar, deeply private person and eminently public citizen, displaying "convincing informality" at some times and "genuinely

elegant stature" at others. However, Lifton's fears of being subsumed within Erikson's work without acknowledgment (one of Erikson's common practices) did not come to pass. Before a large and prominent audience in the nation's capitol, Erikson noted that the protean personality "has been primarily reintroduced by Robert Lifton into our consideration."[23]

Lifton had the last word. When *The Protean Self* came out in 1993, Erikson was very ill, incapacitated, and in no position to read much less respond to Lifton's claims as he had in the past. Lifton praised him effusively in the book for a concept of identity that represented "a gigantic step toward psychoanalytic openness" that was sensitive to changing social currents. But owing to Erikson's loyalty to the Freudian circle in which he was trained, Lifton wrote, his identity theory required an "inner sameness" or fixity that "can be at odds with the radical flux and fluidity of much contemporary experience." Yet Lifton probably sensed that this was an overstatement, and that by the late 1960s Erikson's view of modern identity was hardly at odds with proteanism. When he inscribed my copy of *The Protean Self*, he wrote of "the protean-Eriksonian quest."[24]

V

The sorest point of contention between Erikson and Lifton was over political activism. As a research associate at Massachusetts General Hospital in the late 1950s, Lifton became friends with Harvard sociologist David Riesman. *Tocsin*, an early anti-nuclear war student organization in Cambridge, featured Riesman as an enthusiastic and energetic faculty sponsor. Lifton became active in *Tocsin's* nuclear disarmament campaigns. He attributed this activism to the beginning of his interest in studying the atomic bombing of Hiroshima. He also joined the Physicians for Social Responsibility and worked with other physicians to ease the nuclear threat. Next, Lifton became an early activist against American involvement in Vietnam and worked with Richard Falk, Daniel Ellsberg, and others to document United States war crimes in Southeast Asia. "Beginning with my work in Hiroshima," Lifton noted, "I have come to see advocacy itself as having a necessary ethical and conceptual place in the healing professions." His active political involvement reenforced his "investigative preoccupation" with the fate of survivors in the global tragedies of the twentieth century. He identified with and supported these survivors and felt compelled to "return constantly to my survivor's commitment, if not mission, to place my work in antagonism to war and nuclear holocaust."[25]

Lifton knew that his good friend Erikson shared his anti-nuclearism, his opposition to the American presence in Vietnam, and almost all other positions on which Lifton took active public stands. However, he chided and gently criticized Erikson for refusing to put his beliefs to work in the political arena through public advocacy. To be sure, Lifton praised Erikson for refusing to sign a McCarthyite University of California loyalty oath in 1950. But he was distressed that "during a period of great upheaval in the United States" in the 1960s and early 1970s, Erikson "has generally avoided direct political and social commitments." Indeed, Lifton noted that Erikson was among the few regular participants at the Wellfleet conferences who refused to sign anti-nuclear and anti-Vietnam war political petitions despite Lifton's proddings. He also knew Erikson's record on the Harvard faculty. While sympathetic with campus civil rights, anti-nuclear, and anti-war campaigns in the 1960s, Erikson almost never took public stands, signed petitions, or let his name appear on political advocacy literature. When Lifton proclaimed at the 1970 Wellfleet meeting that the Vietnam war had fundamentally reversed his commitment to his country and Robert Coles heatedly attacked that posture, Erikson (if sympathetic to Lifton) remained silent. Indeed, Erikson's sole public endorsement during this tumultuous interval was to allow his name to be submitted with other prominent Americans supportive of amnesty for Vietnam war resisters.[26]

Erikson disliked it when Lifton pressured him to become an activist. Yet he kept coming to Wellfleet where he usually enjoyed himself even with the political activist records of most participants. Lifton speculated periodically that Erikson was reticent to attack American institutions and political leaders, feeling that they had treated him generously. Indeed, he had worked within institutions like Harvard and the Austen Riggs Center that trained and treated American ruling elites, and his patients included some of the nation's most powerful political, religious, and cultural leaders. It would have been ungrateful to have attacked them publicly; in some cases it might have been therapeutically detrimental.[27]

This relates to the nature of Erikson's Americanism as a very grateful immigrant who felt indebted to the welcoming and wholesome climate he experienced when he arrived in 1933 from an increasingly troubled Europe. Although he had found a profession and established a family in Vienna during the six prior years, he indentified deeply with America as his permanent home. To be sure, McCarthyism, United States nuclear weapons policies, Nixon and Watergate, and especially American military ventures in Hiroshima and in Vietnam had diminished his fervor for his adopted country. "How much of America is My Lai," he wondered at the 1974 Wellfleet meeting. Still, America had given him much by the 1960s and early 1970s, and this went beyond his celebrity status as its premier psychoanalyst and one of its most prominent intellectuals. He identified and empathized from his own past with the loose, unstructured social and emotional lives of many American youths. As he observed, taught, and treated some of them, he had amplified his ideas on the "identity crisis." Erikson had also made the difficult transition for a man in his middle years from German, his native tongue, and had become a superb American author and stylist. Moreover, he developed a keen interest in American cultures—the Sioux and the Yurok, African-Americans from slavery to the Black Panther Party, "mom" in middle class suburbia, and especially American children. Indeed, he viewed Kai, Jon, and Sue—his own children—as thoroughly Americanized and his wife Joan as more American than Canadian. Erikson felt that America had given him all this and more, and he held an immigrant's reserve about criticizing publicly its policies and practices. When I asked his son Kai why Erikson never signed protest petititons at Wellfleet meetings, he simply stated that "It wasn't our way." Kai did not sign either and explained how the immigrant's disposition had passed from father to son.[28]

The matter of political activism therefore promoted a serious tension in the Lifton-Erikson relationship. Yet by the late 1970s and early 1980s even that had begun to ease. Lifton became more accustomed to Erikson's pattern; only bruised feelings resulted by pressing this old man further. Moreover, Lifton felt that the issue of political activism was dwarfed by the very considerable help Erikson was providing him in his new and most difficult of all research projects—the pychology of Nazi doctors who had participated in the Holocaust.

No longer able to write full length books himself, Erikson took an abiding interest in Lifton's task. A German Jewish immigrant, Erikson had written a deep and probing essay on Hitler's appeal among German youth. *Young Man Luther* testified, too, to his abiding concern with the liberating and tyrannic aspects of German culture. Quickly, he detected how difficult it was for Lifton, a Jew trained to be a physician, to listen calmly and to *hear* what Nazi doctors had to say in interviews not only about their barbarities, but what their conduct suggested of the human condition. Commenting on a portion of Lifton's manuscript, Erikson told him that "you have done the nearly impossible, namely, finding a quiet and strong tone for a set of observations which in their emotional substance are really unfathomable." In this way, Erikson explained, "you illustrate forcefully the universality of these events, which cannot be totally buried with the Nazis." Whereas others with whom Lifton talked had difficulty understanding how Nazi doctors could commit atrocities at some times and be decent and caring at other moments, Erikson understood this instantly and helped Lifton to work out the concept of "doubling" to account for it. He convinced Lifton that Nazi physicians at Aushwitz were not displaying a "religious attitude" but "a strong ideological one, which . . . should not be overestimated." He showed Lifton how Nazi rationalizations on the dangers Jews posed genetically was part of the broader human tendency toward "pseudospeciation." Erikson also gave Lifton introductions to German scholars who might facilitate his work, describing him as a "courageous" investigator. Most important, he shared memories with Lifton of life and culture in Germany and Austria, underscoring elements that promoted the Nazi medical and political holocaust. When *The Nazi Doctors* was published in 1986, Erikson was acknowledged for "opening up new dimensions in our dialogue of thirty years." By this point in their relationship, it was difficult to discern tensions over the issue of political activism.[29]

VI

Not long after I learned of Erikson's death in May of 1994, I called Robert Lifton. We discussed some of the errors in the long New York *Times* obituary; he underscored the mistaken claim that Erikson took criticism well. We speculated on the immmediate cause of death and agreed to get together after the memorial service in Harwich, where the Eriksons had moved a year earlier. Lifton did not appear to be as disspirited as I had been.

When we discussed his good friend in the months that followed, Lifton was comfortable and content. He was hurt (if not deeply so) because Joan Erikson had not invited him or other of Erikson's intellectual associates to speak at the memorial service or to sit with family and close friends. But Lifton did speak at a special service at the Harvard Memorial Church in October. There he recalled having chided Erikson on whether he was a Jew or a Gentile, only to hear Erik disarm him with the retort that he was both and that Lifton and Daniel Ellsberg were "Jews who heard the Christian message" in their political activism. It is significant that Lifton admitted at this Harvard service what he had not been able to acknowledge during earlier years of rivalry with Erikson: "Erik was the most creative psychoanalytic mind since Freud." At the annual Wellfleet meeting later that October, Lifton organized presentations around the coming fiftieth anniverary of the Hiroshima bombing and reserved one evening to discuss Erikson. At that time he played a tape recording of Erik presenting at the 1980 Wellfleet meeting on Jesus' Galilean ministry. Lifton underscored the brilliance of that presentation. He concluded the evening by noting that he was modestly troubled because Erik's death came on the eve of the anniversary of Hiroshima. A day later, however, he was his usual upbeat self at Wellfleet and recalled how he and Erikson had once reviewed photographs of early Vienna analysts. Erikson had said that the whole lot of them talked incessantly about sex but did not look like "lady killers." Their verbiage had exceeded their performances. Lifton laughed loudly over this characteristic bit of Erikson humor.[30]

A long and complex relationship was winding down. The surviving member was not disposed to elaborate the major books and ideas of the deceased, for he had his own very full intellectual agenda to advance. If they had not been mentor and student in life, Lifton carried a wealth of fond memories of his old friend. He was willing to speak at every memorial gathering that presented itself to share these memories. Erikson had long emphasized that one gained a full sense of "I" or selfhood only through trusting rapport with another. For decades, Erikson and Lifton had provided each other with just that sort of trusting rapport amidst periodic tensions and disagreements.

Notes

1. Erik H. Erikson (EHE) to Robert J. Lifton (RJL), n.d. (1970), RJL Papers, New York Public Library (NYPL), "some . . . ancestor"; EHE to RJL, December 1959, RJL Papers, NYPL, "unreliable ancestor"; Walter J. Ong to EHE, 5-22-72, E-H (Erikson reply on Ong letter "my student"); EHE to Frederick Wyatt, 12-5-74, Erikson Papers—Houghton Library (E-H), "proceeded . . . dictatorially." RJL, *Explorations in Psychohistory: The Wellfleet Papers* (New York: Simon & Schuster, 1974), 11, "did not cultivate disciples . . ."; "to explore directions . . ." Charles B. Strozier & Michael Flynn, "Lifton's Method," *Psychohistory Review* 20(1992): 132, "quickly transformed . . ."; RJL, "From Analysis to Formation: Towards a Shift in Psychological Paradigm," *Journal. American Academy of Psychoanalysis* 4 (1976): 67, "receptive confrontation . . ."

2. RJL Personal Interview (PI) by Lawrence J. Friedman (LJF), NYC, 4-3-91, "that's my answer." RJL to EHE, 7-19-56, RJL Papers, NYPL, establishing contact with Erikson and noting "a coercive form of psychotherapy."

3. RJL, *History and Human Survival* (New York: Random House, 1970), 14–15, "the beginning of an extraordinary friendship . . ." RJL PI by LJF, 4-3-91; RJL in Joan Erikson-Erik Erikson Recognition Reception, Cambridge, MA., 11-21-91 (tape recording).

4. RJL in JE-EE Recognition Reception, 11-21-91; RJL comment in Wellfleet annual meeting, 10-23-94; RJL PI by LJF, 4-3-91; RJL, *Explorations in Psychohistory*, 12.

5. Betty Jean Lifton in JE-EE Recognition Reception, 11-21-91. See also Betty Jean Lifton, *The King of Children* (London: Pan Books, 1989), 302.

6. Kai Erikson (KE) Tape Recorded Interview (TRI) by LJF, Hamden, 11-7-93. See also KE, *Everything in Its Path: Destruction of Community in the Buffalo Creek Flood* (New York: Simon and Schuster,1976), 168, and RJL & Eric Olson, "The Human Meaning of Total Disaster: The Buffalo Creek Experience," *Psychiatry* 39(1976): 16.

7. RJL to EHE, 10-20-63, RJL Papers, NYPL, on Erikson first coming up with the idea for the Wellfleet gathering. RJL PI by LJF, NYC, 4-3-91, on making Erikson's ideas and presentations the heart of the Wellfleet meeting. See also "Group for the Study of Psychohistorical Process," n.d. (February 1966), E-H., and RJL to EHE, 1-2-66, E.-H.

8. RJL PI by LJF, NYC, 4-3-91; Bruce Mazlish PI by LJF, Cambridge, 2-16-91; "Group for the Study of Psychohistorical Process," n.d. (February 1966), E-H; Gerald Holton TRI by LJF, Cambridge, 2-15-91; Nina Holton TRI by LJF, Lexington, MA. 4-30-91; RJL to EHE, 6-17-68, RJL Papers, NYPL.

9. RJL, "Visit with Erik Erikson in Belvedere, California, March 23, 1973," RJL Papers, NYPL, pp. 1–2 "We embraced. . . ." The Downs child is reported on p. 2.

10. Ibid, 3–5.

11. Ibid, 7–11 on dinner and the evening; ibid., 11 on the Freud-Fliess comparison.

12. Ibid, 14–15.

13. Ibid, 15–16.

14. RJL, *Journal of the American Academy of Psychoanalysis* 4(1976): 63–94, compares Freud's, Erikson's, and his own images quite clearly, especially on 69–71.

15. RJL, *Journal of the American Academy of Psychoanalysis* 4(1976): 90–91, "carries Erikson's principle . . ." See also RJL, "Psychohistory," *Partisan Review* 37(1970), 21, 31–32; Margaret Brenman-Gibson to EHE, 4-6-72 (copy), M.Brenman-Gibson Private Papers, Stockbridge; RJL, "Visit with Erikson in Belvedere," p. 6.

16. RJL commentary on EHE, Wellfleet conference, 10-23-94; RJL PI by LJF, NYC, 4-3-91.

17. EHE, *Childhood and Society* (New York: W.W. Norton, 1950), 370–72 on American physicists. *Newsweek* (Dec. 12, 1970), 88. EHE, "Play, Vision, and Deception" (2d Godkin Lecture), 4-12-72, p. 30, E-H. Janice Abarbanel Lecture Notes, Social Sciences 133, Lecture for 10-20-69, on *Childhood and Society* as pre-Hiroshima in its spirit.

18. EHE, "Wellfleet '74," (n.d.), E-H.

19. RJL, *Partisan Review* 37, p. 30, "characterized by interminable exploration . . ." RJL, "The Self in History," Wellfleet, 10-13-90, elaborated the main lines of what became *The Protean Self* volume. RJL, "Protean Man," *Arch. Gen. Psychiatry* 24(1971): 298–304. RJL, "Protean Man," *Partisan Review* 35(1968): 1–27.

20. RJL, "The Self in History," Wellfleet, 10-13-90, on first observing proteanism with Chinese and Japanese youth. For Lifton on how Eriksonian identity formation is bypassed by the protean personality of out time, see ibid.; RJL, *Partisan Review* (Winter 1968), 13-27; RJL, *The Protean Self: Human Resilience in An Age of Fragmentation* (New York: Basic Books, 1993), 26. See also Howard I. Kushner, "Pathology and Adjustment in Psychohistory: A Critique of the Erikson Model," *Psychocultural Review* (1977): 505, 69.

21. Erikson's notations on RJL, "Protean Man," *Arch. Gen. Psychiatry* 24(1971), 298–304 is found in the Erikson Papers at the Houghton Library (E-H).

22. EHE, *Childhood and Society* (1950), p. 368 *n.* EHE, "On Student Unrest," unpublished brochure, 1969, p. 210, E-H, for his 1968 Bellagio remarks.

23. EHE, "The Jefferson Lectures," 5-2-73 (audiotape, E-H), acknowledging Lifton for reintroducing proteanism. The lectures are published as EHE, *Dimensions of a New Identity: The Jefferson Lectures in the Humanities* (New York: W.W. Norton, 1974) and Jefferson is referred to explicitly as a protean American. See also a telling excerpt from *Dimensions* in EHE, "Thomas Jefferson: Protean Man," *New York Times*, 4-13-74.

24. RJL, *The Protean Self*, 26.

25. Michael S. Kimmel, "Prophet of Survival," *Psychology Today* (June 1988), 46, on Riesman and *Tocsin*; ibid., 48, on the Physicians for Social Responsibility. RJL PI by LJF, 4-3-91 and Telephone Interview, 9-3-92, on his Vietnam activism; RJL, *Journal. American Academy of Psychoanalysis*, 4(1976): 92, "Beginning with my work in Hiroshima . . . ," "return constantly to my survivors. . . ."

26. RJL, *Journal of the American Academy of Psychoanalysis* 4(1976): 92, on Erikson's loyalty oath stand and how he "has generally avoided . . ." and his stand for war resister amnesty. Erikson's avoidance of public advocacy is detailed in RJL PI by LJF, NYC, 4-3-91 and PI, Bowling Green, Ohio, 3-5-93; Kai Erikson TRI by LJF, Hamden, 11-7-93. RJL PI by LJF, 4-3-91, on his 1970 Wellfleet argument with Coles.

27. RJL PI by LJF, NYC, 4-3-91, speculating on Erik being reticent to attack prominent U.S. institutions and leaders.

28. EHE, "Wellfleet—74," E-H. Kai Erikson TRI by LJF, Hamden, 11-7-93.

29. RJL, "The Doctors of Auschwitz: The Biomedical Vision," *Psychohistory Review* 9(1983): 45, on the difficulty of working on *Nazi Doctors*, and 46 quoting Erikson on Nazi "religious attitudes." EHE to RJL, 10-13-81, E-H, "you have done the nearly impossible . . . you illustrate forcefully the universality . . ." RJL at JE-EHE Recognition Dinner, 11-21-91 (tape), on Erikson helping with the "doubling" concept. EHE, "Wellfleet: Lifton," n.d. (early 1980s), E-H, connect-

ing genetic rationalizations to "pseudospeciation." EHE to Kurt Von Fritz, 9-8-78, E-H, typifying introductions to German scholars. RJL, *The Nazi Doctors: Medical Killing and the Psychology of Genocide* (New York: Basic Books, 1986), 540, acknowledging Erikson. RJL PI by LJF, NYC, 4-3-91, on Erikson sharing memories of Germany and Austria, and on tensions with Erikson wholly gone as he completed *The Nazi Doctors*.

30. RJL at Erikson Memorial Service, Harvard Memorial Church, 10-12-94 (tape). RJL comment on EHE at Wellfleet, 10-21-94 (tape); RJL discussion with LJF, Wellfleet, 10-23-94, recounting the Vienna photograph review with Erikson.

12

Mélusine as Feminist: Shape-Shifting in Surrealism

Mary Ann Caws

No hope for synthesis.
René Crevel, *Diderot's Harpsichord*[1]

To think surrealism is to rethink the self. Let's assume this project is at once personal and literary: how do we find ourselves, as readers of this surrealism which willed itself revolutionary in style as in content? It was always, in spite of what we might have thought on an initial reading, a surrealism as personalized as collective. But we must also assume, at the start, that this project will be without possible closure, inconclusive by nature as by choice. It knows there is a war on between a certain contemporary current said to be "objective," and a personal optimism about highly individualizing possibilities.

A common desire for objectivity, alas, frequently and easily wins out over our private selves, the moment we are willing to admit the superior strength of depersonalized structures. Our learned cultural mistrust of anything concerning individual and generally inexplicable emotions can only reinforce our tendency to flee the personal. We flee, often in order to escape toward simpler explicative models, either semiotic or psychoanalytic or anthropological. In the place of the deauthored and deselfed, I would like openly to choose, here and now, and not only in speaking of surrealism, a mode of personal and even emotional relation between suject and object, subject and subject. Even a collective project can become a highly individualized one.

You have to believe it to see it.

Who Finds One Thing Only, Loses

Surrealism knows no more pertinent principle than the freedom to change. So the question arises: what kind of self might we be likely to

151

find and hold on to along the path we are choosing to call surrealist? We know that, if ever we were to find anything at all permanent, we would be in the gravest surrealist danger of fixing ourselves in one attitude, automatically opposed, as efficaciously as tragically, to all the principles of fluidity that surrealism cherishes. We cannot, naturally, give up the spontaneous self and all the possibilities of motion it entails. Like the protean self, the surrealist self has to take its consciousness from drift. Since we know how shape-shifting works, we might wonder in what shape we will be continuing. Rather than finding ourselves, isn't this more strictly losing?

That is not all. This surrealizing person found as a protean self and reader, who might that be anyway? Who could guarantee that it is us and not someone else, some cypher or token person supposed in this idealizing function? To find ourselves, but to find ourselves *other*, and then still other, this is part of the point of the whole surrealist enterprise as it is supposed to work. Any of our *others* is already problematic, to say the least, and already in potential lost to the next, whether it be another person or the most loved text or belief. What do we then get to keep, in this re-creation of the self in movement, detaching ourselves always next from this other other?

Surrealism is, after all, supposed to be positive, after the negativizing Dada experience. We expect and admire that most dramatic detachment of Breton's "Disdainful Confession" in his Dada years. Here he refuses so much that it seems a limit-case of unsettling down: "Formerly," he says, "I only left my dwelling after having said a definitive farewell to everything that had accumulated there as an enveloping memory, everything of myself I felt ready to perpetuate there."[2] His conception of life remains as open to risk later as at this moment. In *Nadja*, he will insist on exposure to everything the street might offer: the world he chooses to dwell in will be "opened to chances, to the most trivial and to the most important," made up of "sudden encounters, petrifying coincidences" and traversed with the flashes of insight these provoke.

There is something about the surrealist state of expectation, the *état d'attente*, that perfectly corresponds to what Adam Phillips stresses in his essays on the uncommitted life in his *On Flirtation*. It is the contingent that can teach us most about ourselves, he says. "Coincidences belong to those who can use them," indeed.[3] The surrealist knows how to see them and use them, and knows how to teach us, in turn, about all that. For that, and that only, is what we get to keep: our redefinition of ourselves. It has to be good enough.[4]

Being Good Enough

Now what mental gestures might we best make, in language and the visual world, as declarations of this credo? How can we declare for ourselves and others, our own openness to the contingent? We have to continue to insist on the initial credo of surrealism, bound to a belief in an objective chance that defines itself as an answer in the outside world to an inner question we didn't realize we had. Such gestures must bear primary witness to our willingness to shift our emotional as well as our mental state.

One of Breton's less well known essays called "First Hand" prefixes a statement about our necessary trust in and encouragement of the emotions by the formal verbal equivalent of a typographical finger pointing, or an arrow aimed at the point: "Never shall we be able to insist enough on this: only by the emotional threshold can we gain access to the royal way; otherwise, the paths of knowledge never lead there."[5] Many are the surrealist texts testifying openly to the emotional sway under which surrealism works, in the wake of romanticism ("We are the tail of romanticism," Breton was inclined to say, adding, "but how prehensile!") So surrealism must be wanting to hold on to something, with its prehensile tail. What it holds on to is its own definition: just as we do.

To reinforce these initial statements about the ways in which one can make a change of self, about the growing up one can do through surrealism, I want to call on the surrealists Louis Aragon, René Crevel, Octavio Paz, and Benjamin Péret, before calling on that child-woman, that mermaid-maiden Mélusine, whose path they will prepare.

For each being, says Aragon in his *Paris Peasant (Le Paysan de Paris)*, there is an image to find that will change the universe, bringing about a great dizziness that will completely alter what is seen, thought, felt. Such faith in a singular image and its attendant emotional state must hold firm against the sort of discouragement Breton faces in *L'Amour fou (Mad Love)* when, walking with his newfound beloved along the streets of Les Halles in the very early morning, he hesitates, saying: "There would still be time to turn back."[6] Breton did not, of course, turn back; but his interior weakening of faith here gives weight to his later meditations on what courage can be, even at its lowest point.

From the standpoint of Breton, Aragon did turn back when he left the surrealist dizziness for political commitment in stasis, including a stasis of language. He felt he should simplify his poetic technique and thought, and did so. What Aragon asks in his "Voyage to Holland," of 1964—in part as an echo to the other voyages to Holland and their invitations extended, such as Baudelaire's[7]—is anguishing and unanswerable except by the self in its question of the emotions:

> Must we reach one day the end of our thoughts
> The end of what we were the end of what we are
> losing the sense
>   Of what we feel we are saying; stopping halfway through   the sentence[8]

René Crevel speaks, in his great essay "The Mind Against Reason," of the links between the emotions and poetry, between poetic revolution and real life, working against convention. That he should have so early on committed suicide invalidates neither his claim on poetry or on life. "Any intelligence that fears the power, the embrace of life, becomes reciprocally incapable of power, of embrace. . . . Moods of the soul have nothing to do with fixed landscapes. Instead of flotsam, jetsam, and wreckage, the emotional flood brings the lively fruits of desire."[9]

Emotion is tied to invention, in this world where language creates the outer and inner landscape. Spaciousness has to be found within the changing self as well as beyond it. Here being and becoming depend on voicing. In his "Draft of Shadows," Octavio Paz examines the relations between the self and its phrasing of possibilities, betwen individual thinking and epic motion:

> I drift away from myself,
> following this meandering phrase,
> the path of rocks and goats.
> . . .
> From my forehead I set out
> Toward a noon the size of time.
> . . .
> I am where I was:
> I walk behind the murmur,
> footsteps within me, heard with my eyes,
> the murmur is in the mind, I am my footsteps,
> I hear the voices that I think
> The voices that think me as I think them.
> I am the shadow my words cast.[10]

The world here is full, the song is large enough to absorb not just the murmur of the mind but the footsteps of the one walking. The shadow cast by language makes room for others, as for the self, for things as for living creatures. The sense of place is strong within the universe of this lastingly contemporary poetry, which is not in drift.[11] More than time-lessness and spacefreeness, it is about the timeful and the spacious, as an intense timefulness and spacefulness develop from the private and pensive forehead. Here the walker-poet can set out "toward a noon the size of time," and know it not to be colorless. Here the positive easily dominates the negative, whether implicit or explicit.

The world that is made through the phrasing and walking-as-making accomodates the self in the kind of rich surrealist plenitude so well represented by Benjamin Péret, for example. His love poetry, which so clearly permits the seeing through another's self, permits so much else besides, in this new-formed universe

> where the pointed breasts of women stare out through
>   the eyes of men
> Today I look out through your hair
> Rosa of morning opal
> And I wake up through your eyes
> Rosa of armor
> And I think through your exploding breasts
> Rosa of black forest drenched with blue-green postage stamps.
> Rosa of cigar smoke
> Rosa of sea foam made crystal
> Rosa[12]

Like Breton's famous "Free Union," where the beloved's attributes are successively celebrated as in the emblemizations of mannerist poetry, Péret's accumulations within the self because of the other, and in the other because of the self, may seem to depend uniquely upon the power of, the fact of, loving. Yet I think they do not entirely do so. Finding or inventing the fullness of the universe through language is what matters most deeply. Paz speaks of a country "Beyond Love":

> Beyond ourselves
> on the frontier of being and becoming,
> a life more alive claims us. (DS, 20–21)

And Breton, saluting the work of Jorge-Luis Borges and his "lucid perplexity" about the world, praises the way in which his self is always and already an other: "Courage, exulting even in its moments of weakness, honing itself anew in each courageous death, is the driving force of this poetry where the 'I' is already intensely 'an other' because it assumes all the exigencies, including that of the inanimate, and can only conceive of itself as their global consciousness." [13] Elsewhere, in an essay gathered in *Perspective cavalière*, the same posthumous collection which includes the essay just quoted, Breton insists on our opposing anything threatening the dignity of our lives, made up of "freedom and love: the whole diamond we are carrying in ourselves" (PC, 166). When Robert Desnos salutes, in the title of his brilliant novel *La Liberté ou l'amour!*, those two terms, even the conjunction shines in its ambivalent glory.

Mélusine's makeup

Mélusine, the surrealist heroine par excellence, is undeniably the feminist model for surrealism at its best, and at hers. [14] One of Breton's most convincing passages in the long lyric essay *Arcane 17* makes an extensive salute to the mermaid, as he reclaims a power to place in woman's hands. It begins:

> Mélusine after the cry. . . . I see no one else who can redeem this savage time. She is entirely woman and yet such as she is today, deprived of her human place, a prisoner of her roots however mobile they are and nevertheless, through them, in providential communication with the elemental natural forces. Woman deprived of her human place, as legend has it, through man's impatience and jealousy. This place can be returned to her only after he has meditated at length on his mistake, a length proportionate to the resulting misfortune. For Mélusine, before and after the metamorphosis, is Mélusine. [15]

A first cry will announce her return to the world, and then a second, announcing childbirth with no suffering, and other miracles. Her uniquely feminine attributes are celebrated: her stomach is like an August harvest, her breasts are like

> ermines caught in their own cry, blinding with the burning coal of their raging mouth. And her arms are the soul of streams singing and perfuming. And under the fall of her hair, with its gilt worn off, are found forever all the distinctive traits of the woman-child, this particular variety which has always captivated poets *because time has no power over her*. (A 17, pp. 93–4.)

She is both composite and shape-shifter, both fish and woman, woman and child. Around her, she undoes all the best organized systems because, like time itself, they have no sway over her. She is invincible *be-*

cause she changes, being the victim of no categorization. She is the perfect model of surrealism, its ideal representation:

> Her complexion disarms any harshness, beginning with those of time, as I don't need to tell her. Even that which strikes her makes her stronger, suppler, clearer in outline, and finally completes her as would the chisel of an ideal sculptor, docile to the laws of a preestablished harmony and which will never find closure because, without any possible misstep, it is on the road to perfection and this road could not end. And even corporeal death, the physical destruction of the work happens not to be an end. Still the radiance subsists, what am I saying, it's the entire statue, still lovelier and possible, waking to the imperishable without losing anything of her earthly appearance, made up of a sublime meeting of light rays. (A, 97)

A legend, yes, but strong as a model for the legendary ability of the female temperament to overthrow what is already too clear and hardened. The Mélusine legend refuses all categorizations, momentary or permanent. Herself the epitome of a shape-shifter, the woman-child exemplifies the power of possibilization for others, the ones who have learned to read surrealism, and the ones who learn later, often from those who have. Upon Mélusine, we can model our openness to contingency and faith in the positive inventions of everyday life. Landscapes, like lives, have to be created before you can hold on to them, even as they change. They are not given, they have to be earned.

And Mélusine is good enough.

Notes

By his enthusiasm on the subject, and by inviting me several years in a row into his graduate classes to speak of it, Robert Jay Lifton brought back into my consciousness a long-ago fascination which André Breton's conception of Mélusine the shape-shifter held for me. She is a true example of Lifton's idea of the protean self, of course. Unlike most of us, she is both mermaid and woman. But making a choice most of us would like to make, she refuses to give up any of her potential. So I see her as the heroine of feminist possibilization in general.

1. René Crevel, *Le Clavecin de Diderot* (Paris: Jean-Jacques Pauvert, Coll. Libertés, 1932), 69. Referred to as CD.

2. André Breton, *Les Pas perdus* (Paris: Gallimard, 1924), 12.

3. Adam Phillips, *On Flirtation: Essays in the Uncommitted Life* (Cambridge: Harvard University Press, 1994), 16. My thanks to my colleague Gerhard Joseph for sharing his discovery with me.

4. My reference is, of course, to Winnicott's notion of the "good-enough" mother, justified by Adam Phillips' reliance on a Winnicottian model.

5. André Breton, *Perspective cavalière*, texte établi par Marguerite Bonnet, (Paris: Gallimard, 1970), 222. Referred to as PC.

6. André Breton, *L'Amour fou*, translated as *Mad Love*, by Mary Ann Caws (Lincoln: University of Nebraska Press, 1987), 45.

7. See Barbara Johnson's study of Baudelaire in *The Critical Difference* (Baltimore: Johns Hopkins University Press, 1980), 24, and *passim*, from which I greatly profited in my "Decentering the Invitation, To Take the Trip," in *Le Centre absent* (passage, métamorphose): En Hommage à Micheline Tison-Braun, Baton Rouge. *L'Esprit créateur* 34(1994).

8. Louis Aragon, *Le Voyage de Hollande et autres poèmes* (Paris: Seghers, 1964), 51.

9. In "Nouvelles Vues sur Dali et l'obscurantisme," René Crevel, *L'Esprit contre la raison* (Paris: Tchou, 1969), 86.

10. "Pasado in claro," from *A Draft of Shadows*, tr. Eliot Weinberger (New York: New Directions, 1972). Referred to as DS.

11. Thus my title "The Place of Poetry, the Poetry of Place," for the discussion of French poetry after the death of Breton in Denis Hollier, *New History of French Literature* (Cambridge: Harvard University Press, 1989), 1023–27.

12. *Benjamin Péret*, ed. Jean-Louis Bédouin, (Paris; Seghers, coll. Poètes d'aujourd'hui, 1961), 107–8.

13. He is here, in "Embers at the foot of Keridwen," speaking of King Arthur's sheild and the art of the Gauls, and Celtic poetry, even as he is speaking of that other Arthur, Rimbaud, for whom, as we remember, the I was always already another: "je est un autre." *Perspective cavalière*, 136.

14. *Mélusine* is in fact the name of the original journal published by the Centre de Recherches sur le Surréalisme. No. 1, from 1979, edited by Henri Béhar, was devoted to "Emission-Réception." It carried a picture of the mermaid and her fountain on the cover.

15. André Breton, *Arcane 17* (Paris: Editions du Sagittaire, 1947), 90–91.

13

The Protean Woman: Anxiety and Opportunity

Cynthia Fuchs Epstein

Wars with guns and wars with words are fought today over conflicts of identity. These battles make ever more dramatic the struggles individuals face over "who" they are and what they might become. And these conflicts go to the heart of age-old questions about the nature of the "self." Social scientists and philosophers have long argued about whether individuals have a "unitary self"—one that is stable, consistent and coherent—or whether the self is composed of many parts, and is changeable. The quest for the basic components of human nature, and its limits and possibilities, has gone on through the centuries and is likely to continue. The search has meaning beyond academic exercise as we can see in political conflicts of identity. Cultural views of the self have important political consequences for individuals and groups. Some views provide a model of freedom (the changing self), and others are based on a model of restriction (the static self).

Robert J. Lifton's model of the "protean self" stands out today as offering a theory that suggests a broad set of possibilities for individuals.[1] Rooted in observation and the experience of a world that is rapidly changing personally and globally, Lifton's model reflects the seeming paradoxes of "odd combinations" of identity elements and subselves, even those which seem "mutually irreconcilable."[2] Dr. Jekyll and Mr. Hyde represented the dark and the good sides of one individual in fiction, but current history suggests that real people are quite capable of vastly contradictory behaviors and transformations stemming from different elements of their selves and the various social roles they play. The most polar extreme is described by Lifton in his searing analysis of the physicians in Nazi Germany who were healers and also killers in the environment of the Third Reich.[3] But although the good and evil components of self may engage our wonder, many other more benign con-

159

tradictory elements of people's selves are also documented by Lifton's case studies.

Contradictory selves are lodged in lives we encounter all the time. Quite ordinary men may be tender lovers but brutal in business, and unremarkable women may be nurturant mothers yet ruthless advocates of bigotry and hatred, as Kathleen Blee's study of women in the Ku Klux Klan has shown.[4] Or shy people may become self assertive, and combative people may become reasoning negotiators when the circumstances of their lives offer or require such behavior. Although this variety is there for all to observe, countless scholars and others are wedded to a model of a constant "self." For many, confronting everyday variety is troubling, and there is a tendency to reconcile discrepancy. Individuals whose selves do not conform to social expectations or prescriptions, or whose personalities seem inconsistent, disorderly, or heterogeneous, face disapproval from others and from within themselves. Such people are often regarded as hypocritical or impaired psychologically; many therefore try to get their disparate selves in order or pressure others to do so. A search for consistency may be human even while inconsistency is normal.

Of course, people differ in regard to their vulnerability to constraints on change. There are, after all, highly gifted adapters—"method actors" of self—self-motivators who are able to change and create new selves; and there are leaden social actors who cling (or are forced to cling) to identities that are set early. But such differences are not necessarily random. Members of some social groups or categories are permitted more diversity and change in their selves than are others; men more than women; urban dwellers rather than small-town inhabitants; artists rather than ministers.

Social norms act on the self to enrich or diminish its potential; with the demand that individuals of certain backgrounds and origins "be" selves and not merely act roles consistent with social expectations. Because new roles often (but not always) create new "selves," individuals are subject to social controls that permit or prohibit their acquisition. Men and women are subjected to these pressures on the basis of their gender, race, social class, and family history. A person is instructed to "be" a woman or "be" a man, not merely to act like one. In the United States a man continues to face pressures to "be" strong, aggressive, ambitious; and a woman is oriented to "be" loving, affiliative, nurturant, and altruistic. These traits are played out in the context of social roles in which they are the prescribed behaviors. The cultural view, of course, is that women and men are only doing what comes naturally.

People "are," suggests Lifton, creatures with potential for "being" complex and doing things they are compelled to do or are attracted to. These behaviors may be consistent, but they may be contradictory. They may enlarge or diminish the person in public evaluation. But the potential, he insists, is wide.

American women today provide evidence for the model of proteanism in human nature. The last few decades have been a field experiment to indicate how variable people's selves—especially women's selves—may be, how changeable. More dramatically today than at any time in history, American women are recognized as publicly and personally complex creatures. The ambivalence that greets these changes also indicates the extent to which cultural and social controls affect the ability to change and to accept the notion of change. And the model that specifies a "self" that is singular and static limits the visibility and comprehension of the many selves American women possess. Men, too are affected by the simplistic model of the unitary self, and often censor others and themselves when they experience complexity or contradiction in their selves, but women find the price of complexity higher, because more societal energy is directed to compelling their conformity.[5]

Only in recent years have some social historians explored the varied and complex lives of women, These explorations have brought us some outstanding biographies of women such as Margaret Sanger, Rosa Luxemburg, Emma Goldman, Anaïs Nin, and Eleanor Roosevelt. All lived multi-dimensioned lives and possessed complex psyches that linked private and public selves of great range and diversity.

However, the lives of less prominent but also complicated women have been made a part of public consciousness. The women whose portraits appear on book jackets do not call out a sense of "everywoman" that others may identify with. They are regarded as unusual, or superwomen; although, many are posed as more to be pitied than honored. Women who presume to add on to their nurturing responsibilities those of breadwinner, organizer, campaigner, speaker, sailor, racer, or warrior have evoked as much distrust as esteem. Today, the high public approval for the traditional roles played by Barbara Bush as First Lady contrasts starkly with the ambivalence expressed toward Hillary Rodham Clinton, a lawyer and political figure as well as the wife of the President. Although men's reputations are more apt to rise as they add activity to activity on many fronts, a woman with many selves is often seen to be failing her duty on some front, or going against her nature, her real woman's self.

Derived from the model of a constant self, a self entwined with one's gender, there is an implied directive for women to keep it simple; to be consistent; to "be there" for others to depend on, and to come home to; to provide the audience. This is seen as "their true nature" and the basis of their "difference" from men. Those who deviate are regarded with hostility or pity; they are not seen as nice people; as real women; or they are seen as overburdened, confused.

These thoughts, of course, run counter to the precepts of a currently popular strain of feminist thought, loosely categorized as cultural feminism. This perspective, with roots in psychoanalytic theory, proposes that women and men possess highly differentiated and persistent identities—selves—that arise through their early experiences in the family— for women, a cluster of traits encompassing a focus on relationships, caring, nurturance; and for men, abstraction and individuation.[6] This view has roots in common stereotypes about men and women that relate men's and women's prescribed activities to their presumed characters. But there is a further fallacy in assuming that internal and external states are necessarily in harmony, as Arlie Hochschild has so perceptively documented in her study of the "emotion work" of airline attendants.[7]

This paper is somewhat of a paradox in its focus on women. Though their opportunities for acquiring complex social roles and accompanying selves is at a high point in history, most women continue to face age-old constraints in shaping their lives. As they move beyond stereotyped visions and behaviors, freed from old restrictive laws and conventions, and into spheres formerly dominated by men, they are subjected to anxiety and opportunity: progress and backlash.

Of course, women have always been jugglers of many roles and many selves as a number of scholars have noted.[8] Through the ages women have had to perform balancing acts in performing their roles as wives and mothers and in doing the multitude of chores historians remind us were typical of the premechanized household.[9] In the past, a woman raised chickens as well as children. She might also work in the fields at harvest, make soap, preserve food and cook for farmhands. Thus women worked at many activities and worked very hard. Even in the plantation household privileged women were caretakers of the sick and managers of their households (and sometimes the entire estate, as was Abigail Adams in the frequently long absences of her husband[10]), and, of course, slave women performed upkeep and production roles for the master, and provider and nurturant roles for their own families.[11] But these multiple tasks all came under the rubric of "women's work" even when women moved into wage labor. Off the farm and into the factory, or in the home factory, as they cut and stitched garments at piece-work wages, women also supervised children and performed housework. And, of course, there were always deviant women who engaged in multiple and contradictory roles. For example, some brought literature into the factory. Some were engaged in politics and organizing reading groups. Some went beyond "women's work" and engaged in union activity. And some were writers and political agitators even as they were lovers and friends. But for the most part their work was subordinate to men's, and rarely did their low wages give them independent lives. Thus, for the great majority, their selves were narrowly characterized by the qualities long associated with womanliness: subordination, deference, nurturance.

But women's capacities clearly are much broader. My own research and experience over the past several decades have led me on a paradigmatic path similar to that posed by Lifton in his evocation of "proteanism." As they moved beyond typical women's roles it has been remarkable to see so many women change their personalities from shy to outgoing, from insecure to self assured, from dependent to autonomous. Emboldened by the civil rights and women's movements many women found they were transforming themselves even as their work was changing the society.[12] Or, denying they had developed entirely new attributes, women nevertheless found they could perform highly contradictory off-stage and on-stage roles.[13]

I found that many women seemed to have such contradictory components of self when I began research for my first study, seeking to explain why so few women chose to work in the professions and explore leadership roles in politics and the business world. Many explanations then current attributed the cause of women's limited public roles to their "nature" or their preferences, comfort, and to the logic of acquiring and playing out traditional roles. Women who acquired such statuses as doctor or lawyer were deviants, socially and numerically, and often were treated as such. They were seen to be taking on selves irreconcilable with those of a normal woman. Nevertheless, while the acquisition of such contradictory combinations of roles created many problems it also engendered many exciting possibilities as their careers progressed.[14] Many of the lawyers I interviewed had been transformed by their experiences. While most of the older women faced discrimination that prevented them from getting fellowships in school and jobs when they completed training, several were extended a helping hand at a crucial moment by a well-placed man or woman (the names of such luminaries as Mayor Fiorello LaGuardia or Eleanor Roosevelt came up); several were given important first opportunities by male partners in the firms they eventually joined; or the circumstance of war caused a shortage of men that gave some women opportunity. Of course, we know today how changes in attitudes have brought such capable women as Ruth Bader Ginsburg and Sandra Day O'Conner to the U.S. Supreme Court after careers marked by serious discrimination in spite of brilliant performances in law school.

Professional women were the focus of my research until the 1980s when I began research on telephone company workers with the sociologist Kai Erikson. The world was changing for these workers in many ways. Affirmative action programs were changing traditional modes of telephone company recruitment, disrupting the networks that brought in family members from particular ethnic enclaves; new technologies were disturbing the basis for competence and evaluation that workers had depended on; and both women and men began to be faced with interlopers of the "other sex" invading their segregated work spheres. But, as it had for lawyers, disruption also brought new opportunities. The dead-end jobs most women had as operators or sales representatives suddenly developed ladders into management positions. And computer technology brought skill into the office rather than where it had been, outside in the cold and up the telephone poles, creating a more level playing field for women to be able to become testers and troubleshooters. The fairly docile labor force of high school-educated, devoted women workers began to change its shape and attitudes. The quiet, dutiful daughters who were taught and compelled to sit upright at their switchboards and to be the "voices with a smile" found new dimensions of self as they thought about supervisory positions, or even "outside work" as installers and repair technicians, formerly entirely male spheres.

Many individuals experienced change; they felt better about themselves, more positive, and sometimes felt like altogether different persons. They demonstrate, as you will read in their words, that when individuals take on more complex selves these enhance their mental health or productive functioning. This is a perspective gathering support in social science studies. Melvin Kohn and Carmi Schooler, for example, found that intellectual flexibility and self esteem directly relate to the complexity of the job one has; Peggy Thoits found that multiple identities lead to psychological well-being; and Rose Laub Coser has shown that as people take on multiple roles in urban life they develop intellectually.[15]

My research findings support these views. They show that as discriminatory practices against women lawyers in the United States were curtailed over the past two decades, the women who assumed demanding and responsible work as attorneys developed self assurance and confidence as they achieved competence in business and courtroom settings, resulting in "new selves." Further, I found that working class women also grew in self esteem as they were given access to jobs made available through affirmative action programs.

But, amid the signs of this success, many of these professional and working class women also expressed anxieties about the changes they experienced. Many others were prevented from the experience of accomplishing proteanism or paid high costs for it. I have noted elsewhere how researchers have neglected the coercive elements that work to limit the choices individuals have in their selection of selves. Conformity to culturally acceptable models restricting change is demanded by gatekeepers—families, employers, and public figures. The cultural models and the demands they make are backed by moral claims and by social controls.[16] For example, women are supposed to be altruistic; thus women who are self-seeking and work-driven in their occupational lives are defined as conforming to a male model or as not being true to who they "really are."

How Jobs Change People

Economic necessity moved married women and mothers into the work force in increasing numbers after World War II, and the trend continues upward. Seventy percent of all mothers are now in the labor force, and women comprise more than 45 percent of the entire labor force.[17] As my research and that of others on women workers shows, a good number reported surprise at how transformative the work experience was.[18] It was not unusual to hear what Carol W., a telephone operator, reported:

> I think I've changed a lot. I feel I can do better for myself now and for my son. . . . I don't have the same friends I had when I grew up. . . . It's different when you have friends that don't work and friends that work. . . . The ones at home spend all day looking at soap operas. . . . When you're out working [you have more to talk about]. I think I have matured more now that I'm working.

And, Barbara E., a maintenance assistant, described her "transformation": "I'm a lot more outgoing now. . . . When I first came to this company I was very quiet and very shy, seldom opened my mouth."

As I wrote in *Women In Law*, the women who went into the legal profession in the 1970s gained confidence from the knowledge that their participation and ambition in the law were bearing fruit. When women were no longer ghettoized in back-room work, writing briefs and doing research, they found they could develop the professional and interpersonal skills that popular wisdom suggested women did not have. For example, they found they performed well negotiating financial deals with clients and arguing in court. They found the work interesting and success possible although most did not have the business backgrounds and role models that their male peers had. In the process they acquired new selves. As one lawyer put it:

> I started out thinking very hard about whether I would be able to do it but the more I did the more capable I felt and the more I developed a clear sense of career goals. I had a fantasy of becoming a judge in the past, but now it seems it is something of a possibility. I am definitely thinking that is what I probably will be in ten or fifteen years.

Some lawyers drew a sense of confidence from juggling many different roles successfully. As three women commented:

> I feel successful this year because I did what I set out to do—to have a baby and still practice law and make some income out of it. As a bonus to that I succeeded in getting some very interesting cases. A year ago I was not feeling very confident.

> I got reviewed this fall with glowing reviews. I got the full bonus for my year. Someone wrote about me they would let me handle any matter and . . . I guess I'm now a different person. I'm an incredibly different person.

> I don't doubt myself so much anymore. Maybe I've developed some of the stupid overconfidence that some of these men have and I speak more forcefully and I just say what I have to say . . . I have come to trust my intuition about things.

Promotion was the key to a new self for many women. Joan B., who became a telephone installer when AT&T was forced to comply with nondiscrimination rules set by the Civil Rights Act of 1964, thereby opening jobs formerly reserved for men, rapidly moved up the ladder. When she was made a foreman (the term she used) she lost her timidity: "I'm not afraid of men anymore. . . . I realize they are no different . . . they're human. . . . I can talk to them."

Not unlike the working class woman who reported finding a surge of self esteem going to work for a large corporation, working in a prestigious firm gave women lawyers confidence. It was not until the mid-1970s that more than a handful of women attorneys were hired by large firms, whose practices were changed after anti-discrimination cases brought against them by law students, the Women's Rights Project of the ACLU and professors at the Columbia University and N.Y.U. law schools. By the mid-1980s women constituted more than 40 percent of law school classes and soon were well over a third or more of the entering cohorts of large law firms. Thus, finally, a woman could be known as a "Cravath lawyer," or a "Weil Gotshal lawyer." One attorney indicated how this helped getting things accomplished.

> I [can] demand certain documents before I will let my clients sign an agreement. The other side just accedes because they realize our clients are paying for us to be meticulous. Then the clients are awed. It is wonderful when not only the client trusts you, but the opposing counsel treats you so seriously. It makes you regard yourself differently.

Another lawyer said that success confronting prestigious lawyers in high-powered cases made her feel in command.

> A client came to me who had problems with a trade agency in Washington. . . . He took me on because he thought I would look at the case from outside the establishment. . . . I turned the whole thing upside down. At first the firm lawyers resented me . . . but they ended up really respecting me. After it was over I sat in the bar at the Mayflower with this 'seat of power' lawyer who told me, 'it's been such a pleasure to work with you and you are terrific.' On the plane coming back to New York I [said to myself]: 'This is the . . . big time and I really can do it!'

As one can see, this acquisition of new selves is highly contingent on the reaction of others. Today, even with wide acceptance of the notion that women can be attorneys, their experiences are not so distinct from their working-class sisters who find that acquiring new roles, venturing into the "male world" or climbing the ladder depends on the support they have from others in their networks and on cultural views they can internalize.

Multiple Roles

It is often thought that the stress women feel is due to the total load of responsibilities they carry. Actually the load is less important than the consistency of the demands on them, and stress often is compensated for by the satisfaction one often can experience from holding multiple roles. Certain role combinations are complimentary and others may cause strains and conflicts in the identities one develops from attachment to those roles.[19] However, conflict and consistency are products of social norms which prescribe "feeling rules" (Hochschild's term) as well behavior for many roles. And, of course, organizations create structures that help or hinder women in performing multiple roles.[20] The conflicts women face as a result of contradictory demands of the norms governing work roles and family roles have been identified and examined a great deal in scholarly writing and in public discourse in the past twenty-five years (although men's problems in this regard have received scant attention). Individuals and institutions respond to these presumed tensions quite differently. For example, many individuals find gratification in being able to express very different selves in the course of a day or in the course of their lives; some may manage to be tough at work but tender at home, or even both tough and tender both at work and in the home.[21]

Workers who were active in their unions, for example, and served as stewards often found gratification in holding two workplace roles. Women (and men) did not find it discordant to have a subordinate rank as a craftsperson and to hold a superordinate post in their union. In fact, many workers were tapped as management material by one company studied, but they frequently refused promotions that would cost them their union posts because they felt that holding the roles of worker and union official gave them more freedom. Claudine G., a feisty shop steward, told of how the men on the job initially resented her transfer into their maintenance administration division, a formerly male domain, but came to respect her because of the way she handled grievances as their union representative. She was a virtuoso of proteanism; not only did she manipulate multiple work roles, but as a white woman married to a black man in a southern city she insisted that her children define themselves as bi-racial, developing their own multiple identities.

Organizational and Technological Change and Changing Self Images

The development of skill is a continuous social process, linked to both the social and technical spheres. But technology has the potential for establishing new roles and offering new opportunities to people—often younger workers and women—who are not wedded to old images of what a particular job entails or who should be working at it.

A switching technician explained that her opportunity to work in a Switch Control Center came about because men who had outside jobs couldn't see themselves working in an office environment:

> When they decided to have a control center, they asked the senior man would he want to go. . . . Naturally, none of the men [who] were out in the field wanted to . . . they wouldn't want to be in an office environment [which they identified as female]. So they all turned it down, so it got down to the junior person . . . me, [and I took it].

In this case, a junior woman employee ended up with a job first offered to senior men. Even though technological changes made outside jobs more vulnerable because fewer workers were required, the senior men were less flexible; they were culturally invested in old work forms that supported their identities as masculine, autonomous, skilled workers, trusted to get the physical job done outside the confines of an office.

This cultural investment in traditional gender ideology causes both men and women to sanction themselves and others when they contemplate nontraditional work or when they are recruited to such jobs within a company.[22] In my studies of lawyers and telephone company workers one could clearly see interactive relationship between cultural norms and people's contemplation of possible jobs.

Sandra, a member of a suburban telephone repair group in New York, commented on why she won't take a job in construction: "Because I don't believe a woman is equal to a man doing that. I don't see myself going into a manhole. . . . I don't see myself. I don't see that."

Other women workers who worked as frame attendants, a job just recently opened to women, reported how they were negatively sanctioned by friends for taking a job not considered traditional for their sex:

> I've noticed with a few friends, either from school or boyfriends, men, they say 'yes, you wear a tool pouch, you lift wire bags and stuff,' and they look at you like you're not a girl anymore, like you're super tough. . . .
>
> . . . basically they think I'm not feminine anymore if I'm cutting my hands . . . getting dirty and carrying tools and so on; its a man's job and what . . . you want to be like a man?

And a lawyer

> There's some people for whom an attractive assertive woman is a sort of nightmare . . . , your greatest nightmare. I'm not safe. I don't look like a man; I don't act like a woman, so I threaten all aspects of them.

A lawyer reported that her mother, a businesswoman, had ambivalent views about her own multiple roles and thus sent mixed messages to her daughter:

> My mother is a businesswoman. But she resents being one. She says she hates her job, but she is successful at it and really loves it. She functions best on the job, but she will tell you that all she really wanted was to be a mother and a housewife. . . . She saw practicing law as unfeminine . . . yet she was so proud when I was admitted to the bar. . . . She'll talk about 'my daughter, the lawyer,' but not in front of me.

Fear of not being attractive to men in their age group is a powerful inducement for many women to conform to conventional gender roles; to keep their "feminine" selves. Marlene, a first-level telephone supervisor, encountered stereotypes about appropriate women's traits in the disapproval of friends who perceived changes in her personality after a promotion: "I had a friend . . . a guy who I was dating who said to me, 'I don't work for you . . . you act like you're at work,' because I was taking the initiative."

Ideological and political commitments often determine whether multiple roles, especially diverse roles (and particularly those seen as inconsistent), are approved or not and whether particular individuals may assume them. Such views make it difficult for women to take jobs that are higher in rank than their husbands, for example. Formal opportunity structures may change because of legislation banning discrimination or economic pressures, but popular views about the appropriateness of specific opportunities for individuals of certain backgrounds may set limits on their ability to take advantage of them.

Some people give up opportunities because of peer pressure not to change and move beyond others in the group, or because of the insecurities and fears of those close to them. A worker in a southern city office described this process:

> I'm sure I was like a lot of other people when I started with the company, being an ambitious person . . . [but I soon got the message from my co-workers] . . . it was like 'all right kid, slow down, you're making the rest of us look bad.'

A law professor told of a woman who gave up a substantial career opportunity to keep peace with her husband:

> She had a chance to go to a big classy firm . . . he didn't talk to her for two months. [Finally] he told her the reason . . . he did not want his wife in a

job with more prestige and attention and more money. She was going to be travelling around the country and meeting people and was going to outshine him. He said it was a double standard and he knew it, but he was not going to change.

Barriers to Mobility

The changes in the self resulting from a new job, one that carries a change in rank, is of particular significance to a person and the community from which the person comes. This is particularly so in cases where promotion was improbable before because of discrimination. With more barriers down, people have to contemplate the possibility not only of adding a role but the self that new role might create. Promotion is a vehicle into a new status with its attendant norms prescribing new behavior and often companion emotions and personality traits. People possess information about the expectations that accompany a new position and can assess whether it will involve changes in the self that match or conflict with the person's view of who they are, or with the expectations of significant others in their families and communities.

Taking a new position in a company may reinforce or change an individual's self-definition. The new position may reinforce or conflict with other "selves" an individual has known, or it may alter the configuration of role identities that support a coherent self-concept. Amy, a telephone operator, speculated on promotion:

It's something I could do. . . . I know this girl who came after I did and she's training for supervisor now. I know I have the brains to do it. I'm not sure I'd like it once I got into it though, because being a supervisor . . . changes your personality.

A number of workers, however, said they had decided to reject the opportunities to become supervisors:

I don't like the person you have to be when you're over people. Your personality has to change and I can't deal with forgetting where I come from and a lot of them . . . their attitudes change. They're very evil and you have to chop down people that you care about. To me, I said that's not worth it. . . .

With the exception of one or two of them their whole personality changes. One of them is now filing for a divorce. I think that because she got the management job it affected her home life.

Conclusion

The pressures and conflicts women often face in their career decisions are a reminder that while change is possible throughout life, and individuals are capable of juggling many roles, deviating from traditional norms is quite difficult. Yet when opportunity presents itself, as it does in a world characterized by many transformations, many women—and men—do brave the consequences and seize the chance to change their lives. Personal anxieties may accompany the norms that restrict one's place in the social order based on gender, race, class, and education. But those who move beyond the boundaries often prosper psychologically and intellectually—becoming protean selves—in a world in which rapid transformations at work and within ourselves have become typical of life experience.

Notes

1. Robert J. Lifton, *The Protean Self: Human Resilience in an Age of Fragmentation* (New York: Basic Books, 1994).
2. Ibid., 50.
3. Robert J. Lifton, *The Nazi Doctors: Medical Killing and the Psychology of Genocide* (New York: Basic Books, 1986).
4. Kathleen Blee, *Women of the Klan: Racism and Gender in the 1920s* (Berkeley: University of California Press, 1991).
5. Cynthia Fuchs Epstein, *Deceptive Distinctions: Sex, Gender and the Social Order* (New Haven: Yale University Press, 1988).
6. Nancy Chodorow, *The Reproduction of Mothering: Psychoanalysis and the Sociology of Gender* (Berkeley: University of California Press, 1978); Carol Gilligan, *In a Different Voice: Psychological Development and Women's Development* (Cambridge: Harvard University Press, 1982).
7. Arlie Hochschild, *The Managed Heart: Commercialization of Human Feeling* (Berkeley: University of California Press, 1983).
8. E.g., Faye J. Crosby, *Juggling* (New York: The Free Press, 1991), and Faye J. Crosby, ed., *Spouse, Parent, Worker: On Gender and Multiple Roles* (New Haven: Yale University Press, 1987).
9. Susan Strasser, *Never Done: A History of American Housework* (New York: Pantheon, 1982); Ruth Cowan, *More Work for Mother* (New York: Basic Books, 1983); Alice Kessler-Harris, *Out to Work: A History of Wage-Earning Women in the United States* (New York: Oxford University Press, 1981).
10. Edith B. Gelles, *Portia: The World of Abigail Adams* (Bloomington: University of Indiana Press, 1992).

11. Elizabeth Fox-Genovese, *Within the Plantation Household: Black and White Women in the Old South* (Chapel Hill: University of North Carolina Press, 1988).

12. See, for example, Cynthia Fuchs Epstein, "Positive Effects of the Multiple Negative: Explaining the Success of Black Professional Women," *American Journal of Sociology* 78 (1973): 912–35.

13. E.g., some strong leaders still felt shy, as we read in Gloria Steinem's self-reflections, *Revolutions from Within: A Book of Self-Esteem* (Boston: Little, Brown, 1992).

14. Cynthia Fuchs Epstein, *Women in Law* (New York: Basic Books, 1981; second edition, Urbana and Chicago: University of Illinois Press, 1993).

15. Melvin L. Kohn and Carmi Schooler, "Occupational Experience and Psychological Functioning: An Assessment of Reciprocal Effects, *American Sociological Review* 38 (1973): 97–118; Peggy A. Thoits," Multiple Identities and Psychological Well-Being: A Reformulation and Test of the Social Isolation Hypothesis," *American Sociological Review* 48 (1986): 174–87; Rose Laub Coser, *In Defense of Modernity* (Stanford: Stanford University Press, 1991).

16. Epstein, *Deceptive Distinctions.*

17. The number of mothers in the labor force is from the *Current Population Survey* (Washington: Bureau of Labor Statistics, 1994), and the number of women in the labor force is from the National Research Council's *Work and Family: Policies for a Changing Work Force* (Washington: National Academy Press, 1991).

18. Epstein, *Women in Law;* Crosby, *Juggling;* Grace Baruch and Rosalind Barnett, "Role Quality and Psychological Well-Being," Crosby, ed., *Spouse, Parent, Worker,* 63–73.

19. Robert K. Merton, *Social Theory and Social Structure* (Glencoe, Ill.: The Free Press, 1948/1968); William J. Goode, "A Theory of Social Role Strain," *American Sociological Review* 25 (1960): 483–96.

20. Hochschild.

21. Thoits; Cynthia Fuchs Epstein, "Multiple Demands and Multiple Roles: The Conditions of Successful Management," Crosby, ed., *Spouse, Parent, Worker,* 23–35.

22. Cynthia Fuchs Epstein, "Tinkerbells and Pinups: The Construction and Reconstruction of Gender Boundaries at Work," Michele Lamont and Marcel Fournier, eds., *Cultivating Differences: Symbolic Boundaries and the Making of Inequality* (Chicago: University of Chicago Press, 1992), 232–56.

14

A Quest of Eternal Life

John S. Dunne

alta fantasia
—Dante, *Paradiso* 33:142

Symbolic immortality is one of the great themes of Robert Jay Lifton's work, from *Death in Life* to *The Protean Self.* Over the years I have often spoken with him about this, from the early days of our little discussion group at Yale in 1972–73. He always underlines the *symbolic* in immortality, and I always want to underline the *real.* I agree nevertheless that immortality is first of all symbolic, and in what follows I talk about the role of imagination in our ideas of immortality. In the end, though, speaking of hope, I want to hint at something real.

Gilgamesh is dead, but his quest is alive and is still going on, the quest of eternal life. I was very moved by his story when I first read the ancient epic some years ago. It spoke to my heart, his realization that he was going to die someday when he saw the death of his friend, his setting out to discover the secret of eternal life, traveling to the ends of the earth to the land of the sunrise, and his coming home wiser but still mortal. I was also reading Heidegger at the time, the essay on death in *Being and Time,* how life opens up before you all the way to death when you realize you are going to die someday. It seemed to me then that Gilgamesh and Heidegger were two ends of a string running from the earliest historic times to the present day and that if I pulled that string tight it would lift many remarkable insights out of history. I began to follow in the steps of Gilgamesh then, going from one figure to another asking each one the questions of eternal life.

I found another string, however, going back just as far as Gilgamesh, farther maybe, on which death is not an issue, because it is thought we live again and again. Instead of two strings, perhaps I should speak of

175

two kinds of thread, one the woof and the other the warp of human times. The other kind of thread goes back to Stone Age peoples who believed in rebirth. For them life passed through the following stages: birth, naming, initiation, death, funeral (including the severing of ties with the dead), and finally rebirth.[1] The severing of ties was necessary, as my grandfather or grandmother after death might return as my newborn son or daughter. The crossing thread, where death is an issue, appears among other Stone Age peoples who maintained ties with the dead—it was from them that the early civilizations evolved on the Nile and on the Tigris and Euphrates, including Erech (whence Iraq), the city of Gilgamesh.

If we maintain ties with the dead, we acquire "the sense of the past,"[2] as Henry James called it, and with that the sense also of the future and withal the sense of time, or of "time's arrow," of movement from past into future, instead of living simply in an endlessly cyclical present. And with the sense of time, death becomes an issue. "Eternal life," Wittgenstein said, "belongs to those who live in the present,"[3] but if we live with a sense of time, of having a past behind us and a future ahead of us, eternal life becomes a quest.

One way of attaining eternal life is by *conquering death.* I think of Mithraism, the great rival of Christianity in the Roman empire, and the central image of Mithraic art, the man slaying the bull, as if the bull were death (as in Hemingway's stories or in Picasso's Guernica). Originally the bull was the constellation Taurus, it has been argued recently,[4] and immortality was sought among the stars—I think of the Bull of Heaven slain by Gilgamesh. Another way is that of Christianity, *overcoming death by undergoing it.* I think of the central image of Christian art, Christ on the cross, or again the bare cross as Christ is risen from the dead. It is thought Mithraism lost to Christianity in part because it was a religion for men only, a soldier's religion, whereas Christianity was for women as well. Actually men's mysteries and women's mysteries both gave way to the Christian mystery of passing through death to life. It may be that overcoming death by going through it is somehow nearer to mortal heart, as Tolkien says of meeting the fair lady Goldberry, "less keen and lofty was the delight, but deeper and nearer to mortal heart."[5]

In the beginning the quest was for a means of prolonging life indefinitely. That is what Gilgamesh sought, to "join the assembly of the gods," to become one of the immortals. But the *Epic of Gilgamesh* proposes the wisdom of accepting death. All along the way he is advised to turn back; one figure after another tells him human beings are mortal, only gods are immortal, and that he should seek a human happiness, "the loved one in your arms, the little ones at your feet." The *Odyssey* too proposes such a wisdom: Odysseus even turns down immortality with the goddess Calypso for a mortal happiness with his human wife Penelope. The quest to prolong life, nevertheless, has lived on apart from the wisdom of the epic tradition. It became one of the three great objects of alchemy: to transmute base metals into gold, to find the cure for all diseases, and to prolong life indefinitely. And these have become the ideals, at least the latent ideals, of science, and thus found their way also into science fiction and fantasy, sometimes in a positive form, as in Giuseppe di Lampedusa's story of the Professor and the Siren, sometimes in negative form, as in Simone de Beauvoir's novel, *All Men Are Mortal.*

Consider the rings in Tolkien's *Lord of the Rings.* The seven rings of the dwarves seem to be linked with the first goal of alchemy, to transmute base metals into gold. The three rings of the elves seem to be linked with second goal, to find the cure for all diseases. The nine rings of men seem to be linked with the third goal, to prolong life indefinitely, but here too the immortality takes a negative form, for prolonging life indefinitely turns human beings into wraiths, the terrible Ring-Wraiths of the story. As for the One Ring that rules them all in Tolkien's story, it is the Ring of Gyges that makes one invisible, according to Herodotus, and gives one power over others, according to Plato. Or again, it is the Ring of the Nibelung that is made by foreswearing love.

Why was the quest to prolong life abandoned in the epics? I think it was because of the discovery of something that Freud rediscovered in the twentieth century, the desire to die. There is the desire to live embodied in the story of Gilgamesh, but there is also the desire to die embodied in the story of the great goddess Innin or Inanna who later becomes Ishtar and is known under many other names besides. (I encountered her myself on the Amazon when I was studying a little chapel there called "The Church of the Poor Devil." Her name is Jemanja or Yemanja and she is identified with the Virgin Mary). Just as the story of Gilgamesh has it that he "set his mind toward the land of the living," so in her story "toward the land of the dead she set her mind."[6] She seeks in the story the land of the dead and then, aided by the god of wisdom, returns to life. If we put the two desires together, to live and to die, we come out with a desire to live a human life, to have a human or mortal happiness.

There is another way, nevertheless, that gradually unfolds in the epics out of the story of the journey through the outerworld, the land of the dead, from the *Odyssey* through the *Aeneid* to the *Divine Comedy.* It is the growing belief in a life after death. It is this journey through the other-world that is the prototype of the journey to other worlds in modern fantasy and science fiction. Dante even calls his own journey "high fan-tasy," *alta fantasia,* in the last lines of the *Divine Comedy.* I don't think he means by that to say his relationship with Beatrice is unreal, even if his meeting with her beyond the grave is, as Borges says, a "meeting in a dream."[7] His journey through hell and purgatory and heaven is reen-acted in modern literature even apart from his faith in a life after death. "Hell, purgatory, and heaven," Luther said, "are like despair, uncer-tainty, and assurance."[8] And so it is possible to conceive of going through hell, purgatory, and heaven on earth. What carries over into fantasy and science fiction is the thought of entering, still alive, into another world.

"Our life is no dream," Novalis says, "but it should and perhaps will become one."[9] Our life is no dream for us now, I think he means, but it should and perhaps will become one for us when we awake from it into eternal life. At any rate, George MacDonald quotes the saying with some such meaning as this at the end of his first fantasy novel, *Phantastes,* where he describes a kind of nightmare journey of soul, and also at the end of his last, *Lilith,* where he describes a nightmare journey from soullessness to soul, or from lovelessness to love. I agree with Tolkien, though, that his best fantasy story is one he wrote in the middle of his life and is now usually counted as a children's story, *The Golden Key.* It is the story of a boy and a girl who become a man and a woman, who pass through death, and who meet again in the other world. What is more, their journey through the other world is described in detail as they go through water, earth, and fire into the rainbow.

I see here an idea emerging of a continuity of life, a life that can live through death. If "hell, purgatory, and heaven are like despair, uncer-tainty and assurance," if we can pass through hell, purgatory, and heaven in this life, then there is a continuity between life on this side and life on the other side of death. At one point in *The Golden Key* the Old Man of the Sea says to Mossy, the boy who has become a man, "You have tasted of death now. Is it good?" "It is good," he replies. "It is better than life." "No," the Old Man said, "it is only more life. . . ."[10] There is a novel by Herbert Read, *The Green Child,* that makes an illuminating contrast with this. In both stories there is a man and a woman who meet and journey together, passing through water and into the earth, but in Read's story they never pass on through fire and into the rainbow, they end up in the kingdom beneath the earth and their bodies entwined with each other in death become like stalagmites or stalactites. Read's is a story of life ending in death, MacDonald's is one of life ending in life. Reading the two stories side by side, we ask ourselves, "Does life end in life, or does it end in death?"

Or better, we can ask "What is our heart's desire?" Is it simply a mortal happiness? Is it rather to prolong life indefinitely and never die? Or is it to live on through death and after? "We each have in us something precious that is in no one else," Martin Buber says. "But this precious something is revealed to us only if we truly perceive our strongest feeling, our central wish, that is in us which stirs our inmost being."[11] It is at once universal, we all have it in us, and in particular, it is in each as in no one else. I imagine all human beings standing in a great circle, and each one is located at some particular point. I am located by what Shakespeare calls the "particulars of my life." On the other hand, there is only one center, and that corresponds to the universal longing of the heart. For each person, therefore, there is a radial path leading from the circumference to the center, what Buber calls "the particular way." As I follow my own particular way from the rim to the center, I get closer and closer to other people, for the paths are all converging on one and the same center. I think of this convergent desire as linked with the loneliness of the human condition, the deep loneliness we feel, the longing to be us alone, to be one.

"When I first came here, I thought sometimes that I would die because of the silence and a loneliness that is in the very air itself," John-lang says in Austin Tappan Wright's utopian fantasy *Islandia*. "For me that loneliness proved to be an anteroom to a more vivid reality than I had ever known before," he continues. "One has to be lonely first."[12] Heart's desire becomes a guiding principle in the stories of Patricia McKillip. "The future—any future," she says in *The Moon and the Face*, "is simply one step at a time out of the heart." And in *The Changeling Sea* she actually uses the phrase "heart's desire" to describe the way into the other world, here the underwater world called the Undersea:

> "To find the path to the Undersea, first find the path of your desire," the spell book said mysteriously. . . . "Call or be called," the spell said. Then: "Many paths go seaward. The path of the tide, the seal's path, the path of moonlight. The spiraled path of the nautilus shell may be imitated. Call or be called, be answered or answer. For those so called, this will be clear to their eyes. For others: You of a certain knowledge, a certain power who wish for disinterested purposes to descend to the Undersea and return, it is imperative that a gift be taken. The gift must be of the value—or seem of the value—of the traveler's life. It may become necessary to make the exchange in order to return to time."

"A gift—it says I need—," Kir says later. "Ah," Lyo said, shaking his head. "That's for mages. You have your heart's desire; that should be your path. You are the gift."[13]

Still, the heart's desire is not just the longing for another world, and thus somehow for death, but also for the longing for life. It is the synthesis of the desire to live and to die. "Do not seek death. Death will find you. But seek the road which makes death a fulfillment," Dag Hammaraskjold tells himself in his diary *Markings*.[14] For me the road which makes death a fulfillment is the radial path that leads to the heart's desire, the particular way that leads from the point on the human circle where "the particulars of my life" have located me to the center where all human paths converge. "He used often to say there was only one Road," Frodo says of Bilbo at the beginning of Tolkien's *Lord of the Rings*, "that it was like a great river: its springs were at the very doorstep, and every path was its tributary"[15] That is another image of the convergence of human paths. There is also the song that is the theme song of Tolkien's song cycle, "The Road goes ever on and on." Where does the Road lead? That is the question. Or what lies at the center where all human paths converge?

There is an answer in the cycles of storytelling. There is a twofold emergence and separation that has taken place in time. There is the emergence of the human race and its separation from the rest of nature. Then there is the emergence of the individual and the separation of the individual from the rest of humanity—thus the deep loneliness that has come to light, especially in the diaries and autobiographies of modern times. This twofold emergence and separation points backward to a time when all things were once at one, and it also points forward to a time when the individual will be reunited with humanity and humanity with nature or with God. So there are four cycles of storytelling. The first cycle is "once upon a time," when we were at one with the birds and the animals, when, as David Guss says, we knew "the language of the birds."[16] Then there is the second cycle when the human race emerged and separated from nature. Then there is the third cycle, the one we are in now, when the individual emerges and separates from the rest of humanity. And then finally there is the fourth cycle, still to come, that of the reunion of the individual with humanity and of humanity with God. This last is a stage of things often imagined in fantasy and science fiction, from Olaf Stapledon's *Star Maker* to Richard Bach's *One*.

When I ask myself the question "What for me is the road which makes death a fulfillment?" I find my answer in the mystics talking about union and reunion, "the road of the union of love with God."[17] When I read those words in San Juan de la Cruz, I thought to myself, "This is my road!" Now I am talking again about my own radial path to the center, my own particular way. But the words may also cast light on the center itself, that it is a union of love with God and with humanity. Or they may cast light on "the one Road" that Tolkien talks about, like a great river, its springs at every doorstep, every path its tributary. The primordial unity, spoken of in storytelling, is one of knowledge, us knowing "the language of the birds" and the languages of all living beings. The ultimate unity is one of love, of a union or reunion of love with God and with all others. But then there is a knowledge that comes of love. "It is the nature of love," Master Eckhart says, "that it changes us into the things we love."[18] We become what we love and so we come to know.

"We listen to our inmost selves," Buber says, "and do not know which sea we hear murmuring."[19] I wonder if the sea we hear murmuring is a deeper life that will survive our death. I wonder if our life after life is what is now our inner life. There are two rhythms in life, like the two rhythms of the sea: there is the surface rhythm of the things of life entering and passing like the waves are breaking on the shore. I can live simply according to the surface rhythm of things coming and going, or I can live according to the deeper rhythm of knowing and loving. The things of life are the situations and the persons of the life, as in a play where there is a cast of characters, the persons, and then a sequence of scenes, the situations. Love and knowledge are the basic relations to the things. In love we go out to the things of life, "It is the nature of love that it changes us into the things we love." In knowledge we take the things of life into ourselves, what we know of someone or something we have within us.

There is a rather strange fantasy novel by David Lindsay, *A Voyage to Arcturus*, where there is a kind of imagery for the deeper life, a pulsating rhythm like a heartbeat and flashing lights like strobe lights. It is said that a rock group of the Sixties called The Velvet Underground were planning to make the story into a rock opera just at the point when the group fell apart. But you can easily imagine the rock opera with the mysterious rhythm becoming very insistent and the strange flashing lights, strobe lights indeed, coming up again and again in the course of the action. At one point in the story there is not only the rhythm but also a strange music that culminates in the light:

> While he was standing there, anxious and hesitating he heard the drum taps. The rhythmical beats proceed from some distance off. The unseen

drummer seemed to be marching through the forest away from him. . . .
At the same time a low, faint music began. . . . The music rose to crescendo.
The whole dim, gigantic forest was roaring with sound. The tones came
from all sides, from above, from the ground under their feet. . . . A strange
brightness began to glow in front of them. It was not daylight, but a radi-
ance such as he had never seen before, and such as he could not have
imagined to be possible.[20]

Can the deeper life of love and knowledge survive death? Is death
simply the passing of the things of life while the life of relation continues
on? "Death is the side of life that is turned away from and unillumined
by us," Rilke says. "We must try to achieve the greatest possible consciousness of our being, which is at home in both these immeasurable
reams and is nourished inexhaustibly by both." He is envisioning a life
that lives on both sides of death. The circuit of this greater life, as he
sees it, is like the circulation of the blood. "The true pattern of life
extends through both domains, the blood with the greatest circuit runs
through both," he says. "There is neither a This-side nor a That-side but
a single great unity in which the beings who transcend us, the angels,
have their habitation."[21] The arteries carry life from the heart of the
universe to us, the veins carry life back from us to the heart of the universe. There is a great to-and-fro of life, of love and of knowledge.

We experience the deeper life most intensely when our life is taken
out of our hands. I think of two recent narratives. One is *Beyond the
Mirror* by Henri Nouwen, describing the accident that happened to him,
being hit from behind by the outside rearview mirror of a passing van
as he was walking along a road, and then his experience in intensive
care, his life being taken out of his hands, like passing beyond the mirror in stories (Lewis Carroll, George MacDonald, Jean Cocteau), passing
through into the otherworld. The other is *Journeys in Dream and Imagination* by Arthur Lundkvist, "the hallucinatory memoir," as he calls it, "of
a poet in a coma." He too tells of the experience of his life being taken
out of his hands, but without any faith in a life beyond. "I know I am
travelling all the time,"[22] he begins. He is in his hospital bed, and he is
traveling all the time, but only "in dream and imagination," or is it
"beyond the mirror?"

Here I think of the combination of willingness and hope that is often
seen in people recovering from terminal disease. When there is only a
willingness to die, there is a peaceful death; when there is only a hope
to live, there is often a recovery, a "remission" as doctors say. I have
observed this myself, particularly in one friend who was struggling with

a terminal blood disease, fighting against it with a hope that became ever more desperate until finally she accepted death, telling herself "It's okay to die! It's okay to die!" and with that immediately went into remission and began to recover. It is that strange combination, willingness and yet hope, that Kierkegaard in *Fear and Trembling* calls "faith."

If we can hope even in the face of death, I conclude, while at the same time accepting death, we can often recover, though not indefinitely I suppose. Finally we do come to die. Is there still hope even then? That is the question of the deeper life. I have found a distinction that Jean Giono makes very helpful here, between *espoir*, the masculine noun for "hope" in French, and *esperance*, the feminine noun for "hope," or perhaps we could say in English, "hopefulness."[23] It is the difference between a hope that is set on a specific thing and a hope (fullness) that is open to whatever may come. What if I come to death with this combination, a willingness to die and a hope to live that is an open-ended hope, a hopefulness? I get the feeling of something like this open-ended hope in a central passage in Tolkien where he has the main characters of his story ask the question, "What kind of story are we in?":

> "I wonder what sort of a tale we've fallen into?" Sam said. "I wonder," said Frodo. "But I don't know. And that's the way of a real tale. Take any one that you're fond of. You may know, or guess, what kind of tale it is, happy-ending or sad-ending, but the people in it don't know. And you don't want them to."[24]

Notes

1. Cf. G. Rachel Levy, *The Gate of Horn* (London: Faber & Faber, 1948), 65. See my discussion in *A Search for God in Time and Memory* (New York: Macmillan, 1969), 14–15.

2. This is the title of Henry James' last and unfinished novel, *The Sense of the Past* (New York: Scribner's, 1917 and 1943), a strange story of travel in time.

3. Ludwig Wittgenstein, *Tractatus Logico-Philosophicus*, trans. by D. F. Pears and B. F. McGuinnes (London: Routledge & Kegan Paul, 1961), 147.

4. David Ulansey, *The Origins of the Mithraic Mysteries* (New York: Oxford University Press, 1989).

5. J. R. R. Tolkien, *The Lord of the Rings* (London: George Allen & Unwin, 1976) (one volume edition), 138.

6. See my discussion of the story of Gilgamesh and that of Innin in *The City of the Gods* (New York: Macmillan, 1965), 1–14. I have a discussion of Gilgamesh also in *Time and Myth* (Garden City, NY: Doubleday, 1973), 7–15. I describe my

encounter with Jemanja in *The Church of the Poor Devil* (New York: Macmillan, 1982) (see especially note 36 on p. 162).

7. Jorge Luis Borges, "The Meeting in a Dream" in his *Other Inquisitions,* trans. by Ruth L. C. Simms (New York: Washington Square, 1966), 101ff.

8. Luther says this in Thesis 16 of the famous *Ninety-Five Theses.* See my discussion in *A Search for God in Time and Memory,* 79.

9. Novalis quoted by George MacDonald, *Phantastes* and *Lilith,* with intro. by C. S. Lewis (London: Victor Gollancz, 1962), 180 and 420.

10. George MacDonald, *The Golden Key* (New York: Farrar, Straus & Giroux, 1967), 68–71. Compare Herbert Read, *The Green Child* (New York: New Directions, 1948). See my comparison of the two novels in *The House of Wisdom* (San Francisco: Harper & Row, 1985), x–xi and 1, 3, 10 and 60.

11. Martin Buber, *The Way of Man* (Secaucus, NJ: Citadel, 1966), 18. See my discussion in *The Peace of the Present* (Notre Dame and London: University of Notre Dame Press, 1991), 7.

12. Austin Tappan Wright, *Islandia* (New York: Farrar & Rinehart, 1942), 876.

13. Patricia McKillip, *The Moon and the Face* (New York: Berkeley, 1986), 88, and *The Changeling Sea* (New York: Ballantine, 1988), 118 and 128.

14. Dag Hammarskjold, *Markings,* trans. by Leif Sjoberg and W. H. Auden (New York: Ballantine, 1985), 138.

15. Tolkien, *The Lord of the Rings,* 87.

16. David M. Guss, *The Language of the Birds* (San Francisco: North Point, 1985), especially xiv–xv on the four cycles of story. See my discussion of the four cycles in *The Peace of the Present,* 71–72.

17. Saint John of the Cross (San Juan de la Cruz), *Dark Night of the Soul,* trans. by E. Allison Peers (Garden City, NY: Doubleday, 1959), 34.

18. Master Eckhart quoted by Martin Heidegger in *Poetry, Language, Thought,* trans. by Alfred Hofstadter (New York: Harper & Row, 1975), 176.

19. Martin Buber, *Ecstatic Confessions,* ed. by Paul Mendes-Flohr, trans. by Alfred Hofstadter (New York: Harper & Row, 1975), 176.

20. David Lindsay, *A Voyage to Arcturus* (originally published in 1920) (London: Sphere, 1980), 150–54.

21. Rainer Maria Rilke, *Selected Letters 1902–1926,* trans. by Ann B. Weissman and Annicka Planck (New York: Four Walls Eight Windows, 1991), 23.

22. Artur Lundkvist, *Journeys in Dream and Imagination,* trans. by Ann B. Weissman and Annika Planck (New York: Four Walls Eight Windows, 1991), 23. Compare Henri Nouwen, *Beyond the Mirror* (New York: Crossroad, 1990).

23. Jean Giono, *The Man Who Planted Trees* (Chelsea, VT: Chelsea Green, 1985), 50–51 (afterword by Norma L. Goodrich). See my discussion in *The Homing Spirit* (New York: Crossroad, 1987), 69.

24. Tolkien, *The Lord of the Rings,* 739.

15

The Second Scar

Richard Sennett

Robert Jay Lifton's psychoanalytic writings have constituted a unique provocation for students of modern society; he has challenged us to look for puzzles of collective sentiment, to explore group emotions which have no clear names; he has made sociologists, political scientists, and historians search harder for meaning than our own disciplines might prompt us to do. Lifton's work on the "protean self" has been a guide for me in the following essay, which explores some of the sources and virtues of the protean self in Western culture. In this essay, I have not used Lifton's vocabulary, however, for the phenomenon he describes psychoanalytically as a protean self appears socially in many guises, in the figure of the wanderer or the foreigner, in the experience of displacement or estrangement, in post-modern theories of the de-centered self. Nonetheless, I hope Robert Jay Lifton will find in "The Second Scar" the marks of my great esteem for him and his work.

The Second Scar of Oedipus

The foreigner is perhaps the most threatening figure in the theatre of society. An outsider calls into question society's rules, the sociologist Georg Simmel believed; the foreigner exposes the sheer arbitrariness of society's script, which insiders follow thinking its lines have been written by Right, Reason, or God.[1] Yet this cannot be the whole story. For the foreigner may also gain another knowledge through his or her own exile denied to those who remained rooted to home, knowledge about living a displaced life. And this knowledge Western civilization, from its very origins, has honored, if painfully.

The exile's knowledge about living a displaced life shapes, for instance, the first two of Sophocle's Theban plays, which the playwright makes dramatically apparent in two scars on King Oedipus' body. *Oedipus Rex* turns on a fact which seems of little artistic interest in itself—just a cog in the machinery of the plot. The king's ankles bear a scar as a result of a wound he received as a child; the very name "Oedipus" in Greek means "one with pierced ankles." The king has wandered, lost touch with his origins; when the characters in the legend come to the point where they must know the king's true identity, they are able to recover this truth by looking at his body. The process of identification begins when a messenger declares, "your ankles should be witnesses."[2]

Were the evidence King Oedipus seeking not about incest, we might pay more attention to his scar. Despite the great migrations in his life, his body contains permanent evidence about who he "really" is. The king's travels have left no comparable signatures upon his body. His migratory experience counts for little, that is, in relation to his origin; in his origins lie his truth. Indeed, it is a commonplace that among the polis-proud Greeks, exile, dispossession, migration have been of far lesser account than the marks of origins and of belonging. One thinks of Socrates' refusal of exile as evidence of the belief that even death as a citizen was more honorable than exile. Or of Thucydides' remark that foreigners have no speech—by which he meant that their speech counts for nothing in the *polis*; it is the chattering of those who can't vote.

Yet the marks on Oedipus' ankles will not be the only marks on his body. He will answer the wounds others made on him at the beginning by gouging his own eyes out. The second wound balances the first; the first wound marks his origins, the second marks his personal reckoning of his life. Twice-wounded, he has became a man whose life can literally be read in his face. When Freud wrote about Oedipal guilt, this second scar seemed the end of the story. Yet in Sophocles drama, this tragic, willed act sets in motion a new phase in the life of the King.

Oedipus sets out again into the world as an exile, thinking that perhaps he could return to his origins, to the mountain, "*my* mountain, which my mother and my father while they were living would have made my tomb,"[3] yet this return is not to be. As *Oedipus at Colonus* opens, he has come instead to the deme (village) of Colonus, a mile northwest of Athens, where the Delphic oracle has told him he will die instead; the prophecy will in turn be fulfilled differently than he had imagined at the opening of the play. The two wounds on Oedipus' body are thus a scar of origins which cannot be concealed and the wanderer's self-inflicted scars which do not seem to heal: unlike Freud's image of guilty consummation, Sophocles tells the story of a life which cannot stand still.

The Greeks would have understood Oedipus' unending journey as resonant with the Homeric legends, particularly the legend of Odysseus. In Greek practice, later to be codified in Roman law, there were certain circumstances in which foreign exile was in fact honorable, more honorable that Socrates' way; *exsilium* entitled the person convicted of a capital charge to choose exile instead of death, a choice which spared friends and family the shame and grief of witnessing one's execution. Sophocles introduces to *Oedipus at Colonus* a moral dimension to the very act of migration in depicting Oedipus as a figure who has been ennobled by his uprooting. But how, precisely, has that happened?

At a haunting moment in *Oedipus Coloneus* Oedipus tries to tell the young Theseus what he has learned in his exile:

> Dear son of Aegeus, to the gods alone it happens never to die or to grow old; all else is confounded by almighty Time. The strength of the land wastes away, and the strength of the body; faith dies and faithlessness comes to be, and the same wind blows not with constancy either in the friendships of men or between city and city. To some now, and to others later, the sweet becomes bitter and then again pleasant. And if in Thebes it is now fair weather for you, Time in his course will break to pieces the present pledges of harmony for a small word's sake.[4]

The speech seems to foreshadow Simmel's image of the outsider as a man possessed of a threatening knowledge: *nomos* is not truth; ordinary things, in themselves, are illusory. And yet Oedipus does not speak to Theseus in despair. Since the king blinded himself, he has not lost faith in the world, but rather seen it in a new way, as a place of provisional loves, of temporary attachments, of insecurity. In his blindness, Oedipus has accepted the world on these terms, they are all he or Theseus can hope for; Oedipus dies at Colonus at peace. The second scar has led him to dwell in the world, uncertainly, painfully, yet aware.

Something of that same knowledge informs the Judeo-Christian tradition.[5] The people of the Old Testament thought of themselves as uprooted wanderers. The Yahweh of the Old Testament was himself a wandering god, his Ark of the Covenant portable and, in the theologian Harvey Cox's words, "When the Ark was finally captured by the Philistines, the Hebrews began to realize that Yahweh was not localized even in it. . . . He traveled with his people and elsewhere."[6] Yahweh was a god of time rather than of place, a god who promised to his followers a divine meaning for their unhappy travels.

Wandering and exposure were as strongly felt to be the consequences of faith among early Christians as among Old Testament Jews. The author of the "Epistle to Diognatus" at the height of the Roman Empire's glory declared that

> Christians are not distinguished from the rest of humanity either in locality or in speech or in customs. For they do not dwell off in cities of their own . . . nor do they practice an extraordinary style of life. . . . They dwell in their own countries, but only as sojourners. . . . Every foreign country is a fatherland to them, and every fatherland is a foreign country.[7]

This image of the wanderer came to be one of the ways in which Saint Augustine defined the two cities in *The City of God*:

> Now it is recorded of Cain that he built a city, while Abel, as though he were merely a pilgrim on earth, built none. For the true City of the saints is in heaven, though here on earth it produces citizens in which it wanders as though on a pilgrimage through time looking for the Kingdom of eternity.[8]

This "pilgrimage through time" rather than settling in place draws its authority from Jesus' refusal to allow His disciples to build monuments to Him, and His promise to destroy the Temple of Jerusalem. Judeo-Christian culture is thus, at its very sources, about experiences of displacement.

Yet no more than Oedipus do these Judeo-Christian homilies preach sheer renunciation of the world. If ordinary social relations do not reveal divine purposes, they nonetheless are morally important. In the world we must learn to accept ourselves and each other as insufficient creatures, unfinished works. We can attain closure, if at all only in another life. By uprooting ourselves, in spirit or in fact, from our daily circumstances we might come to such realizations of our finitude. This wound of displacement is the Judeo-Christian version of the second scar: we deprive ourselves of rootedness that we can became consequent human beings.

The two scars on the body of King Oedipus represent a fundamental conflict in our civilization between the truth-claims of belonging and origins versus the truths discovered by displacement and wandering. The second scar is not so much a dismissal of society as a hard lesson about how to live with its rules, customs, and beliefs. Only by a painful act of self-denial or self-injury can one come to experience the nomos as the problematic, uncertain reality it is.

This ancient conflict has taken on a new form in the modern world. On the one hand, the "disenchantment of the world" of which Max

Weber wrote has meant that people experience the arrangements of society as mere conventions which can be changed at will. On the other hand, and perhaps because living in a truly disenchanted condition is more than most people can bear, modern society has generated a deep need to deny the ethical dimensions of disenchantment conveyed by the second scar. Community, identity, roots: these human relations represent borders to be sealed rather than boundaries to be crossed. The passion for closure appears not only in nationalistic and ethnic strife, but also, within gentler states, in experience of sexual, religious, and racial differences—as though truth lay in finding out who we "really" are, as though our lives lay in the secrets of Oedipus' first scar. The notion that we might traverse the complexities of society only by willing painful ruptures in ourselves seems in turn truly foreign and strange.

Though historians today are rather perversely suspicious of dates, the Revolution of 1848 marks a moment in which the modern passion for identity, roots, and origins bursts forth in Western culture, a passion declared for community especially in its nationalist form, at the expense of the estranging journeys of self-tranformation. In these nationalist explosions of 1848, the native—using that word in its largest sense—rebuke the foreign.

The Revolution of 1848 lasted four months, from February to June of that year. It began in Paris, but by March its repercussion were felt throughout Central Europe, where movements sprang up proclaiming the superiority of national republics over the geographic parcellings of territory made by dynasties and diplomats at the Congress of Vienna in 1815. Events had something of the same combustive character as did the disengagement from Russian hegemony which spread across these same nations in the last four months of 1989.

The generation of 1848 also marks a contrary implosion in modern culture as well. After the revolutionary fervor subsided, something like a knowledge of the second scar appeared in the arts, a research into the possibilities and consequences of displacement, an enquiry into how the everyday could be made strange. The ensuing conflict between modern art and society is one way in which our own time still echoes the passions of the Homeric legend, the tragic playwrights, the prophets of the old Testament and the early Christian believers.

The Native Self

It may be a truism that all societies fear outsiders, an ethnocentrism which the psychoanalyst Erik Erikson calls incisively "pseudo-speciation," meaning the propensity to treat those unlike oneself as not really human. In the nineteenth century nativity—that core identity with which one seemed born—became a highly self-conscious cultural construction, however, as self-conscious an effort as must be the desire to render the everyday world strange and foreign. It is certainly true that the voices heard in 1848 throughout Europe celebrating place, blood, and inherited ritual were not those of men and women who had learned suddenly to speak. The tangled history of nationalist sentiment was as old as the nation-state. Yet in 1848 those who spoke about nations had to account for new ways of speaking about society, principally in the emerging domain of anthropology, and even more sought to relate the sentiments of blood and soil to that most modern of all discourses— discourses about the self. As Isaiah Berlin has shown in his study *Vico and Herder*, the eighteenth century thought in anthropological ways which would be rejected in the nineteenth century. In the eighteenth century, the word "native" had two meanings which we continue to employ today, but lacked one meaning which the nineteenth century created. In the *Encyclopedia*, Diderot used "native" as an adjective to describe any person's origins; he used the noun "native" to describe a non-European. (Montesquieu would make a play on this second usage in *The Persian Letters* by having his Persians treat the Parisians like aboriginal natives.) Lacking in these usages was the sense that natives were the ancestors of Europeans—the native was an Other, rather than a kinsman. Prior to Darwin, early-nineteenth-century English and French accounts of Inuits, Laplanders, and Africans described native peoples as the first humans out of which civilized Europeans evolved to their present glory—for reasons these early ethnographers could not really explain. These accounts, moreover, connected the world of the European peasantry to "savage" life abroad; to be civilized meant to live in a court or a town.

The savants of the Enlightenment earlier employed their own anthropological understanding for the most liberal of reasons; they sought to affirm the dignity of human differences. To Herder, in Berlin's words, ". . . it is [people's] differences that matter most, for it is the differences that make them what they are, make them themselves."[9] This assertion that human beings are culture-specific was in the eighteenth century more than a plea for taking sheer anthropological variation seriously. It was an attack upon what we call today "Eurocentrism." Voltaire believed that "It is terrible arrogance to affirm that, to be happy, everyone should become European."[10] In different places, different people find different ways to attempt happiness, that most difficult of feats.

To Voltaire, the knowledge that others do not die of foods we are afraid to eat, that others in fact find happiness in tasting them, ought to give us pause about our own convictions, indeed ought to arouse our desire to taste the unknown. The perception of differing values ought make the perceiver more cosmpolitan. That perception about aboriginal natives then crossed to the usage of "native" as an adjective describing any person's birthplace. The best hopes of 1789, for instance, drew upon this cosmopolitanism; one did not have to live in Paris, or to be French, to believe in the liberty, equality, and fraternity proclaimed in the French Revolution. In Kant's *Reflections of a Universal Citizen of the World* of 1784, the philosopher argued that the capacity for reasoned political judgement develops when a person learns to feel at home and derives stimulation among a diversity of people; This "universal citizen" learns corespondingly what is common to them all, aboriginal Indian, Persian, Pole, and Frenchman alike.

European powers had for generations practiced imperialism in the name of destroying aboriginal peoples as heathens, devils, and animals, justifying the carnage by religious doctrines of "pseudo-speciation." The contrary eighteenth-century celebration of natives, as in Rousseau's writings about the "noble savage," constituted in fact a bitter play on words. Rousseau seems to have been much struck by the stuffed figure of an American Indian in full ceremonial dress who was put on display in Paris by a taxidermist in 1741; the taxidermist had posed the Indian in a pensive mood. This "savage" Rousseau imagined to be a man whose reflectiveness was more acute and profound than the be-wigged, gossipy, thoughtless Parisians who came to the taxidermist's shop. The Noble Savage stood, like Kant's citizen of the world, for a more universal, deeper humanity, a personage freed of the petty habits and the moral blindness which passed for civilization.

Whereas Herder understood something ahead of his time: the perception of difference might make people more ethnocentric, since there is no common humanity to which they can jointly appeal. Nativism in turn would create blindess and indifference towards others—a blindness justified by conceiving of the native as a man or woman innocent of the world. The natives who appear in Manzoni's writings on the Italian peasantry after 1848 have crossed into that innocent territory, for instance. Sometimes Manzoni does indeed depict them to be like Rousseau's noble savage—self-conscious and knowing: removed from the cities which were the seats of Austro-Hungarian power, they have guarded the democratic values of an earlier, free Italy. More often Manzoni writes as Tolstoy will later write, claiming the peasantry is morally superior because peasants have no awareness of themselves in time and history, are free of the gnawing poison of too much thought, of thinking beyond the confines of life as it is given. Manzoni's "man of the soil" does not look in the mirror of history; he simply lives.

The politics of this cultural movement used a new language of legitimacy transcending the views of those who had earlier argued for constitutional regimes, democracy, or other political ideals in their homelands, echoing the eighteenth-century ideals of the American and French Revolutions. The language of the Slavophiles or the Sons of Attica represented the triumph of an anthropology of innocence over the worldly politics of difference. In 1848, the revolutionary nationalists rejected the very idea of a nation as a political creation because they believed that a nation was enacted instead by custom, by the manners and mores of a *volk*; the food people eat, how they move when they dance, the dialects they speak, the precise forms of their prayers, these are the constituent elements of national life. Law is incapable of legislating these pleasures in certain foods, constitutions cannot ordain *fervent* belief in certain saints: that is, power cannot make culture.

The loathing of intellection and self-consciousness—characteristic of so much modern intellectual culture—coagulated in this rhetoric of nationalism. As I have tried to show elsewhere, by 1848 the self as a psychological phenomenon had become a political issue, for a labyrinthine self-consciousness, a burdened self-hood, seemed the mark of a rotten social order, and it seemed possible that political action could lighten that burden.[11] The man or woman of the city appeared to carry the heaviest psychological burden. A century before 1848, Rousseau had imagined, in his *Letter to D'Alembert*, that those who fled towns would become more introspective and self-knowlegeable human beings, like the Noble Savage. In 1848, the burdens of selfhood are to be lifted, in the towns and in the countryside alike, through recourse to images of an unknowing innocence. The Romantic movement had inflated the realm of individual sensation and reflection to a moral condition; the revolutionaries proposed to deflate it by a return to the native, collective self.

The new anthropology crossed with this psychology in 1848 in visually sophisticated ways. In the posters calling for national unity composed in the spring of 1848 by Chodluz and others, for instance, the People are shown responding to the call for uprising dressed in work clothes, or in peasant costume. In the revolutionary posters of 1790 and 1791, poster artists frequently dressed the poor in military uniforms or in the colors of their political clubs; two generations later, in responding to a great historical event, the People do not dress for the occasion. Nor in the posters of 1848 are the masses given especially dramatic expressions of rage or patriotic zeal: everything is done to signify that the people are not self-conscious, just being themselves. Gone, indeed, are even the allegorical, classical figures who emblazoned the posters of the revolutions of 1830, such as Delacroix's "Liberty Leading the People." For the revolutionary nationalists of 1848, the unawareness of the *volk* of itself, its lack of a mirror, was a source of virtue—as against the vices of self-consciousness and self-estrangement of the cosmopolitan bourgeois whose mental outlook is upon a diorama of mirrors which reflect back endless hesitations and second thoughts. The native self would be liberated from all this.

This crossing of anthropology and psychology in the concept of a native self supported a renewed sociological emphasis on the truth of origins, the truth of the first scar. The seeming spontaneity and lack of cosmopolitan self-consciousness of natives renewed that emphasis first through denying history's hold over a people's inherent character. Petofi's appeals for a Magyar revolt exclude from whatever it is to be a "real" Magyar the centuries-long interaction of Magyars with the Turks, Slavs, and Germans, though these historic encounters in fact colored the practice of religion, created a complex cuisine, and altered the structure of the Hungarian language itself. In place of this history, Petofi preached a version of Magyar-ness as if from generation to generation it had been both unchanging and self-sustaining.

The ingredients of the native self which crystallized in radical thought in 1848 secondly gave a corresponding, fixed geographic imperative to the concept of culture: habit, faith, pleasure, ritual—all depend upon enactment in a particular territory. This is because the place which nourishes native culture rituals is a place composed of people with whom one can share without explaining, that is, people like oneself. Both the time and soil of the true native are freed of the cursed turns and inner questioning of the cosmopolitan.

The eighteenth-century code of national honor would have found this celebration of everyday life degrading. In that older code, you placed a foot soldier—whether mercenary or not, French or not—in a blue-and-red flannel uniform fitted with gold braid, epaulets, and stamped ceremonial buttons. No matter that it was a useless costume or worse than useless during military engagement, no matter that he might be starving in barracks; this ceremonial robe gave him a place in something greater and grander than himself, it glorified his condition as a Frenchman. Similarly, in peacetime monarchs like Louis XIV sought to legitimate their policies through elaborate ceremonies, the "progresses," "turnings" and "audiences" threw into dramatic relief the glory of the state, its magnificent constructions elevated far above, if "unnatural" in relation to, the sphere of everyday life.

The ideology of the native self preached by Kossuth, Manzoni, Garibaldi, Mieckewitz, or Louis Blanc—that a people should glory in themselves as they ordinarily were marketing, feasting, praying, harvesting—meant that honor was to be found in an anthropology of authenticity rather than of arbitrary signification. Native rituals, beliefs, and mores represent forms of being rather than doing, to make Heidigger's distinction, embodied in time-tested and permanently cohering form, inseparable from native territory.

We may recognise in this rough sketch beliefs which overflowed in 1848 about nativity and true identity the origins of many twentieth-century totalitarian practices. Modern totalitarian states capitalize upon the virtues of the native self, legitimated repressive institutions as reflections of that selfhood impulse rather than as constructions which might be problematic and in need of constant discussion; civil police or neighborhood revolutionary committees, for instance, can be declared permanant organs of spontaneity, seeming only emanations of what "everybody" wants welling up from the folk-life. Yet to think about the legacy of 1848 in terms of totalitarianism alone clouds our understanding of how the quest for a native self continues to permeate more democratic forms of life.

Nineteenth-century aspirations established the modern ground-rule for having an identity. You have the strongest identity when you aren't aware you "have" it; you just are it. That is, you are most yourself when you are least aware of yourself. This doctrine of spontaneity-as-truth has served as much as a touchstone in the arts as in everyday life; it diminishes our pleasure in sheer artifice for its own sake, and makes the practice of courtesy seem fake.

Perhaps more consequently, the belief in a native self has infected what Americans have come to call multi-culturalism. The terms on which cultural differences appear in our society are not those which Voltaire imagined, the appearance of differences which stimulate people to cross borders of identity. Rather, these borders are increasingly sealed, as though the sexual, racial, religious, and ethnic differences between people constitute native distinctions. Of course it has become common to criticize gays, blacks, and radical feminists for having become separatist in their thinking and behavior; it is highly unusual, however, for the people making these criticisms to speak of gay impulses in themselves, or—seemingly even more bizarre—moments when they become black. The dominant culture speaks instead of inclusion and absorption, offers in place of the disturbances of difference the balm of assimilation, as though that dominant center is more fundamental and solid, as though those who differ must seek to return to native ground.

Yet 1848 also set in motion the forces which would lead modern culture to draw again on the passions of the second scar through entirely modern means. The failed revolution set in motion profound doubts about the stability and certainty of everyday life, that *nomos* which the nationalist revolutionaries celebrated. This subsequent *critique de la vie quotidienne*, to use Henri Lefebrvre's phrase, appeared most strongly the arts. But that artistic impulse to dislodge the everyday, the rooted, and the fixed also appeared among some revolutionaries who had to make sense of their own lives as permanent exiles. More largely, the political upheavals of our own time reflect our need for Oedipal knowledge of the second scar, as we continue to struggle with the scar of nativity.

Notes

This essay is the first part of a longer work in progress.

1. cf. Georg Simmel, "The Stranger," in Kurt Wolff, ed., *The Sociology of Georg Simmel* (Glencoe, Ill.: Free Press, 1956).

2. Sophocles, *Oedipus the King*, as translated by David Greene (Chicago: University of Chicago Press, 1954), p. 55; original, *Oedipus Tyraneus*, Loeb: 1030–1035.

3. *Oedipus the King*, p.73; *Oedipus Tyraneus*, 1453.

4. Sophocles *Oedipus Coloneus* (Cambridge, Mass.: Loeb Classical Library), 607–620.

5. In the following four sentences I have taken the liberty of paraphrasing myself; they appear in Chapter Three of my new book, *Flesh and Stone: The Body and the City in Western Civilization* (New York: Norton, 1994).

6. Harvey Cox, *The Secular City*, rev. ed. (New York: Macmillan, 1966), 49.

7. Translated and quoted in Jaroslav Pelikan, *Jesus through the Centuries* (New Haven: Yale University Press, 1985), 49–50.

8. Augustine, *The City of God*, trans. by Gerald G. Walsh, S. J., et al. (New York; Image, 1958), 325.

9. Isaiah Berlin, *Vico and Herder: Two Studies in the History of Ideas* (London: The Hogarth Press, 1976), xxiii.

10. Berlin, *op. cit.* 197–98.

11. See Richard Sennett, *The Fall of Public Man* (New York: W. W. Norton, 1993), 154–73 and 224–36.

16

The Japanese Psyche: Myth and Reality

Takeo Doi

Robert Jay Lifton and I have been friends since he came to Japan as a young medical officer of the American Air Force in the early 1950s. I followed closely his emergence in the ensuing years as a prominent scholar studying men and women caught in various extreme situations peculiar to our age, just as he witnessed my own attempts to combine Japanese heritage with American learning.

One could perhaps question the legitimacy of talking about the Japanese mind. One may say that there is no such thing as the Japanese mind, or, if there is, it is not yet proven, for there exist only individuals who are called Japanese. Naturally there is a great variety among them and one should not generalize from selected samples. That is the criticism raised by scholars of the empiricist persuasion against the indigenous studies of the Japanese mind, which have become popular in recent years. My own work is often mentioned as one example of these indigenous studies. In reply, I say that it is legitimate to talk about the Japanese mind, just as it is legitimate to talk about the American mind. There are phenomena which require explanation in terms of the group mind, such as the differences between cultures or the historical development of various nations. I admit that such explanation would be hypothetical or, one might even say, fictive. However, this does not invalidate the explanation, since any explanation about any subject is hypothetical in the last analysis, and the validity of a hypothesis hinges upon how much it can explain.

Any discussion of the Japanese mind—or the American mind for that matter—involves a value judgment. Consider, for instance, Allan Bloom's famous *The Closing of the American Mind*, a severe indictment of cultural decay that seems to be eating away at the American mind today. Along the same line, though totally different in approach, is Christopher Lasch's *The Culture of Narcissism*. Interestingly enough, there are no

197

such books written by Japanese authors regarding the Japanese mind. Quite the reverse, almost all recent studies of the Japanese mind seem to emphasize its unique qualities. Indeed, this tendency is so marked that it has invited some strong reaction, mostly from abroad. Peter N. Dale, for example, in *The Myth of Japanese Uniqueness*, is a particularly caustic critic, arguing that the recent studies by Japanese authors are all inspired by a nationalistic fervor which betrays "a diffuse sense of inferiority to the West."[1] Dale may have a point. But he is also much too ideological, for he equates the West with "mature modernity," while he condemns Japan's modernity as a facade which masks ineradicable feudalism. Surely Japan went through transformation under the pressure from the West in recent centuries.

No wonder then that there have been repeated attempts to reflect upon the true status of Japan as a nation or a culture in order to recover the Japanese identity. Hence, the recent studies of Japan by Japanese authors tend to be tinged positively in sharp contrast with the portrayal of the West by certain western scholars. I grant nevertheless that it may be unwise to use the word "unique" in describing the different qualities of the Japanese mind, because it might appear that we are implying that the Japanese mind is unrivaled and beyond comparison. If so, this would call to memory the xenophobic nationalism that swept through prewar and wartime Japan. The term "unique" may even seem offensive when the "uniqueness of the Japanese" is proposed as an explanation of Japan's remarkable transition from a completely shattered nation to a great economic power in mere decades. This smacks of ethnocentrism and such an ethnocentrism, whether by the West or Japan, is wholly unacceptable.

So let us be clear that if the Japanese mind is unique, it is only in the sense that any nation or any person is unique. But then, one should not suppose also that there is nothing in common, say, between the Japanese mind and the American mind. We are all human, first and foremost. There are more features in common that bind us than there are differences that separate us from one another. In other words, I do not subscribe to cultural relativism, which dictates that any culture should be judged only on its own terms, that it cannot and should not be tampered with, and that it should not be criticized from the outside. It seems to me that cultural relativism and ethnocentrism are two sides of the same coin. Indeed, why should I be talking about the Japanese mind to non-Japanese if it concerns us Japanese alone? I am not presenting the Japanese mind as a curiosity, as something beyond comprehension, and certainly not as an enigma. I present the Japanese mind as food for thought, just as the American mind has been for Japanese thought all these years.

If I should name one psychological trait characteristic of Japanese people, I would say that it is the dependent posture that works like oil in interpersonal relationships. I am not saying that Japanese are more dependent than Americans in some biological or psychobiological sense. We are equally dependent; however, it is the emphasis on dependence that distinguishes Japanese from American and is a most prominent feature of the Japanese mind. Let me explain how I came to this view. When I first came to the United States for study in 1950, I was immediately struck by the dramatic difference between the way people in Japan relate to one another and the way Americans relate to one another. I realized that the difference lies in the appreciation of dependent relationships in Japan and the lack of this appreciation in the United States.

This observation, it seemed to me, is borne out by the existence of a special vocabulary in Japanese to express various phases of emotional dependence. While I do not want to go into details of the language, it should be noted that the word *amae* plays a pivotal role in the lexicon of Japanese dependent relationships. *Amae* refers primarily to infant psychology in that it indicates what an infant feels toward its mother when it wants to come close to her and hold her. This fact led me to the following conclusion. The dependent relationships the Japanese seem to enjoy must be an extension of one's original dependency toward one's parents. It can be further concluded that it is possible to study child rearing in light of *amae*. Actually this idea was put into practice by my friend, the late Dr. William Caudill, cultural anthropologist and pioneer in a cross-cultural study of Japan and the United States. He and his assistant, Mrs. Helen Weinstein, selected a matched sample of thirty three-to-four-month-old Japanese and American infants and studied the interaction of those infants with their mothers. The conclusion they drew from this study is extremely interesting:

> American infants are more happily vocal, more active, and more exploratory of bodies and their physical environment, than are Japanese infants. Directly related to these findings, the American mother is in greater vocal interaction with her infant and stimulates him to greater physical activity and exploration. The Japanese mother, in contrast, is in greater bodily contact with her infant, and soothes him toward physical quiescence, and passivity with regard to his environment. Moreover, these patterns of behavior, so early learned by the infant, are in line with the differing expectations for late behavior in the two cultures as the child grows to be an adult.[2]

This observation is highly indicative of the differences between American and Japanese patterns of communication. Americans are conditioned from the very beginning of life to associate human contact with verbal communication, whereas Japanese tend to emphasize nonverbal communication in everyday transactions. This characteristic of the Japanese people, in my view, is related to the psychology of *amae*. In the interaction between mother and infant, the mother, of course, *can* verbalize feelings while the infant cannot. *Amae* describes that nonverbal feeling which the infant experiences in its emotional dependence upon the mother. In other words, through *amae* the Japanese demonstrate their appreciation of (and emphasize) what ordinarily passes unspoken in everyday communication.

There is, however, one important distinction about the vocabulary of *amae*: it describes an emotion but in itself is not emotive like the English word "love." One could even say that, for Japanese, verbal communication is something that accompanies and supplements nonverbal communication, not the other way around. Perhaps that is why Japanese often impress foreigners as not properly communicative, not as straight and forthright as they should be. This comes about because Japanese are extremely sensitive to the feeling surrounding interpersonal relationships and tend to neglect verbal communication.

In this connection, one might note a difference between what Japanese understand by a close relationship and its American equivalent. Japanese feel that with a close friend or lover or spouse one does not have to say much; they are happy simply being together and will not waste time in just talking. In fact, one way the Japanese characterize a close relationships is that it is one in which two people can be comfortably silent together. It seems to me that Americans are quite different in this respect; being close to someone means being able to talk with that person to one's heart's content. It is not that Japanese do not enjoy talking. They do at times, but in the closest of relationships silence will prevail over talk as the surest form of intimacy.

In the same context, you may notice Japanese shyness—reluctance, really—about demonstrating affection in public. Lovers, spouses, or parents and children do not embrace or kiss in public simply because they do not want to make public what should remain private. Only shaking hands among the Western forms of greeting has become somewhat fashionable nowadays—besides traditional bowing—particularly among city people; but this still is done less frequently than in the West. These patterns of social behavior derive from the Japanese propensity for estimating at first meeting how much one can or should be dependent and deferential toward the other.

The preference of Japanese for nonverbal communication also goes

together with the well-known Japanese fondness for group and communal interactions, for nonverbal communication is workable only among
those who know each other intimately. And what Japanese value most
in group life is the sense of belonging. Actually, the very purpose of
socialization is to gain this sense of belonging, which is inculcated in
children from the very early stage of life. No wonder, then, that Japanese
love group life, which they generally experience as supportive and not
as constrictive. Of course, a group can be constrictive; however the Japanese style of group control is not authoritarian, not really from the top
down. The notorious consensus-building proceeds inconspicuously
from the bottom up. Also, one must remember that the Japanese identification with a group is never meant to be total: Japanese do experience
conflict between individual interests and group life. How to manage
such conflict is no small matter to a Japanese.

The question of how to manage this individual-vs.-group conflict is
related to the problem of ambivalence, which in the technical parlance
of psychiatry means the co-existence of opposite feelings toward the
same object. It was Freud who popularized the theory that ambivalence
is inherent in human nature. Even if it is accepted that ambivalence is
universal, there are individual differences and, I strongly suspect, cultural differences as well in the ways of coping with it. It seems to me that
Westerners, and possibly Chinese, tend to apply a certain principle in
resolving conflict, thereby putting aside ambivalence. In other words,
they try not to reveal ambivalence to outsiders. Japanese, on the contrary, seem to dwell on ambivalence and may at times even appear to be
playing with two opposite feelings.

This is where the Japanese classical duality of *tatemae* and *honne* comes
in. *Tatemae* indicates the rules of whatever group one happens to belong
to and *honne* one's personal considerations for belonging to such group.
Japanese observe *tatemae*—the social obligation—as long as it contains
honne. But when it no longer does, they feel entitled to act out *honne*—to
act on the previously unstated interests. It is this pattern of behavior that
is usually interpreted as Japanese unscrupulosity, a Japanese distaste for
confrontation or preference for ambiguity. It is this pattern that often
gives Westerners the impression that Japanese are two-faced and oppor-
tunistic. In more neutral terms they can be said to be relativistic and
flexible; and of course, depending upon circumstances, this can also be
interpreted as a sign of weakness or shrewdness.

Do these *tatemae/honne* concepts apply to Americans? I think they do,
in spite of the appearance that defies such duality. But whichever of the
two aspects is adopted, Americans vigorously justify it; Japanese do not.

I am inclined to say that even when Japanese reject *tatemae*, its influence somehow lingers and serves as a kind of buffer. I think it is this which often disguises Japanese aggression, whereas American aggression tends to be direct and naked, if justified at all. Or should one say that it is direct and naked because it is justified?

I think the attitude of the Japanese toward ambivalence very much affects their relationships with foreigners. If they show their ambivalence to each other, they will naturally manifest it even more toward foreigners, in turn inviting foreigners' ambivalence. The upshot of all this is that they may not be really liked by foreigners in spite of an ardent desire to be liked. This, incidentally, explains the rather poor performance by Japanese in international diplomacy. In particular, they do not seem to be able to exert leadership in the arena of international politics. But how can they when they have the same problem in domestic politics? This is the root of the Japanese problem which so vexes Americans.

Lastly, I would like to say few words about the function of the emperor in Japan. I understand that the funeral of the *showa* Emperor attracted much coverage of this subject on American television. According to the present Constitution, the emperor is the symbol of the unity of Japan as a nation; this definition seems to make sense in the light of what I have said before. There is much division and tension in Japanese society in spite of the professed homogeneity, because such homogeneity is permeated by ambivalence. The emperor is said to unite a nation, not with power, but with his status as the symbol of national unity. He is not even emperor in the original sense of the word, even though Japan waged past imperial wars in his name. He is essentially a tribal chief with an added religious function. In fact, he is totally dependent, like an infant, upon his subordinates. Yet he is accorded the highest rank—an acknowledgment of the dignity of dependence.

One might say that this paradox comes from a myth, and I say, surely, it is a living myth. It is widely perceived that Japanese, compared with Westerners, can be naively, sometimes blindly, trusting toward fellow human beings—so much so that Japanese as a whole are often labeled as too paternalistic for a modern nation, which arouses negative reactions from Western critics like Peter Dale. But this fact of public life is not something fabricated or politically maneuvered into being. I am not saying that everything is right about this myth. The fact is that it was much inflated in prewar and wartime Japan, and the emperor was exploited by the militarists just as the trusting population was abused. Thus, when the *showa* Emperor became the focus of attention all over the world because of his illness and subsequent death, there arose a renewed interest in his culpability as a war criminal. It has also been remarked upon in this connection that Japanese, in general, do not seem to talk about their war guilt as much as they should, as Germans do. But I wonder if war guilt applies only to defeated nations. I also wonder if there is any nation that wallows in national guilt.

It does not follow, however, that Japanese negate guilt because they do not talk about it openly. I think the *showa* Emperor was certainly aware of his culpability and must have felt truly grateful that he was not tried openly. He simply did not wish, however, to let his personal feeling be known. Japanese are simply diffident, or inhibited, when it comes to guilt or any other private matter. You might say that it also could be an expression of their ambivalence. Certainly, it exemplifies their distaste for confrontation or their preference for silence. Whether good or bad, this is the Japanese mind.

I do not know if the Japanese mind will change in the foreseeable future or if it should change. Japanese talking about their guilt openly and unabashedly! I, for one, have to say that I hope the soul of Japan will not change.

Notes

1. Peter N. Dale, *The Myth of Japanese Uniqueness* (London: Croom Helm; Oxford: Nissan Institute for Japanese Studies, 1986).

2. William Caudill, "Mental Care and Infant Behavior in Japan and American," *Psychiatry* 32(1969):12–43.

17

Symbolic Immortality in Modern Japanese Literature

David G. Goodman

Having now written and taught about the effects of the bombing of Hiroshima and Nagasaki on Japanese culture, and having authored several other books in both English and Japanese that apply a psychohistorical perspective to the study of Japan, I think it is fair to say that my encounter with Robert Jay Lifton upon my return in 1967 from my first trip to Japan, my studies with him as a Yale undergraduate, and my subsequent intermittent but continuous dialogue with him over the course of nearly thirty years have had a far-reaching impact on my life and work. I could say a great deal about how *Death in Life* influenced my study of Japanese plays on Hiroshima and Nagasaki, about how *The Nazi Doctors* affected the way I dealt with Japanese anti-Semitism in *Jews in the Japanese Mind*, or how early essays like "Youth and History: Individual Change in Postwar Japan" and "Protean Man" served me in my writing in Japanese. Here, however, I would like to comment on the 1979 volume *Six Lives/Six Deaths: Portraits from Modern Japan* and the implications it has had for my general understanding of modern Japanese literature.

Six Lives/Six Deaths grew out of collaborative work Lifton did with the Japanese critic Katō Shūichi[1] and their student Michael Reich at Yale in 1974–75. The book essentially interprets Katō's intimate knowledge of Japanese literary history in the light of Lifton's psychohistorical model.

Lifton's basic psychological insight is that human beings require a sense of continuity beyond death in order to function in a healthy and effective manner. According to Lifton, human beings need to achieve a sense of "symbolic immortality" in one or more of five possible modes: biological, creative, theological, natural, and transcendent. We all require, that is, an organic sense that we will symbolically survive our own death through our biological offspring or biosocial affiliation, through our creative works, through the saving grace of an immortal God, or through identification with changeless nature. Alternatively, we need to vacate the problem of death altogether by an experiential transcendence of the dichotomy of life and death. Lifton has argued that the failure to achieve this sense of mastery over death—feeling that we are going nowhere (stasis), that we are isolated from any larger community or source of meaning (separation), and that our life is devoid of any organizing principle (disintegration), feelings that he describes as "death equivalents"—is the underlying precipitant of much mental disease.

Six Lives/Six Deaths combines this perspective with Katō's sociohistorical understanding of the development of modern Japanese culture. As he presents it in his *History of Japanese Literature*, Katō sees modern Japanese intellectual culture as the product of more or less distinct generations of writers and intellectuals who responded in diverse ways to the particular historical challenges of their time. This approach comports well with Lifton's emphasis on shared themes in his psychohistorical work.[2]

Six Lives/Six Deaths treats only six individuals, but it has suggested to me a comprehensive interpretation of modern Japanese culture as an evolving series of responses to the shared psychological quest for symbolic immortality in a bewildering and disjointed age. It seems to me that modernity in Japan has been characterized by an attenuation of the authoritative traditional paradigms of symbolic immortality, especially those deriving from Buddhism, and the consequent need for individuals to improvise their own personal ways of coming to terms with death. I read modern Japanese literature as the public record of these improvisations and as a guide to the psychological experience of being Japanese in modern times.

The Meiji Paradigm of Life and Death

In the intercalary fourth month of 1868, immediately after it assumed power, the new Meiji government of Japan decreed that henceforth all funerals would be conducted according to Shinto practice. This was a monumental change for Japan, where for more than a millennium Buddhism had been an essential component in the way the Japanese dealt with death. The imperial family itself belonged to the Shingon sect of Buddhism, and its members were cremated according to Buddhist rites. Indeed, as recently as 1866, the funeral of the Emperor Kōmei had been conducted according to Buddhist ritual practice.[3]

The point of the Meiji edict was to assert the new government's hegemony over the world of the dead as well as the living. It was an attempt to put an end to a period of painful flux in Japanese attitudes toward death, and, since it dictated the shape of Japanese struggles to achieve symbolic immortality, it defined one of the principal dynamics of Japanese culture through the Second World War.

The attenuation of Buddhist authority had begun at the end of the sixteenth century, when Toyotomi Hideyoshi had defeated the monks of the Tendai sect on Mt. Hiei and put a decisive end to Buddhist military power. Under the Tokugawa regime, which ruled the country from 1600 to 1868, Buddhism continued to fare badly. The Tokugawa government patronized neo-Confucianism, which stressed the virtues of loyalty and rationalism, and it exploited Buddhist institutions to control the population, forcing everyone in the country to register with a local Buddhist temple. By the late eighteenth century, the Buddhist establishment was embattled to say the least, and fiction writers like Ueda Akinari were lampooning the vestiges of Buddhist belief among the masses.

There was also a concerted effort on the part of certain feudal domains within the Tokugawa state to extirpate Buddhism outright. In the early years of the Meiji period (1868–1912), these efforts became national in scope, and by the mid-1870s, one Japanese scholar has estimated that as many as two-thirds of the Buddhist temples that had existed in Tokugawa Japan had been destroyed by government-sanctioned violence. In the 1860s, some Buddhist clerics were predicting an imminent government ban on Buddhism in Japan, and while such a proscription never materialized, an order formally disestablishing Buddhism was issued in 1868.[4]

The attenuation of Buddhist authority, and with it the authority of the prevailing paradigms of life and death, precipitated a major crisis in Japanese culture. In 1825, the nativist ideologue Aizawa Seishisai decried the "spiritual crisis" that gripped the country and asserted that spiritual weakness made Japan vulnerable to ideological subversion by the West. There were also strong signs of malaise among the general population. Intense religious questing led to the establishment of numerous new salvific cults (*shinkō shūkyō*). Chiliastic riots fraught with demands for "world renewal" (*yonaoshi*) were a prominent feature of the mid-1860s; and an antinomianism manifested in transvestitism and hysterical, trancelike behavior was common, bespeaking an expectation among the Japanese masses that an apocalyptic "end of days" was close at hand.[5]

The Meiji Restoration of 1868 resolved Aizawa's "spiritual crisis" by fiat. By disestablishing Buddhism, banning Buddhist funerals, and through numerous other measures, the new Meiji government asserted that henceforth the sole approved route to symbolic immortality for the Japanese would be identification with the emperor and assimilation to the biosocial unit of Japan he incarnated.

The new Meiji paradigm of life and death did not emerge fully formed but evolved over time, the product of intense cultural negotiation during the first two decades of the Meiji period. Shinto extremists fell from favor, a nationalistic "New Buddhism" (*Shin Bukkyō*) emerged, and an eclectic national ideology was formulated. This new ideology was articulated most succinctly and authoritatively in the Imperial Rescript on Education of 1890, which became the catechism of Japanese school children through the end of World War II. It blended nationalistic Shinto, Confucian, and modern statist elements and unequivocally asserted that the emperor was the sole guarantor of Japanese posterity. He transcended time and place and was the repository of all transhistorical values. The imperial institution was, the Rescript asserted, "coeval with heaven and earth," and the Imperial Way was "infallible for all ages and true in all places." To identify with the emperor and the values he personified was consequently the only true way for the Japanese to conquer death. Conversely, political dissent threatened the nation's link to posterity and was consequently condemned as immoral.[6]

Literary Responses to the Meiji Paradigm

All of this had a profound impact on the development of modern Japanese culture, and the history of modern Japanese literature can be seen as a series of attempts to come to terms with the problem of human mortality and with the Meiji orthodoxy that had been fabricated to solve it.

Initially, there were four responses to the Meiji paradigm. The first was the affirmative response of authors like Mori Ōgai (1862–1922) and Natsume Sōseki (1867–1916), the two undisputed giants of Meiji literature, who wrote works immediately following the death of Emperor Meiji in 1912 that explicitly affirmed the official paradigm. In works like "The Abe Clan" (1913) and *Kokoro* (1914), Mori and Natsume respectively affirmed the legitimacy of the suicide of General Nogi Maresuke, who had killed himself on the day of the emperor's funeral in a final act of fealty and atonement to his lord.[7] In *Kokoro* especially, the central character, known simply as Sensei (Master), mimics Nogi's suicide in a self-conscious attempt to break the logjam of his life, which he describes as a living death. With his suicide, Sensei sees himself joining General Nogi in affirming the immortalizing power of the emperor. The chapters on Nogi and Mori in *Six Lives/Six Deaths* deftly analyze the psychology of this affirmative response.

There were dissenting responses to the Meiji paradigm as well, however. The first was the theological response of Uchimura Kanzō (1861–1930), the most influential Japanese Christian of the twentieth century. Uchimura's Christian faith was conceived from the outset as an alternative to the Meiji orthodoxy. His famous refusal to bow before the Imperial Rescript on Education in 1891 was an overt rejection of the Meiji paradigm. Where Meiji orthodoxy stressed that fealty to the emperor and participation in the extended family of the Japanese state was the only way for a Japanese to transcend his or her mortality, Uchimura emphasized the existence of a divine source of eternal life who transcended all temporal power. It was God, not the emperor, Uchimura wrote in 1895, who "will save me in Heaven at last."

Eventually, Uchimura did bow to the Imperial Rescript, and throughout his subsequent life he was tormented by the painful tension between his particular identity as a Japanese and his transcendent identity as a Christian. He described this tension most poignantly in "Two J's," which he wrote in English in 1925.

> I love two J's and no third; one is Jesus, and the other is Japan.
> I do not know which I love more, Jesus or Japan.
> I am hated by my countrymen for Jesus' sake as *yaso*, and I am disliked by foreign missionaries for Japan's sake as national and narrow.
> No matter; I may lose all my friends, but I cannot lose Jesus and Japan.[8]

Painful as it was, however, this tension also served Uchimura as a source of creative energy, which he used to establish an original Japanese Christian theology known as "Churchless" (*Mukyōkai*) Christianity. This original theology had an immense impact on modern Japanese intellectuals, not the least of whom was Masamune Hakuchō, who is profiled in *Six Lives/Six Deaths.*

The second alternative to the orthodox Meiji paradigm was socialism, which emphasized human creativity as the premier immortalizing principle. While much of prewar Japanese socialism was influenced by the social gospel of nineteenth-century Protestantism, it was the secular socialism of Kōtoku Shūsui (1871–1911) that represents this alternative most clearly. Kōtoku was a disciple of Japan's first translator of Rousseau,

Nakae Chōmin, the subject of another portrait in *Six Lives/Six Deaths*, and a follower of the Russian anarchist Peter Kropotkin. His socialism was adamantly anthropocentric and provided an essential source for the subsequent development of Marxism in Japan.

Kōtoku's greatest contemporary literary devotee was the poet Ishikawa Takuboku (1885–1912), who identified closely with Kotoku, copying and annotating his defense of his anarchism in his *Letter from Prison*. "The attitude of the writer toward humanity cannot be one of detachment," Ishikawa wrote in his *Romaji Diary*. "He must be a critic. Or a planner for mankind."⁹

The Meiji government recognized the challenge presented to Meiji orthodoxy by Kōtoku and his anarchistic brand of socialism, and they saw to it that he was executed in February 1911 for allegedly plotting to assassinate the emperor. Whether or not Kōtoku was actually guilty of the charge, it certainly had psychological truth, for the socialism he espoused, which saw human salvation as the result of human labor, not fealty to the imperial state, posed a potentially lethal threat to the emperor as supreme immortalizing principle. The Marxist economist Kawakami Hajime, whose life is described in *Six Lives/Six Deaths*, was an intellectual descendant of Kōtoku's who elaborated his perspective.

The transcendent individualism of the novelist Shiga Naoya constituted the third alternative to Meiji orthodoxy. Shiga, who is known in Japan as the "patron saint of the novel" (*shōsetsu no kami-sama*), was obsessed with the problem of death. He continuously asked what possible meaning life could have in the face of cosmic entropy and inevitable human demise, and his work can be construed as a lifelong quest for a means to solve this conundrum. In the short story "At Kinosaki" (1917), a writer who has been injured in a train accident observes the meaningless deaths of creatures in nature while recuperating at a hot springs resort and asks why any living thing should struggle to survive. Twenty years later, in his magnum opus, *A Dark Night's Passing* (1937), Shiga systematically tests and rejects the biological, theological, and creative modes of symbolic immortality, finally concluding that the dichotomy of life and death is a false one. "I came to realize," he says in "At Kinosaki," "that there was no great difference between life and death"; and in the final pages of *A Dark Night's Passing*, Shiga's protagonist, in a state of near-death rapture, comes to the same realization. Shiga thus voided the problem of human mortality and offered the special mode of experiential transcendence by each individual as an alternative to Meiji orthodoxy.

Questing Between the Wars

Historical dislocations brought about by rapid social change compounded the problems faced by the Japanese and stimulated writers to new innovations. Not only did no leader emerge with the unifying charisma of the Emperor Meiji following his death, but Japanese society had changed in fundamental ways, presenting new complexities. By 1940, more Japanese lived in Tokyo alone (6.78 million) than had lived in all Japanese cities in 1890. The number of students enrolled in universities had increased more than twenty-five-fold, and Japan had developed into a military and industrial powerhouse with a far-flung overseas empire. Japan won the Sino-Japanese war (1894–95), defeated the Russians (1904–05), annexed Korea (1910), dispatched 72,000 troupes to Siberia (1918–22), invaded Manchuria (1931), and went to war with China (1937). In this environment, the exhortations and prescriptions of the Imperial Rescript on Education rapidly lost their consensual character and became the centerpiece of a dogmatic ultranationalist ideology.

It fell to the writers and intellectuals of the interwar period to sort out these dizzying changes and identify possible new sources of immortalizing power. Once again, there was a multiplicity of responses. Some, like the dyspeptic Nagai Kafū (1879–1959), responded with nostalgia for the earlier, simpler lifestyle of the Tokugawa era. Convinced that he could never fulfill the role of the modern intellectual as defined by engaged writers like Émile Zola, and equally sure that the ambitions of other Japanese intellectuals to do so were quixotic or worse, Nagai sought his immortality in identification with the eternal, albeit inconsequential, pleasures of the Edo dilettante.

Akutagawa Ryūnosuke (1892–1927) tried to apprehend the modern Japanese experience in his work and experimented with a wide variety of literary forms and styles, but he was ultimately frustrated by his inability to formulate it definitively. "Reality" and "truth" eluded him as they did the characters in his most famous story "In a Grove," which became the basis for Kurosawa Akira's 1950 film masterpiece *Rashōmon*. He came to experience his society as a dystopia, which he described with loathing in his novel *Kappa* (1927).[10] When, in poor health and complaining of "a vague sense of uncertainty," he took his own life on July 24, 1927, Akutagawa may have been making a last, desperate effort to impose some coherence on his disintegrating world.

Tanizaki Jun'ichirō (1886–1965) avoided Akutagawa's fate by combining the latter's modernist intellectualism with Nagai Kafū's nostalgia to produce an empowering new aesthetic. Tanizaki's youthful impulse was to reject everything Japanese and emulate the West, but by the early 1920s he had become thoroughly disillusioned with the shallow life Westernized Japanese culture produced. He rejected the values of growth, power, and adaptability upon which modern Japan was founded, and in their place he forged a new aesthetic that stressed the virtues of decay, eros, and inadaptability (conceived as abnormality or perversity). He articulated this new aesthetic most explicitly in his essay "In Praise of Shadows" (1934), but its most succinct formulation appears in the 1948 novel *The Makioka Sisters*, where he compares the beauty of a firefly hunt with a cherry blossom party. Tanizaki does not reject cherry blossom viewing, the epitome of Japanese aesthetic pleasures, but he argues that the "dark, dreamy child's world" of the nocturnal firefly hunt has an incomparable beauty of its own. With defensive self-deprecation, Tanizaki portrayed his preference for the shadowy, decaying world of the Japanese past over Westernization as a form of perversity or masochism, but he rejected criticism of his stance, arguing in his 1929 novel *Some Prefer Nettles* that there was simply no accounting for taste. Bolstered by his new aesthetic, Tanizaki proceeded to translate the eleventh-century classic *The Tale of Genji* into modern Japanese not once but three times, thus identifying himself with the immortal tradition of Japanese literature while at the same time renewing it for future generations.

With varying degrees of success, Nagai, Akutagawa, and Tanizaki attempted to transform their age through art. The dramatist Kishida Kunio (1890–1954) and the novelist Kawabata Yasunari (1899–1972), who won the Nobel Prize for literature in 1968, were conservatives who had no such ambition. Instead of transforming it, they sought to capture in a spare poetic idiom the sense of disintegration, loss, and emptiness that characterized their time. Beauty, in their view, was intimately related to this sense of loss and to the profound sadness it engendered.

In the fifty plays he wrote between 1924 and 1935, Kishida Kunio obsessively described the loss of patriarchal authority and the sense of dislocation and paralysis that accompanied it in modern Japan. Divine salvation, he suggested in *A Diary of Fallen Leaves* (1927), following his mentor, the devoutly Roman Catholic French director Jacques Copeau, may be the only hope for human beings mired in the sin of their own imperfection. And when he said in the founding manifesto of the Literary Theatre Troupe (*Bungakuza*) in 1937 that he wanted to produce "a theatre for the soul," he was probably speaking in more than metaphorical terms. Salvation of the soul and a theatre devoted to that end was Kishida's central concern.[11]

Kawabata Yasunari's religiosity was more typically Japanese and centered on the concept of *mujō*, the impermanence of things. For Kawabata, who became so familiar with death as a child that he was nicknamed the "master of funerals" (*sōshiki no meijin*),[12] the transience of human life was the ultimate reality, making all human effort seem an exercise in futility (*torō, mudabone-ori*). Unfeeling but not necessarily hostile nature was truth, and submission to it was salvation. Thus, in the final scene of Kawabata's most famous novel, *Snow Country* (1947), the dilettante Shimamura is overwhelmed by the enormity of the universe as he contemplates the beauty of the corpse of Yoko, the woman who has personified death for him and who has now come to manifest it.

All of these responses were effective on the artistic and personal level, but none suggested a practical politics. The proletarian literary movement was the only sustained attempt in the prewar period to create a literature that proposed that human salvation depended upon the perfection of human society through politics. Kobayashi Takiji's 1929 novel *The Factory Ship*, generally regarded as the best work of proletarian fiction, describes life and working conditions aboard a crab-canning boat operating off the Russian coast and advocates worker solidarity as a political solution to the problems of modern Japan.

The state reaction to this political alternative was swift and cruel. On February 20, 1933, Kobayashi was beaten to death while in police custody. Four months later, on June 10, two members of the Japanese Communist Party Central Committee publicly recanted their Marxism, and a mass defection of Communists to ultranationalism ensued. Forced to give up the more mechanistic aspects of their Marxism and confront the ambiguities of their situation, some leftist writers like the poet Oguma Hideo actually improved following this repression,[13] but in general the mass left-wing about-face (*tenkō*) of the mid-1930s represented an abandonment of historical creativity and responsibility in favor of ethnic nationalist irrationalism. It removed the last obstacle to the vulgarized version of the Meiji paradigm promoted by the Japanese military, which asserted paradoxically that the ideal way for a Japanese to live a meaningful life was to die for the emperor.

The Postwar Situation

The Japanese surrender of August 15, 1945, signaled not only the defeat of Japan's military regime but the disqualification of the paradigm of life and death that had evolved since the Meiji Restoration and that had served as the centerpiece of the ultranationalist ideology used to justify the war. The emperor, guarantor of Japanese posterity, had proven to be all too fallibly human, a fact he acknowledged in publicly denying his divinity on January 1, 1946. In a sense, the Japanese people were spun back to the situation they had faced in the early nineteenth century, when ambiguity in their immortalizing systems had become insupportable and had precipitated a "spiritual crisis." The more than 700 new religious cults with more than 375,000 clergy that appeared in Japan by the early 1950s were indicative of the fact that a similar situation obtained in the early postwar period.[14]

Some writers, like Sakaguchi Ango (1906–55) and Dazai Osamu (1909–48), embraced the sense of anomie and debasement that came with defeat. They took it as a sign that the old moral paradigm that had led to war had been deposed and a new, more humane one could be fashioned in its place. Indeed, debasement was one of the principal themes of literature in the early postwar period, and Sakaguchi's essay "On Debasement" (1946) developed this theme:

> To be alive is the only miracle. In the sight of our ancient generals lined up and led before the war crimes tribunal, men who had not even been able to cut open their stomachs to save their honor, we discover a splendid vision of humanity bestowed on us by the end of the war. Japan lost the war and the way of the *samurai* has perished, but we have been born for the first time as human beings through the true womb of debasement. Let us live and be debased! This alone is the correct way—there are no other easy paths to salvation.[15]

The themes of death and rebirth "through the true womb of debasement" articulated so clearly in this mordant essay are repeated in Dazai Osamu's novel *The Setting Sun* (1947), where a sexual union between a member of the deposed Japanese aristocracy and a grotesquely debased novelist produces moral renewal conceived explicitly as a fulfillment of both the promise of Christian salvation and Marxist revolution.

> Recently I have come to understand why such things as war, peace, unions, trade, politics exist in the world. I don't suppose you know. That's why you will always be unhappy. I'll tell you why—it is so that women will give birth to healthy babies. . . . Even if Mary gives birth to a child who is not her husband's, if she has a shining pride, they become a holy mother and child. I disregard the old morality with a clear conscience, and I will have as a result the satisfaction of a good baby. . . . To give birth to the child of the man I love, and to raise him, will be the accomplishment of my moral revolution.[16]

The themes of death, rebirth, and moral renewal are given a political dimension in the work of the humanistic writers of the *Sengo-ha* or "Post-war School." Typical is Ōoka Shōhei's *Fires on the Plain* (1951). The main character in this extraordinary war novel is a soldier named Tamura who is separated from his unit and is depicted fleeing U.S. forces through the jungles of the Philippine island of Leyte, struggling to survive. Like the characters in Shiga Naoya's work, Tamura asks continually why he should struggle to live in the face of inevitable death, but he also asks an additional question: what keeps human beings moral in such extreme situations? This question is formulated in terms of the temptation Tamura feels to commit cannibalism. While others around him are doing so, however, Tamura resists the temptation to eat human flesh, and after the war he asks what force in the universe made this resistance possible. His experience in the Philippines convinced him that such a force exists, but he can only identify it in the most tentative way:

> If, at the very moment I was about to fall into sin through my pride, I was struck on the back of my head by that unknown assailant . . .
> If, because I was beloved of God, He vouchsafed to prepare this blow for me in advance . . .
> If he who struck me was that great man who on the crimson hilltop offered me his own flesh to relieve my starvation . . .
> If this was a transfiguration of Christ himself . . .
> If He had indeed for my sake alone been sent down to this mountain field in the Philippines . . .
> Then glory be to God.[17]

Tamura pens these lines while confined to a mental institution. He has been driven into an asylum in part because of his frustration with Japan's postwar political movements, which failed to transform these ultimate concerns into a meaningful politics.

Kurosawa Akira (b. 1910) also belongs to the *Sengo-ha* group, and his film *Ikiru* (To Live, 1952) similarly links human immortality to morality conceived in terms of socially responsible behavior. The film concerns a petty bureaucrat named Watanabe who is dying of cancer and has just six months to live. He is known as "Mr. Mummy" because he has lived his life as if he were already dead, disconnected from others and insensitive to the society he is pledged to serve. In a final effort to invest his life with meaning, Watanabe becomes a social activist, transforming both his life and his society in the process. The intense encounter with death in *Ikiru*, as in *Fires on the Plain*, is thus translated into a profound moral sense and a conviction that morality is only meaningful insofar as it is expressed in socially responsible action.

This concatenation of morality and sociopolitical activism as an immortalizing schema was preponderant among liberal intellectuals in the postwar period, but it was by no means universal. The major alternative was proposed by the novelist and playwright Mishima Yukio (1925–1970), who refused to accept the demise of the emperor system as the authoritative immortalizing principle in Japanese culture. Little influenced by the strains of socialism and Christianity that informed the *Sengo-ha* group, Mishima, the subject of the final portrait in *Six Lives/Six Deaths*, concluded that without the emperor there could be no such thing as a meaningful death for a Japanese. And since he wanted desperately to end his own life, Mishima's motives for rehabilitating the imperial paradigm were urgently personal as well as philosophical. This intersection of personal psychological needs with the general requirements of the historical moment provided the basis for a powerful, fundamentalist (what Lifton calls "restorationist") reformulation of the Meiji paradigm.

Mishima did not begin with this alternative fully formed in his mind but developed it gradually. In his 1959 novel *Kyoko's House*, he recorded the personal process of elimination by which he had settled on the notion of the emperor as the premier vivifying principle of Japanese culture. In his subsequent works, beginning with "Patriotism" in 1960, he methodically developed linkages among the emperor, beauty, and eternal life. His final tetralogy, *The Sea of Fertility*, continued to explore reincarnation and other death-transcending ideas. By the time he committed dramatic suicide at the Tokyo headquarters of the Japanese Self-Defense Force in November 1970, demanding a restoration of the emperor to power, he had all but single-handedly resurrected the Meiji paradigm as a viable avenue toward immortalizing the self. Mishima's political-philosophical position enabled his death; and his death served to ratify his political philosophy.

By the 1960s, there were thus two paradigms of life and death competing in Japan: the paradigm that stressed politically responsible action born of the defeat and elaborated by the *Sengo-ha* writers, and the paradigm that emphasized assimilation to vitalizing cultural archetypes, especially the emperor, championed by Mishima Yukio and other conservatives. Japanese literature, especially drama, regularly juxtaposed these two paradigms, and works like Satoh Makoto's *Nezumi Kozō: The Rat* (1969) depicted history as a dialectic driven by the interaction of these alternative immortalizing regimes. Transhistorical figures who defied death and transcended time appeared in droves on the Japanese stage in the 1960s, bespeaking a pervasive concern in Japan with eschatological issues. These figures ranged from the immortal Kaison in Akimoto Matsuyo's *Kaison the Priest of Hitachi* (1964) to John Silver in Kara Jūrō's John Silver plays (1968–70) and the Beatles in Satoh Makoto's *My Beatles* (1967). Identification with and assimilation of these immortal archetypes was recognized as the indigenous Japanese way of overcoming death, but the playwrights criticized this avenue, recognizing that it was politically irresponsible, for identification with an immortalizing deity meant abandoning historical responsibility.[18]

Ōe Kenzaburō, who won the 1994 Nobel Prize for literature, elaborated this pattern in the novel. From his earliest stories, "Lavish Are the Dead" (1957), which concerns a university student's employment in a morgue, and "Prize Stock" (1958), which begins in a crematorium. Ōe has been explicitly concerned with the individual's confrontation with death. As the youngest member of the *Sengo-ha*, he has insisted that he is committed to the immortalizing power of political activism. In works like the novel *A Personal Matter* (1964) and the documentary *Hiroshima Notes* (1965), he argues that reality compels one to live responsibly. The realities that particularly concern him are the personal tragedy of his son Hikari, who was born with severe brain damage, and the historical tragedy of Hiroshima. Only through a new humanism, the commitment to the survival of one's fellow human beings, Ōe argues, can one survive oneself.

But Ōe seems not to be entirely convinced by this argument, for he frequently juxtaposes it with an indigenous regime of eroticism, beauty, and historical abandon not unlike the one Mishima Yukio espoused. Ōe recognizes the seductive power of this regime, and he depicts it in the hidden valley in Shikoku, where many of his works are set. In novels and stories from *The Silent Cry* (1967) and "The Day He Himself Shall Wipe My Tears Away" (1972), Ōe's work has been characterized by a tension between these two immortalizing regimes. In the 1980s, this competition evolved into a quest for spiritual salvation, and, drawing on William Blake, Dante, and others, Ōe's works have become increasingly mystical, introspective, and religious.

Coming of age in a period of affluence and removed from the trauma of World War II, younger authors like Murakami Haruki (b. 1949) and Yoshimoto Banana (b. 1964) have wanted to avoid the weighty metaphysics of both Mishima and Ōe. Nevertheless, they have continued to be concerned with the same underlying problem. As Murakami puts it in *A Hard-Boiled Wonderland at the End of the World* (1985), the dreams of previous generations no longer have a hold on him and his generation; they will fashion their own dreams, their own world, their own relationship with the living and the dead. And in her slight, pleasant novella *Kitchen* (1987), Yoshimoto's protagonist communicates matter-of-factly with the dead in a sort of shamanistic elegy reminiscent of ancient Japanese literature. These authors continue to grapple with questions of death and the continuity of life, but they are notable for their freedom from the psychological complexes and sense of political mission that characterized the older postwar writers.

A Continuing Dynamic

The question of who has the right to define the paradigms of life and death remains open and politically sensitive in Japan today. On August 15, 1985, the fortieth anniversary of Japan's World War II surrender, for example, Prime Minister Nakasone Yasuhiro, accompanied by fifteen cabinet ministers and 172 Diet members from the ruling Liberal Democratic Party, visited Yasukuni Shrine, the institutional expression of the Meiji paradigm, the center of wartime State Shinto, and the shrine where the souls of Japan's war dead, including Class A war criminals, are enshrined. With this act, Nakasone, who as head of Japan's Self-Defense Agency in the late 1960s had encouraged Mishima Yukio's neomilitarist fantasies, became the first sitting prime minister to visit the shrine on the day of the surrender, and he removed any ambiguities about his intention to reassert the government's right to regulate death as well as life by making a constitutionally questionable contribution to the shrine from state funds. In a related incident three years later, the Japanese Supreme Court upheld the government's right to apotheosize as a Shinto god a member of Japan's Self-Defense Force who had died in an automobile accident in 1968 over the strenuous objections of his Christian widow.[19] As has been the case since the Meiji period, in other words, Japanese governments continue to try to extend their control over the realm of the dead, and their efforts are resisted by Christians and others who have alternative immortalizing strategies.

The modern Japanese predicament thus remains basically unchanged and the task of defining appropriate and satisfying methods for achieving symbolic immortality will continue to occupy Japanese writers into the future.

Notes

1. The Japanese names in the body of this essay are given in the Japanese order, surname first. In the notes, surnames follow given names.

2. Shūichi Katō, *History of Japanese Literature*, Volume 3: *The Modern Years*, tr. Don Sandereson, (London: Macmillan, 1979).

3. James Edward Ketelaar, *Of Heretics and Martyrs in Meiji Japan: Buddhism and Its Persecution* (Princeton: Princeton University Press, 1990), 44; Helen Hardacre, *Shinto and the State* (Princeton: Princeton University Press, 1989), 11.

4. Martin Collcutt, "Buddhism: The Threat of Eradication," in Marius B. Jansen and Gilbert Rozman, eds., *Japan in Transition: From Tokugawa to Meiji* (Princeton: Princeton University Press, 1986), 143. Tamamuro Fumio of Meiji University announced his findings regarding the destruction of Buddhist institutions during the Tokugawa period at the Meiji Studies Conference sponsored by the Edwin O. Reischauer Institute of Japanese Studies at Harvard University on May 8, 1994. See also Joseph M. Kitagawa, *Religion in Japanese History* (New York: Columbia University Press, 1966), 199–203; and Ketelaar, *Of Heretics and Martyrs in Meiji Japan*, passim.

5. George Wilson, "Pursuing the Millennium in the Meiji Restoration," in Tetsuo Najita and J. Victor Koschmann, eds., *Conflict in Modern Japanese History: The Neglected Tradition* (Princeton: Princeton University Press, 1982), 186–87. George Wilson, *Patriots and Redeemers in Japan: Motives for the Meiji Restoration* (Chicago: University of Chicago Press, 1992). John W. Dower, ed., *Origins of the Modern Japanese State: Selected Writings of E. H. Norman* (New York: Pantheon Books, 1975), 343–55.

6. The text of the Imperial Rescript on Education can be found in Ryusaku Tsunoda et al., eds., *Sources of Japanese Tradition*, vol. 2 (New York: Columbia University Press, 1964), 139–40. The best description of the creation of Meiji ideology is Carol Gluck, *Japan's Modern Myths: Ideology in the Late Meiji Period* (Princeton: Princeton University Press, 1985).

7. A list of translations of Japanese literary works may be found in Japan P.E.N. Club, ed., *Japanese Literature in Foreign Languages, 1945–1990* (Tokyo: Japan Book Publishers Association, 1990).

8. Kanzō Uchimura, "Two J's," in Tsunoda et al., eds., *Sources of Japanese Tradition*, vol. 2, 349.

9. Takuboku Ishikawa, "The Romaji Diary," in Donald Keene, ed., *Modern Japanese Literature* (New York: Grove Press, 1956), 216.

10. I am grateful to Koon-ki T. Ho for the characterization of Japanese society as a "dystopia" in Akutagawa's *Kappa*.

11. See David G. Goodman, ed. and tr., *Five Plays by Kishida Kunio* (Ithaca, N.Y.: Cornell East Asia Program, 1989).

12. Donald Keene, *Dawn to the West: Japanese Literature in the Modern Era, Fiction* (New York: Holt, Rinehart and Winston, 1984), 787.

13. See David G. Goodman, ed. and trans., *Long, Long Autumn Nights: Selected*

Poems of Oguma Hideo, 1901–1940, Michigan Monographs Series in Japanese Studies, 3 (Ann Arbor: University of Michigan Center for Japanese Studies, 1989). For another example, see Sakae Kubo, *Land of Volcanic Ash*, tr. David G. Goodman, Cornell East Asia Papers, 40 (Ithaca: Cornell East Asia Program, 1986, 1993).

14. Ichirō Hori, *Folk Religion in Japan: Continuity and Change*, ed. Joseph M. Kitagawa and Alan L. Miller (Chicago: University of Chicago Press, 1968), 217–18.

15. This translation is adapted from Brett de Bary, "Five Writers and the End of the War: Themes in Early Postwar Japanese Fiction," Ph.D. diss, Harvard University, 1978, 147.

16. Osamu Dazai, *The Setting Sun*, tr. Donald Keene (New York: New Directions, 1956), 172–73.

17. Shōhei Ōoka, *Fires on the Plain*, tr. Ivan Morris (Rutland, Vt.: Tuttle, 1967), 246.

18. For translations and an analysis of these plays, see my *After Apocalypse: Four Japanese Plays of Hiroshima and Nagasaki* (New York: Columbia University Press, 1986; Ithaca: Cornell East Asia Program, 1994); and *Japanese Drama and Culture in the 1960s: The Return of the Gods* (Armonk, N.Y.: M. E. Sharpe, 1988).

19. Details and a sensitive analysis of these incidents may be found in Norma Field, *In the Realm of a Dying Emperor: A Portrait of Japan at Century's End* (New York: Pantheon, 1991).

18

Reflections on the Self of Homo Hippocraticus and the Quest for Symbolic Immortality

Phyllis Palgi (with Joshua Dorban)

"Doctors are born, not made." (young Israeli physician)

"Just as a human being must be taught to be a doctor, a doctor must be taught to be a human being." (elderly Israeli physician)

This paper is about Western physicians in general, and the Israeli variant in particular. Half a century has passed since World War II. Medicine during this time has experienced unprecedented changes. The extraordinary new life-prolonging capabilities of medicine and the invention of revolutionary reproductive techniques have dazzled the minds of physicians no less than those of the public. However, ethical dilemmas and social paradoxes appeared in the train of these developments, concomitant with the obvious striking benefits. Like the cynical form of the old aphorism which says "every silver lining has a cloud," there is now evidence of an undercurrent of professional uneasiness and confusion shadowing the feelings of excitement generated by these medical innovations. The surfacing of such doubts gives urgency to the theoretical questions raised in this paper, because they have far-reaching practical implications.

Western medicine traces its history as far back as the fifth century B.C., when the appearance of the Hippocratic School on the Aegean Isle of Cos signified a new and critical stage in medical thought. The culmination was an almost clear-cut breakaway from the dominance of the pre-existing supernatural philosophy of disease and illness. Natural explanations of disease were presented for the first time in terms of a defined

221

school of thought. Because of the unique role of Greece in the history and growth of Western civilization, biomedical thinking became an organic part of Western thinking and vice versa. Ackernecht, the medical historian, named this revolutionary approach medicine's declaration of independence, although the actual body of scientific knowledge at that time was minimal. Concomitantly, much of the appeal of the Hippocratic school was derived from the fact that, while it was biomedical, it was not merely focused on the disease, but as in the older medical tradition, was oriented to the patient in his or her total environment. This led to its becoming better known and appreciated in wider circles. The encompassing orientation of the Hippocratic School was further strengthened by the code of ethics prescribing the behavior of the physician with colleagues, pupils and patients.

During the last two millennia, the persona of Hippocrates grew in stature and gained mythical dimensions, despite historical transformations making zigzagging inroads into the evolving medical philosophy and practice. Hippocrates became the uncontested primeval Father of Modern Medicine. A picture of him as a thoughtful, serious and distinguished man began to appear in medical books. No concrete evidence, however, proving his actual existence has yet been found, let alone details of his appearance. Most medical historians tend to give the benefit of the doubt to the view that Hippocrates, the 'great man,' did exist. Historical accuracy, however, is not the issue here because the power lies in the public symbol and not in the facts. Sherwin Nuland, a writer and surgeon, reflects on the illustrious place of Hippocrates in medical history and legend when he compares the controversy about his authenticity with that of the polemics surrounding the authorship of Biblical texts, or with arguments on whether, in fact, Jesus had ever existed. Nuland writes, "Tradition is a persuasive teacher, even when what it teaches is erroneous. It tells us that all of the Hippocratic writings are the work of one author. It says the same of the Pentateuch of the Old Testament, and yet hard literary evidence denies such a claim as forcefully for the former as it does for the latter."[1]

Worldwide ritual keeps alive the mythical and historical past. At graduation ceremonies of most medical schools, students swear allegiance to adapted forms of the Hippocratic Oath, which represents the quintessence of the rules of professional behavior towards colleagues and students, and of the ethical principles from the Hippocratian Corpus.

Hippocrates as a symbol seems to fall somewhere between Erikson's concept of spiritual 'great men' and Lifton's historical or mythical heroes who appear at the time of fundamental historical shifts (1983).

While Hippocrates has been enshrined as the Father of Medicine, there is, however, no accompanying narrative or drama suggesting oedipal rivalries. It is not surprising that the description of Hippocrates as a physician is congruent at the ideal level with that of the modern professional medical self. He was wise, protective and essentially human. He admitted his mistakes and demanded 'post-mortem' discussions on patients who had died. Unlike some culture heroes who in their greatness may cast a giant shadow over ordinary mortals who would like to emulate them, Hippocrates in his modesty remains an attainable ideal—a model for everyday action and a dream which may come true for each and every physician. Thus, today, one Israeli gynecologist says with conviction "It is only through one's mistakes that one learns," and continues, "When I was appointed as head of the department, my first move was to introduce sessions on 'blunders.' My aim was to teach and not to blame." In the same spirit, an Israeli pediatrician claims "In medicine, knowing what you don't know is even more important than the knowing."

For many human beings there can be no parental fantasy more satisfying than that of the figure of the primeval ancestor of modern medicine. Hippocrates came to represent the ultimate good in society without being divine. In writings attributed to him, he admitted his imperfections and warned against the potentially dangerous power that accompanied his professional knowledge as a healer. If Hippocrates, the wise patriarch, never existed in flesh and blood, the need was strong enough for the collective imagination to give birth to him to fulfill a symbolic role for posterity. Following Lifton's view that "the self is one's inclusive sense (or symbolization) of one's own being" (1993), so the medical professional self may be viewed as the public symbol of the guardian of health, for the community.

Being a Doctor in Israel

The healer in the Jewish tradition has always been accorded a special place. The professional self of the Israeli physician draws its power from the classical traditions shared by all doctors but also gains inspiration from the equally ancient Judaic heritage. The earliest definition of the doctor in Judaic terms is that the doctor (traditionally male) is the appointed messenger and instrument of God. While the source of the healing power is considered sacred, actual medical practice is next only to godliness. Medicine, having been sanctioned by Biblical and Talmudic law, has been regarded for centuries as a spiritually endowed vocation and always had an important bearing upon the professional self of the physician in Jewish communal life. In Israel, the orthodox allow their sons to attend secular medical schools but they must bear in mind that "first comes God and then you—the doctor" or "behind every small doctor there is a large angel." In this sense the Judaic heritage is in perfect tune with the Hippocratic philosophy. In both cases the doctor is expected to know that he is not divine although medicine still carries mystical overtones. The original Hippocratic oath, for instance, was sworn in the name of Apollo, Aesculapius and other minor gods and goddesses.

Numerous doctors in our ongoing study on physicians in Israel reported that they came to medicine not because of direct parental pressure but they themselves began to feel as if it was almost a mystic inevitability that they should become physicians. A pensioner, close to 80 years old, said that if he does not lay hands on one patient a day, then he does not feel he is alive.

Two physicians, one Israeli born and the other originally from South Africa, had wanted to become musicians. Their fathers had been doctors. The two sons had achieved prominence in the medical profession yet spoke wistfully about their love for music. Both summed up that to be doctors was their fate: it was "bashert" (Yiddish for "it was fated").

Characteristic Features of Israeli Society

Historically, a number of rather extraordinary characteristics of modern Israel have played a decisive part in shaping its medical culture. The absorption within a short period of an unusually large number of immigrant and refugee physicians, from Europe in particular, and the organization of medical services within non-profit institutions which has its roots in early socialist ideology have given a special character to Israeli medicine.

In spite of the social complexity and tensions from internal ideological clashes, there are themes that emerge clearly in Israeli life. Four extant imperative features are a strong sense of belonging, cultural diversity, national security and evocative memories of the Holocaust. First, the doctors as a group have a very prominent social presence but do not, however, constitute a prosperous elite within the country. Their high visibility together with their positive integration into the country is due to the intricate interweaving of historical circumstances with the symbolic role of medicine in Israel and its style of practice. The number of doctors per capita of the population is among the highest in the world. Furthermore, the doctors are fully available to the entire public through the national health scheme with services which are organized in a network style, fanning out from central hospitals to small neighborhood clinics throughout the country. The vast majority of physicians are full-time employees but many "moonlight" after hours to supplement their relatively modest monthly paycheck. Israel is known for its large number of doctor visits per patient, especially among the lower earning and less educated. Working as public employees, the doctors cannot choose their clientele. All these factors contribute to the overall process of Israelization of physicians through the strong tie of the individual doctor to the larger society.

With regard to cultural diversity, the nonselective and unprecedented rate of growth of a culturally heterogeneous population through mass immigration means that not only patients, but also physicians come from all five continents. The result is that they, too, have to go through the process of cultural adjustment. Medical anthropologists have been interested in the problem of communication between physicians and their ethnically different patients. Few, however, have addressed the situation in which the physician population is culturally heterogeneous and includes many immigrants.

The third feature, a strong sense of solidarity and the sensitivity associated with wars which have dogged Israel's entire history, has contributed to producing an army which is essentially a citizen's army and as such, has become an organizing epithet within the culture. A popular culturally prescribed story of a medical miracle told by doctors is often presented in something like the following way: "Here was this very sick baby (or severely injured young boy). I did everything humanly possible to save him but I didn't know what his chances were for the future. Years later, I meet this tall healthy young soldier and find out that he was that very sick baby. . . . It is such a wonderful feeling."

Another story, recurring in different forms, is about successful medical improvisation at the front line: "It was during the War of Liberation. I had only just graduated. This young soldier had a bullet in his throat. I found some piping lying around. . . . We are both alive today to tell the story."

An army commander told how he envied the doctor at the front. "I was doing the shooting" he said "while the doctor under fire cut, cleaned, drained, stitched and put an injured but live body on the helicopter."

However, there are also the exceptions. In a discussion about doctors in the army, a combat officer told, "It was the Yom Kippur War . . . , the bullets were flying, one of my men was lying there bleeding. The young doctor paralytic from fear, couldn't function. I aimed my gun at him and shouted: 'Get on with your job.' He was shocked into action."

Physicians are conscripted and do regular reserve duty like others, with one significant difference—they serve only in their own profession. This privilege is not granted to other professionals. In other words, doctors are like all other citizens—except for their profession.

The fourth, and in some sense unique feature of Israeli culture is the omnipresence of the Holocaust experience. Its influence on doctors is subtle, deep and special. A number of the older generation of doctors are Holocaust survivors themselves like many patients their age. The experiences of these Israeli doctors during the Nazi occupation ranged from surviving on false papers or incarceration in labor camps to being prison doctors in concentration camps. The tendency was to draw a veil over their European wartime experience and only refer to it in an oblique fashion. A Polish-born physician remembers for forty-five years the story of how he admitted to hospital a patient with severe abdominal pains who had managed to survive Auschwitz. He thought the patient should be "opened up" but the professor in charge did not agree. The next day the patient was dead. To this day the doctor cannot forgive himself for not fighting for his opinion. It haunts him that the patient survived a concentration camp only to die because of a medical mistake.

The Holocaust as a Metaphor

The Holocaust has become a controlling metaphor in diverse domains of life in Israel. Its deep symbolic meaning, seared onto the Israeli collective psyche, is the fusion of life and death. The Holocaust in itself represents death while Israel represents new life, and the two have merged.

The annihilation of millions of Jews generated, paradoxically, in Israel, a life-force for survival, for building and recreating. The tragic historical event intensified the pursuit of every possible mode of symbolic immortality offered by the culture. Extracting such meaning from the Holocaust is possibly the only way of gaining psychological reparation from such an event. In this way, death has symbolically become inseparably linked with revitalization. In modern Israel, war deaths in particular, but in fact deaths of all young people, are immediately endowed with publicly proclaimed meaning. The centrality of collective dominant themes such as the need for heroic measure for the survival and perpetuation of new life, places the physician in a key symbolic position. Being an Israeli physician has become a powerful cultural symbol which exists on both the personal and social levels. Physicianhood is constantly recreated by each individual doctor and thus serves simultaneously as the crystallization of a solution to inner personal conflicts and as an expression of a socially transmitted message.[2]

Healing and Impairment

For historical and ideological reasons as well as because of a deep sense of admiration for medical excellence, the Israeli medical establishment has hitched its wagon to the star of American medicine. Paradoxically, America, which is renowned for having the most scientifically advanced and technologically sophisticated medicine in the world, is the main source of the pessimistic reports about the confusion which has penetrated the Western medical profession self.[3] By the seventies, a new diagnosis had been added to the American medical nomenclature—"The Impaired Physician Syndrome." Medical conferences in America are now a regularity and seek means of both preventing and dealing with problems of substance abuse, marital strife, suicide and other stress symptoms found among physicians. The general tenor of research on the subject is that the solid buttress of the medical professional self is no longer impervious. As yet, no such signs of a physician impairment syndrome has been discerned in Israel but because of the close relations with American medicine and because of reports of growing stress among physicians from England as well, we raised the question of whether these disturbing disclosures should be seen as "the writing on the wall" for the Israeli doctors. A prime goal of the Israeli study was to examine how the doctors actually felt about their own profession. With an eye to the future and in the youth-oriented spirit of the country, we now focus on the self-perceptions of younger doctors who are in the formative process of trying to organize their jostling subselves, particularly their professional and personal ones, into a core self.

Here are some typical thoughts expressed by young physicians:

> *A surgeon:* "It is a unique profession, particularly my specialty. In our ward you are dealing with the very life of a human being . . . you receive a child who was blue and now he walks out of the operating theater and his pink color has returned. Its a question of existence and non-existence. There is no other field like it."

Internist: (son of a doctor) "Its a profession that has everything. . . . The doctor has influence over life and death in a way that does not exist in any other profession in the world. James Bond and doctors have something in common. They have the power to kill. . . . One small injection will do it."

Gynecologist: "I think that it is the most beautiful profession that exists in the world. I know that nuclear physics is interesting and important, but for me, medicine is it. With all this, the doctor in Israel gets very little encouragement from the medical bureaucracy."

Family physician—woman doctor. "I feel that medicine is a lofty profession. I don't mean to say that I have distinction. I am referring to the profession as a whole."

Anesthiologist: "Medicine becomes your life. The power and the responsibility accompanies you every hour of the day wherever you may be. Another point is that poor financial rewards don't affect your love for your work. A bus driver wouldn't remain in his job if he thought the pay to be inadequate."

The essence of these quotations is clearly the belief in the uniqueness of the profession, which gives its members, by belonging to it the possibility of achieving a personal sense of being special. This specialness incorporates a sense of mastery and responsibility which is also congruent with the ideal concept of self in the Western world. However, the satisfaction acquired through medical mastery and responsible acts is never free of struggle and pain, which are aggravated when the physician faces failure.

Memories

We asked the doctors to recount special memories from their medical careers. The dominant theme of the 300 memories told to us was that of facing death. Doctors of all age groups shared sadness, anger and feelings of helplessness at the death of a young person. The male doctors, particularly the young ones, were much more dramatic when describing their heroic saving of lives through practicing high-standard medicine. Women doctors, particularly young Israeli graduates, also spoke of excellence in medicine but spent more time on affective themes like personal devotion to and identification with the patients and their families.[4]

Taking an overall view of the contents of their memories, the doctors may be divided into three main groups. One group recalled only successes, another only failures, and the largest group made valiant efforts to balance success and failure. Failure was invariably a synonym for the death of a patient. One physician added sadly, "Every doctor has his own cemetery."

Irrespective of how they represented themselves, all perforce had to wrestle with two fundamental medical dilemmas: first, whether their behavior in any way fell below the line of the irreducible responsibility expected of a physician when there was a "failure," and second, whether they can protect themselves against becoming "wounded" themselves. The most appealing feature of the medical professional self is that it has the potentiality of connecting with something that immortalizes, a life outside the physician's own, a life that may outlive that of the healer. Yet, *powerful as the professional self may be, it has not, on its own, created sufficient mechanisms to deal with the so-called failures.*

It is a humbling experience to know that the vulnerability of healers is a time-honored human dilemma. Again, one may return to ancient Greece and find Chiron, the most celebrated of the mythic centaurs as the early formative symbol of the ubiquitous wounded healer. He was known for his wisdom, gentleness, and particularly for his power of healing. Yet, ironically when he became severely wounded he was not able to heal himself. He only gained relief from his excruciating pain by renouncing his divine immortality handing it over to Prometheus, who too became released from his suffering and then was honored as the founder of human civilization. Chiron became mortal, but through his therapeutic act and sacrifice Prometheus gained immortality.

An analysis of this myth reveals the complexity of the dynamics involved in the physician's confrontation with life-and-death issues. The myth records the dramatic shift from the healing process as the sole property of gods to a natural process which trained mortals can comprehend and master. The vulnerability of the healer who may also one day become a patient is regarded as both the symptom and the means for its cure throughout the course of human interaction. We contend that the modern physician, like Chiron, through being engaged in the therapeutic process, is strengthened to cope with his own vulnerability by breathing life into others and thus ensuring his or her own symbolic immortality.

Notes

1. Sherwin B. Nuland, "The Doctors . . . ," *Biography of Medicine* (New York: Vintage, 1988).

2. Phyllis Palgi and Joshua Dorban, "The Formation of Cultural Symbols and Their Therapeutic Function for the Individual: Clinical Illustrations From a Case Study of the Mourning Process of an Israeli War Orphan," *Ethos* 23 (June 1995): 2.

3. Sharon R. Kaufman, *The Healers Tale* (Madison: University of Wisconsin Press, 1993); Melvin Konner, *Medicine at the Crossroads* (New York: Pantheon, 1993).

4. Gender emerged from the study as a subtle and complex issue which is growing in importance with the increasing number of women medical students. The implications of this trend will be discussed in a forthcoming publication.

19

Illicit Stories

Peter Brooks

Robert Jay Lifton has given us a body of work remarkable for its combination of theoretical penetration and humane commitment. It has been influential across many areas of thought and inquiry. My own attention to the place of victims' narratives at the law no doubt has distant roots in Lifton's thinking about survivors and the tales they tell—though in the present instance, I will argue, the *place* of such tales may be at issue. "Illicit Stories" represents a piece of work-in-progress attempting to cross-cut between law and literature, with a particular interest in instances where the law foregrounds the importance of constructing and construing narratives. Here, I focus especially on the role of listeners in determining how a story goes together, and what it means: on how stories take effect in listeners'—primarily juries'—reaction to them or participation in them. While Lifton has not turned his attention to issues of legal storytelling, I trust he will recognize here the kind of concerns that he has done so much to illuminate.

Listen for a moment to Chief Justice William Rehnquist, delivering the Opinion of the Court in *Payne v. Tennessee* (1991):

> Inside the apartment, the police encountered a horrifying scene. Blood covered the walls and floor throughout the unit. Charisse and her children were lying on the floor in the kitchen. Nicholas, despite several wounds inflicted by a butcher knife that completely penetrated through his body from front to back, was still breathing. Miraculously, he survived, but not until after undergoing seven hours of surgery and a transfusion of 1700 cc's of blood—400 to 500 cc's more than his estimated normal blood volume. Charisse and Lacie were dead.
>
> Charisse's body was found on the kitchen floor on her back, her legs fully extended. She had sustained 42 direct knife wounds and 42 defensive wounds on her arms and hands. The wounds were caused by 41 separate

231

thrusts of a butcher knife. None of the 84 wounds inflicted by Payne were individually fatal; rather, the cause of death was most likely bleeding from all the wounds.
Lacie's body was on the kitchen floor near her mother . . .

[111 S.Ct. 2597 (1991), at 2602]

I give only an excerpt from the long narrative with which Rehnquist begins his Opinion. At a level of jurisdiction—the Supreme Court of the United States—where what is at issue concerns constitutional principles and jurisprudential policy, one may be somewhat surprised by so circumstantial a story. Storytelling in Supreme Court decisions in fact seems more common in dissenting opinions, where the "facts of the case" are sometimes used to argue that the majority has overlooked relevant circumstances. Most often, the Opinion of the Court dispenses with the facts in dry and summary fashion, in order to reach underlying principles, and to maintain the all-important rule that appellate jurisdictions don't second-guess the triers of fact. Juries hear and interpret stories; appellate courts simply make sure that the rules of the game have been observed in the telling of these stories.

Yet Rehnquist in *Payne* makes a point of telling a circumstanced story of the scene of the crime, and its sequels, in grisly detail, and setting this story at the head of his opinion. Why is this? As one reads on in the Opinion, the bloody scene in the apartment in Millington, Tennessee, seems to bear little relevance to the principle under consideration. He is giving us the narrative of the crime scene as it was discovered by the police, and reported during the trial that found Pervis Tyrone Payne guilty of murder in the first degree. Whereas what's at issue in *Payne v. Tennessee* is another story, that of the effect of the murder on surviving family members: the story known as a "Victim Impact Statement" introduced, not during the adjudication of Payne's guilt, but only *after* that determination, when the jury was called upon to determine whether or not Payne should be executed. Was the State within its constitutional rights in introducing, during this "sentencing phase" of the trial, a "Victim Impact Statement," largely based on the testimony of Charisse's mother, Mary Zvolanek, and largely concerning the continuing distress of the surving child, Nicholas? The Supreme Court here rejects Payne's contention that introduction of the Victim Impact Statement (VIS) during the sentencing phase of a capital case constituted a prejudicial violation of his rights under the Eighth Amendment ("cruel and unusual punishment"), and thus overrules the Court's holdings just four and two years earlier, in *Booth v. Maryland* (1987) and *South Carolina v. Gathers* (1989).

Rehnquist's grisly narrative of the crime scene thus is basically irrelevant to the issue under debate, and indeed essentially gratuitous. But it has a certain rhetorical appropriateness in that it places before us, through a kind of displacement, the powerful *effects* of narrative that will be at issue in Victim Impact Statements. It makes a kind of preemptive strike, as if to say: you who may doubt the relevance of the narratives introduced by the prosecution when the jury deliberates on the death penalty for murderers must listen to this. Such are the stark events in this story. After listening to this tale—which was part of the trial record itself, and thus certainly is licit to tell—tell me in turn if you can get over it. Can you then pretend that there is some sequel to this story, some consequential part of it, that should not be heard? Can you—in the manner of the majority of the Court in *Booth* and *Gathers*, and the dissenters in *Payne*—claim that the jury should be insulated from such truths? After such knowledge, what forgiveness? After listening to this story, there is no turning back. To reiterate: Rehnquist isn't giving us here the story told by the incriminated VIS. He's giving a story which the jury heard during the deliberative phase of the trial, thus something legally unrelated to the Court's decision on the use of the VIS. But by presenting this first story in such gory detail, he's asking you to find the subsequent introduction of the Victim Impact narrative harmless, and any attempt to exclude it a pathetically misguided avoidance of realities, or a perverse sympathy with the monstrous criminal.

I must here be more precise about the issue involved in *Payne*, as in *Booth* and *Gathers*. Victim Impact Statements are a relative innovation in criminal law—the Maryland statute at issue in *Booth* dates from 1986—which aim to present for the jury's consideration at the sentencing phase of a trial information about the full consequences of the criminal act, including economic loss and physical injury suffered by the victim, change in personal welfare or familial relationships, need for psychological services, and other information "related to the impact of the offense upon the victim or the victim's family that the trial court requires." [*Booth v. Maryland* 107 S.Ct. 2529 (1987), at 2531]. The "Victim's Rights Movement," dating from the late 1960s, has become potent enough that most states now allow the prosecution to introduce some form of victim impact evidence at the sentencing of the defendant. As Justice Antonin Scalia writes in his dissent in *Booth*, "Recent years have seen an outpouring of popular concern for what has come to be known as 'victims' rights.' . . . Many citizens have found one-sided and hence unjust the criminal trial in which a parade of witnesses comes forth to testify to the pressures beyond normal human experience that drove the defendant to commit his crime, with no one to lay before the sentencing authority the full reality of human suffering the defendant has produced—which (and *not* moral guilt alone) is one of the reasons society deems his act worthy of the prescribed penalty" [at 2542]. Scalia thus summarizes the political force behind the mandate for VIS, and the argument that since the defense is allowed to introduce mitigating evidence, the prosecution should be able to counter with this kind of aggravating evidence.[1]

The problem arises in the particular context of homicide, where the victim has suffered ultimate harm. Does it make sense to go beyond this ultimate harm—the death dealt to the victim—to include the collateral harms inflicted upon others, essentially the surviving members of the victim's family? And can such evidence be introduced into a capital sentencing deliberation where, as Justice Lewis Powell writes in the Opinion of the Court, "the jury is required to focus on the defendant as a 'uniquely individual human bein[g]' " [at 2534, citing *Woodson v. North Carolina*, 96 S.Ct. 2978 (1976)]. Capital sentencing must, by the Court's own holdings, consider any mitigating circumstances that may make the criminal less liable to execution. Should it also consider circumstances that tend to aggravate his culpability? Is there such a thing as aggravated murder, or is murder in the first degree itself an ultimate case? Is the kind of information supplied by the VIS relevant to a determination of this culpability? And is the introduction of a VIS unduly inflammatory, thus likely to produce violations of the Eighth Amendment's prohibition of "cruel and unusual punishment"?

The Court in *Booth* argues essentially that in "the unique circumstance of a capital sentencing hearing," the VIS is irrelevant, since it does not focus on the character of the defendant, but rather on the character and reputation of the victim and the effect on his family, which "may be wholly unrelated to the blameworthiness of a particular defendant" [at 2533–34]. The VIS in effect introduces the wrong story, in the wrong place. The murderer may after all not even know that his victim has a family. The jury will in this case be imposing the death sentence because of factors about which the the defendant was unaware, and that were irrelevant to the decision to kill. Part of this argument— that concerning the murderer's possible knowledge of the victim's circumstances, and of the "full range of foreseeable consequences" of homicide, as related to the murderer's blameworthiness—seems to me less than wholly persuasive in the present context because it might be applied to the use of the VIS in all sentencing decisions, not merely in capital cases. More pertinent is the Court's point that the nature of the victim, and of the victim's family, has no bearing on a judgment of the murderer's blameworthiness. As the Court states, the decision on capital sentencing ought not to turn on perceptions that the "victim was a sterling member of the community rather than someone of questionable character" [at 2534]: a life taken is a life taken, and it should not matter, morally, whether the victim was a bank president or one of the homeless. As Justice John Paul Stevens argues in his dissenting opinion in *Payne,* "if a defendant who had murdered a convenience store clerk in cold blood in the course of an armed robbery, offered evidence unknown to him at the time of the crime about the immoral character of his victim, all would recognize immediately that the evidence was irrelevant and inadmissible" [at 2626]. Evidence of this kind "can only be intended to identify some victims as more worthy of protection than others. Such proof risks decisions based on the same invidious motives as a prosecutor's decision to seek the death penalty if a victim is white but to accept a plea bargain if the victim is black."[2]

The Court in *Booth* also argues that capital sentencing should not depend on the degree to which the victim's family has been articulate in its expression of grief and harm—as it very much was in this case. There is a variability in the narratives provided by Victim Impact Statements—in the effectiveness, indeed, of their impact—that must make their influence on sentencing open to suspicion. Consider, as a kind of limit case not mentioned in either *Booth* or *Payne,* the situation of a murder victim who had no surviving relatives or friends. Such a victim would be bereft of any VIS. He would be essentially unnarratable, a zero-degree victim. Without a story, he would, in relative terms, be less a victim, though equally dead.

Finally, the Court in *Booth* notes also how difficult it would be for the defendant to attempt to rebut the evidence presented in Victim Impact Statements. What kind of counter-story could be introduced to contest these narratives of grief and rage? As Justice Thurgood Marshall concludes in his dissent in *Payne*—effectively summarizing Justice Powell's majority opinion in *Booth*—"the probative value of such evidence [VIS] is always outweighed by its prejudicial effect because of its inherent capacity to draw the jury's attention away from the character of the defendant and the circumstances of the crime to such illicit considerations as the eloquence with which family members express their grief and the status of the victim in the community" [at 2620]. The VIS gives the wrong story, defined as a story in the wrong place, diverting attention from the right place to illicit questions.

What is the "illicit" story introduced at Booth's sentencing? The Maryland statute in question provided that the victim's family members could be called to testify during the sentencing phase, or else the VIS, prepared by the State Division of Parole and Probation, could be read to the jury. This was the procedure used with *Booth,* and the Appendix to the Supreme Court's decision gives us the text, detailing the reactions of son, daughter, and granddaughter to the discovery of the bodies of Irvin and Rose Bronstein, stabbed to death in the course of a robbery for money to buy drugs. The VIS is mainly concerned with the mental states induced in the survivors by the murder, the consequent depression, fright, sleeplessness, the feeling that their lives have been permanently changed by this tragedy. Much of the VIS unfolds in *style indirect libre,* indirect discourse summary of emotional affect. For instance, concerning the daughter:

> They didn't have to kill because there was no one to stop them from looting. Her father would have given them anything. The murders show the viciousness of the killers' anger. She doesn't feel that the people who did this could ever be rehabilitated and she doesn't want them to be able to do this again or put another family through this. She feels that the lives of her family members will never be the same again. [at 2538]

The effectiveness of such a passage—as novelists since Flaubert, at least, have understood—results from its effacement of the mediating narrator, its claim to render impersonally, without mediation, the thoughts and feelings of the individual subject. The anonymous author of the VIS comes forward only at the end, in a peroration all the more telling in that she has let the story "tell itself" up to that point:

> It became increasingly apparent to the writer as she talked to the family members that the murder of Mr. and Mrs. Bronstein is still such a shocking, painful, and devastating memory to them that it permeates every aspect of their daily lives. It is doubtful that they will ever be able to fully recover from this tragedy and not be haunted by the memory of the brutal manner in which their loved ones were murdered and taken from them. [at 2539]

"It is doubtful that . . .": at this phrase, one wants to ask—as Roland Barthes does of some narrative statements in Balzac—"who is speaking?"[3] In the absence of a clear answer, the phrase appears to be proffered on behalf of the reader, as the reader's judgment. The conclusion reached by this anonymous employee of the Department of Parole and Probation appeals to an impersonal, and therefore irrefutable, construction, one devoid of specific human agency, endowed with all the power of the *doxa*, the truth invested with general societal authority.

One must imaginatively recreate the VIS of *Booth* at the moment of its enunciation, as the jury weighs whether or not the defendant is to be executed. Consider, in this context, Justice Byron White's dissent on the matter of "[t]he supposed problems arising from a defendant's rebuttal of victim impact statements" [at 2541]. There is nothing in the Maryland statute that prevented the defendant from attempting to rebut the VIS, writes White. He adds: "Petitioner introduced no such rebuttal evidence, probably because he considered, wisely, that it was not in his best interest to do so." The remark appears either disingenuous or obtuse. How would one go about rebutting a narrative of inconsolable grief? Perhaps, on the model of the Marquis de Sade, by the argument that murder merely furthers the destructive work of nature herself, and thus cannot be considered contrary to a natural morality? But the point is really that certain narratives—particularly narratives of the irreparable, of what cannot be undone—are not susceptible of rebuttal. To speak of the possibility of rebuttal of what is recounted in the VIS appears as a misunderstanding of the nature of narrative and the ways one listens to it, receives it, the way it makes an effect. No more than those listeners on board the ship *Nellie*, anchored in the Thames estuary, who have listened Marlow's tale in *Heart of Darkness*, can the members of the jury neutralize the VIS with a counter-story. Once told, certain darknesses do not dissipate.

It is somehow characteristic that *Booth* and *Payne*, which worry about the relevance of impact stories told in certain crucial contexts, manage to proliferate strange hypothetical narratives of dubious relevance. For instance, Justice White in his *Booth* dissent, announces: "There is nothing aberrant in a juror's inclination to hold a murderer accountable not only for his internal disposition in committing the crime but also for the full extent of the harm he caused; many if not most persons would also agree, for example, that someone who drove his car recklessly through a stoplight and unintentionally killed a pedestrian merits significantly more punishment than someone who drove his car recklessly through the same stoplight when no pedestrian was there to be hit" [at 2540]. The logic of this narrative analogy is by no means clear, since in the case under consideration the "pedestrian" is clearly dead, unintentional manslaughter is not at issue, and the contested story concerns expressions of grief and loss by the survivors of that unanalogical pedestrian.

Justice Scalia, in his dissent, replays the theme, with variations: "It seems to me, however—and, I think, to most of mankind—that the amount of harm one causes does bear upon the extent of his 'personal responsibility.' We may take away the license of a driver who goes 60 miles an hour on a residential street; but we will put him in jail for manslaughter if, though his moral guilt is no greater, he is unlucky enough to kill someone during the escapade" [at 2541]. This narrative precisely begs the question before the Court, which concerns what is to be considered relevant "harm," and introduces a new variable—moral luck or unluck—which, when brought to bear on the question of capital sentencing, would seem to require considerably deeper ethical analysis than the narrative of the speeding car allows. Apparently feeling the need to produce an analogy more appropriate to a capital case, Scalia goes one better in the next paragraph: "If a bank robber aims his gun at a guard, pulls the trigger, and kills his target, he may be put to death. If the gun unexpectedly misfires, he may not. His moral guilt in both cases is identical, but his responsibility in the former is greater." To be sure, but that notion of "responsibility," once again, has nothing to do with the survivor stories at issue in the case.

But the prize for wildly extrapolated and impertinent narratives in *Payne* must go to the usually sober Justice David Souter in his concurring opinion. He contends that much of what is contained in a VIS must inevitably come out during the "guilt phase" of the trial, and thus that excluding it from the sentencing phase is an improbability, to the extent that the holdings of *Booth* would logically require empanelling a separate jury for the sentencing phase. (Stevens in dissent dismisses such an interpretation of *Booth* as "entirely unwarranted," at 2630.) To make his point, Souter tells a lengthy story involving "a minister, unidentified as such and wearing no clerical collar" who is robbed and killed while his wife and daughter look on from a parked car. The jury will learn from the surviving wife and daughter that he was a minister "on an errand to his church" since this is part of the relevant contextual evidence. And what if the minister's daughter "had screamed 'Daddy, look out,' as the defendant approached the victim with drawn gun": in that case, the murderer would have known before pulling the trigger that the minister had a daughter, a fact which then should be morally relevant in judging his decision to kill [at 2616–17]. While one may be sympathetic to Souter's conclusion that "*Booth* promises more than it can deliver" [at 2618] in that the sentencing phase can never be wholly insulated from the guilt phase of a trial, his hypothetical minister-*cum*-family man is quite wide of the mark of the specific effect of the VIS at the moment the jury, having determined guilt, is considering the magnitude of punishment.

I cite these randomly proliferating narratives generated by the opinions in *Booth* and *Payne* because they point to the Supreme Court's problem in handling an issue that has to do with the relevance and the effect of narratives, the rules concerning their presentation to listeners. As in the case of confessions, the problem is one of narrative rules. In *Miranda v. Arizona,* the Court had to decide when the story of a suspect's inculpation began—thus when his Fifth Amendment right to silence could be invoked—whereas in *Booth* and *Payne* it must decide when the story of the crime ends, the limits of its retelling. More specifically, *Booth* and *Payne* consider, with contradictory results, rules about how, when, and by whom narratives can legitimately be heard.

In my view, the problem is most succinctly disposed of by Justice Stevens, in his *Payne* dissent, when he writes: "Evidence that serves no purpose other than to appeal to the sympathies or emotions of the jurors has never been considered admissible" [at 2626]. But I want to suggest that this statement is by no means unproblematic, since the kind of dispassionate hearing that it proclaims for juries may itself be at contest. Consider the case of *California v. Brown* (1987), which again concerns the penalty phase of a capital trial, and whether or not the Eighth Amendment has been violated. At issue here is not a VIS, but a jury instruction. In the trial of Brown, found guilty of rape and murder, the judge instructed the jury that in determining Brown's sentence it should consider and weigh the aggravating and mitigating circumstances, but that: "You must not be swayed by mere sentiment, conjecture, sympathy, passion, prejudice, public opinion or public feeling" [107 S.Ct. 837 (1987), at 838]. Brown was sentenced to death. The California Supreme Court reversed the sentence on the grounds that federal constitutional law "forbids an instruction which denies a capital defendant the right to have the jury consider any 'sympathy factor' raised by the evidence when determining the appropriate penalty" (at 839, quoting the California Supreme Court). In a 5–4 decision, the Supreme Court of the United States reversed and remanded, upholding the jury instruction.

The debate between the majority opinion, written by Chief Justice Rehnquist, and the dissenting opinions written by Justices William Brennan and Harry Blackmun, turns on the word "sympathy" in the jury instruction. Since in the sentencing phase of a capital case a jury must consider all mitigating evidence—evidence intended to induce consideration of "compassionate or mitigating factors stemming from the diverse frailties of mankind," as the Court held in *Woodson v. North Carolina*—is the instruction not to be swayed by sympathy a violation of the defendant's rights? Does it ask the jury to listen to his story in the wrong way? Rehnquist's opinion turns on what a "reasonable juror could have understood the charge as meaning" [at 839, citing *Francis v. Franklin* (1985)]. This "reasonable juror," like the "common reader" who used to be invoked in literary criticism, is supposed to reject singling out "almost perversely" the word "sympathy" from the nouns that accompany it [at 840]. The reasonable juror is also supposed to read the "mere" that stands at the head of the list of considerations to eschew as applying to all items on the list. In the sentence: "You must not be swayed by mere sentiment, conjecture, sympathy, passion, prejudice, public opinion or public feeling," place "mere" before each noun. "We think a reasonable juror," writes Rehnquist, "would . . . understand the instruction not to rely on 'mere sympathy' as a directive to ignore only the sort of sympathy that would be totally divorced from the evidence adduced during the penalty phase" [at 840].

In dissent, Justice Brennan shows himself to be a fierce close reader. Rejecting the notion (advanced in the brief for the State) that the instruction merely bars " 'untethered sympathy' unrelated to the circumstances of the offense or the defendant," Brennan claims that "the instruction gives no indication whatsoever that the jury is to distinguish between 'tethered' and 'untethered' sympathy," and finds that the Court's interpretation of the reasonable juror's interpretation is based on an "implausible construction" [at 843]. The construction he has in mind is first of all grammatical and syntactical. He rejects Rehnquist's insistence that the reasonable juror would read "mere" as applying to "sympathy":

A juror could logically conclude that "mere" modified only "sentiment," so it is by no means clear that the instruction would likely be construed to preclude reliance on "mere sympathy." In order for "mere" to be regarded as modifying "sympathy," as the Court contends, "mere" must be read to modify all the other terms in the instruction as well: conjecture, passion, prejudice, public opinion, or public feeling. By the Court's own logic, since "mere" serves to distinguish "tethered" from "untethered" sympathy, it also serves to distinguish "tethered" from "untethered" versions of all the other emotions listed. Yet surely no one could maintain, for instance, that some "tethered" form of prejudice relating to the case at hand could ever be appropriate in capital sentencing deliberations. Indeed, the Court describes the nouns accompanying "sympathy" in the instructions as "no more than a catalog of the kind of factors that could improperly influence a juror's decision to vote for or against the death penalty" [*Ante*, at 840]. The single word "mere" therefore cannot shoulder the burden of validating this antisympathy instruction. [at 843]

Brennan's virtually deconstructive reading of Rehnquist's efforts to limit and control a "reasonable" reading of the instruction results in his construction of a juror disoriented and misled by the instruction. "While we generally assume that jurors are rational," writes Brennan, "they are not telepathic" [at 844]. He goes on: "The vast majority of jurors thus can be expected to interpret 'sympathy' to mean 'sympathy,' not to engage in the tortuous reasoning process necessary to construe it as 'untethered sympathy.' " Thus is Rehnquist's reasonable juror turned into a tortuous heremeneut.

For the dissenters in *California v. Brown*, the grammatical, syntactical, and interpretive issues are crucial because so much is at stake. As Brennan writes further, "The defendant literally staked his life in this case on the prospect that a jury confronted with evidence of his psychological problems and harsh family background would react sympathetically, and any instruction that would preclude such a response cannot stand"; "it is highly likely that the instruction eliminated his only hope of gaining mercy from his sentencer" [at 849]. As both Rehnquist and Brennan understand, listening sympathetically or unsympathetically makes all the difference in the meaning and the result of the story told. Though neither offers much in the way of analysis of "sympathy," both sense that it is crucial in determining the reader's or listener's response to the narrative message.

Sympathy is notoriously a slippery concept. It implies the capacity to participate in the suffering of another (*sym-pathos*) and, more generally, to feel a like emotion, to experience "fellow feeling," to put yourself in another's place. It became a key concept in the Enlightenment's concern with the foundations of a secular humanist ethics: both the cornerstone of ethics (for Rousseau, for instance) and something more problematic and worrisome because of the potential for theatrical enactment and deception implicated in the concept. As David Marshall writes in explication of Adam Smith's discussion of sympathy in his *The Theory of Moral Sentiments*: "For Smith, acts of sympathy are structured by theatrical dynamics that (because of the impossibility of really knowing or entering into someone else's sentiments) depend on people's ability to represent themselves as tableaux, spectacles, or texts before others."[4] As Smith himself puts it:

Though our brother be upon the rack, as long as we ourselves are at our ease, our senses will never inform us of what he suffers. They never did, and never can, carry us beyond our own person, and it is by the imagination only that we can form any conception of what are his sensations. Nei-

ther can that faculty help us to this any other way, than by representing to
us what would be our own, if we were in his case. . . .

By the imagination we place ourselves in his situation, we conceive ourselves enduring all the same torments, we enter as it were into his body,
and become in some measure the same person with him and thence form
some idea of his sensations, and even feel something which, though weaker
in degree, is not altogether unlike them. His agonies, when they are thus
brought home to ourselves, when we have thus adopted and made them
our own, begin at last to affect us, and we then tremble and shudder at the
thought of what he feels.[5]

If the recreation of what another feels depends to this extent on the
imagination, and on representation of another's feelings, resulting in a
powerful reaction based on "the thought of what he feels," it is evident
that the capacity of sympathy to bridge the boundaries between separate
subjectivities is matched by its capacity for manipulation, its susceptibility to a theatrical staging. Sympathy may be a trope—the opposite of
irony, which creates distance—that appears to abolish distance. In Rousseau's critique of theatrical representation (in his *Lettre à d'Alembert sur
les spectacles*), the artificial simulation of emotions by actors on the stage
creates a powerful affect which can cause the spectator to lose his or her
moral compass, and enter into an essentially immoral participation. In
another twist on the argument, Diderot's *Paradoxe sur le comédien* suggests that the most accomplished actor is the one who is most distanced
from the emotion to be simulated because his detachment allows him
to create that emotion from the point of view of the spectator, who alone
matters. Sympathy may in this conception be the most artificial of emotions, the creation of a pure fiction.

California v. Brown does not enter into any such analysis of sympathy,
but one nonetheless senses that the Court has trouble dealing with the
place and consequences of sympathy in the jury instruction because it
understands that sympathy is, affectively and almost epistemologically, a
slippery concept. To what extent do we want a jury to change places,
imaginatively, with the criminal defendant? To what extent to we want
jurors to use their imagination to represent the suffering of the defendant and, through representing to themselves what it would be like to
be in his place, to "tremble and shudder" at what he must feel? The
majority and the minority in *California v. Brown* evidently split on this
issue— ultimately in large part because of their differing views about the
morality of the death sentence itself. It is perhaps Justice Blackmun who
most overtly acknowledges that sympathy may be a useful and necessary
concept to place before the jury not in spite of but precisely because of

its emotional appeal. "While the sentencer's decisions to accord life to a defendant at times might be a rational or moral one, it also may arise from the defendant's appeal to the sentencer's sympathy or mercy, human qualities that are undeniably emotional in nature" [at 849–50]. Blackmun thus replaces sympathy in its more optimistic Enlightenment context, as one of the altruistic components of human nature. "[W]e see in the sentencer's expression of mercy a distinctive feature of our society that we deeply value," writes Blackmun [at 850]. Thus a jury instruction that the jurors must not be "swayed" by sympathy "well may arrest or restrain this humane response, with truly fatal consequences for the defendant."

I dwell on the problem of the "antisympathy instruction" debated in *California v. Brown* because it touches so closely on the issue of what juries are to listen to, and how they are to be asked to listen, that is at stake in the victim impact statement cases, and indeed throughout the law. Trials are pre-eminently a place of narrative construction, from the moment of the discovery of the scene of the crime (so detailed in Rehnquist's *Payne* opinion), through the making of hypotheses about its commission (what the genre of the detective story is all about), through the construction of the competing narratives of prosecution and defense, and on to the rereading and reinterpretation of these narratives by appellate jurisdictions, which are especially charged with making sure that the rules of storytelling have been properly observed. The rules of evidence, including the rules of what must be excluded as evidence, are all about "fairness" in the way stories are constructed. And it is perhaps obvious but also important to note that all the narrative constructions, and all the rules governing them, eventually and ultimately must be conceived and judged from the point of view of the listeners to the stories told, that is, from the point of view of juries.[6] For it is the judgment of this listener, empowered by society to judge the stories told and to impose sanctions, including the ultimate sanction of death, that alone counts. What juries listen to, and how they listen to it, is of fateful importance.

Notes

1. For a useful summary of the history of the Victims' Rights Movement, and the various cases involving VIS, see Michael Ira Oberlander, "The *Payne* of Allowing Victim Impact Statements at Capital Sentencing Hearings," *Vanderbilt Law Review* 45(1992): 1621.

2. See the issue of *South Carolina v. Gathers* [490 US 805 (1989)], where the fact that the murder victim, Richard Haynes, was found to be carrying a voter registration card and a religious tract known as the "Game Guy's Prayer" was introduced by the prosecutor during Gathers' sentencing as evidence of the fine character of the victim. The Supreme Court of South Carolina overruled Gathers' death sentence on the basis of *Booth*, and the Supreme Court of the United States affirmed, in a 5–4 decision, with Justice Scalia offering a dissent in which he called for overruling *Booth*.

3. Roland Barthes, *S/Z* (Paris: Editions du Seuil, 1970), 145–46, 157–58.

4. David Marshall, *The Surprising Effects of Sympathy* (Chicago: University of Chicago Press, 1988), 5.

5. Adam Smith, "Of Sympathy," *The Theory of Moral Sentiments*, eds. D. D. Raphael and A. L. Macfie (Oxford: Clarendon Press, 1976), 10.

6. In *Post v. Ohio*, 486 US 367 (1988) (cert. denied), the Court refused to consider a case in which victim impact evidence had been introduced during capital sentencing because sentencing was performed by a three-judge panel, not a jury, and judges could be considered immune to illicit emotional appeals. Justices Marshall and Brennan dissented.

20

Life in Death

Noel Walsh

As I have followed the developments in Lifton's work over the years, I have become increasingly interested in applying his theories to my own clinical work. The subject matter which he has explored is often extraordinary and horrific (for example, *The Nazi Doctors*) and frequently seems remote from the less dramatic experiences of the psychiatric consulting room. The psychiatrist, faced as he is with so much individual suffering is often tempted to flee from the pain and suffering of his patients. It is easy to dismiss Lifton's work, with its fascinating and extraordinary subject matter, as being removed from clinical practice. Yet these same struggles with death, mortality and anxiety are not only the province of the Vietnam veteran, the victim of torture, or the concentration camp survivor; they are the bread and butter of the consulting room. The recent increase in research in the area of psychological reactions to trauma—post-traumatic stress disorder and the like—only serves to underline the importance of Lifton's work. I would like to illustrate the importance of death-related imagery and other Liftonian concepts in the therapy of psychological reactions to the kinds of traumas—road accidents, muggings, and hold-ups—that impinge on our everyday life and so frequently present to the psychiatrist.

The theme of death is ever-present in Lifton's work and is a major preoccupation of the patient who has suffered any sort of trauma. In order to understand how Lifton talks about this theme it is useful to look at the concept of "death-imagery." Lifton's concept draws on the work of Susanne Langer. For Langer, the image is both "a genuine conception" and "a carrier of a whole cargo of feeling," central to the whole symbolising process.[1] Langer implies that the image is indispensable in the process of the specifically human attributes of symbolisation and meaning. The image is not static, but dynamic, and includes a plan or schema for enactment. In this sense the image can be described as being a part of the phenomenon of intentionality. For the human subject, faced with the inevitable traumas bound up with birth and existence, the image is essential in dealing with these traumas.

The infant's earliest inchoate imagery is directed toward connection with the other, and with a sense of movement and integrity of his own body. This is associated with a positive sense of life and vitality. Death imagery, on the other hand, is associated with a threat to the integrity of the organism and with stasis and disintegration; the origins of this death imagery are the precursors of the fear of death and are associated with death anxiety. The experience of birth is the infant's first encounter with such threats and gives rise to his death imagery. Birth has two components, extrusion and emergence. Extrusion is the biological separation from the mother. The infant's body is passively forced through the birth canal to the outer word with all its new stimuli and sensations, and the cutting of the umbilical cord is its final separation from its former lifeline. Thus birth is bound up with the negative imagery of loss, separation and physical stress, but also with the positive imagery of emergence, the first experience of individuation, autonomy, movement, vitality and a new form of existence.

The infant has innate behavioural systems which direct it towards proximity and attachment to the mother or other caregiver. It is this early attachment which lays the rock-bottom foundation for a sense of trust, invulnerability and self-esteem. Deficiencies in the nurturing process due to either maternal shortcomings or genetic deficiencies in the infant, or a combination of both, may lead to a dominance of negative imagery that includes disintegration and stasis in contrast to the positive imagery of attachment, integrity and movement. The dialectic of positive (life) and negative (death) imagery is reflected in the different phases of development, from oral, anal and oedipal stages, through adulthood, old age and death. Each individual, depending on which point in the life cycle he may find himself, will have built up a psychological balance sheet in which positive biographical assets will favour life-enhancing imagery, or biographical deficits will be linked to death imagery. Trauma, particularly in early childhood and infancy will alter this "balance sheet" in favor of death imagery, and each further trauma will call into question the subject's death and life imagery.

For Lifton the death encounter is shattering because the victim's prior images, symbolism or inner forms cannot absorb or integrate the threat of the annihilation of the self. Hence the diminution of the actuality of the sense of self which Lifton calls psychic numbing. The depersonalisation and derealisation so frequently seen in traumatised individuals bear witness to this numbing and to the inadequacy of words in describing and processing the event. Lifton's concept of the traumatic process can be usefully compared with the Lacanian notion of the imaginary, the symbolic and the real, the three registers which are knotted together to designate the subject's relation to others, to his own history, and to his desire.[2] Lacan distinguishes the *real* from reality. The *symbolic* register is that of language, which delimits and defines our subjectivity. The *imaginary* is the identity which we assume for ourselves (illusory though it may be), the ego, how we conduct ourselves in everyday life. The *real* is what cannot be imagined or spoken of. It is best understood as that which falls out of language, but which only exists because of the inadequate language to which we are subject. The Freudian example of the fort-da game is the quintessential example of the tension between the real, symbolic and imaginary. Freud described the cotton reel game of his nephew who tried to cope with painful separation from his mother by creating a game (imaginary) and using the words *fort* and *da* (*gone* and *here*) to master his anxiety. However the real of mother's absence is experienced at a level which is deeper and more inaccessible than any game or words can describe. That is why the fort-da game is repetitive; it is because it doesn't work. In metaphysical language this real is the onto-logical level or the level of being in which we all participate. Because it defies language it is traumatic. However the real can also be manifested in what is good, what provokes wonder, what is beautiful, what is yet to be discovered, what Kierkegaard has called the "passion for the pos-sible."

The real both presupposes and grounds the nature of the imaginary and the symbolic registers. When we contemplate the vastness of the universe on a moonlit night, reflect on the mighty powers of nature, listen to Mozart, read about the theory of relativity, respond to a great work of art or literature, or take note of the parallels of symbolic pat-terns of human thought from diverse cultures and civilizations we are in the presence of a creative power emanating from the inaccessible real. The nature of the real is an onto-theological question and raises the issue of the extent to which any particular theory of human psychology is open or closed to a transcendental dimension in life or death.

Separation from the mother raises the question of *desire*. The child not only desires mother's proximity but wants to be the desire of mother herself, to be everything for her. In this imaginary preverbal world the child wants to be the phallus of mother which she lacks but desires. It is later, if all goes well, that the father, as metaphor for Law, prohibition of incest, and promise, intervenes and forces the renunciation of the child's omnipotent desire to be everything for mother. It is in accepting that renunciation, and the lack which it implies, that the child can move to a position of having a limited desire of his or her own, which can be symbolised and expressed in language. This is the crux of castration. It is this experience which also enables the child to form its subjectivity in terms of its future sexuality. For Lacan, desire is insatiable (unlike biological needs) and our relationship to the symbolic order requires the giving up of the illusion of completeness and unity as experienced in the imaginary relationship to the mother. Lacan expresses this in the "formula," "there is no Other of the Other," the "Other" designating both language and the mother, who is the initial bearer of that code. Desire can be characterised as a tension between an archaeology which is an ongoing regressive pull back to the infantile archaic and symbiotic world, and the teleology of ongoing progressive and synthetic striving towards future fulfilment. For Lacan, castration is inextricably bound up with desire.

The precursors of death equivalents—extrusion from the mother's womb, and the loss of the breast at weaning—are balanced by increased individual independence. From learning increased neuromuscular control and bodily integrity (in the anal phase), the child must go on to negotiate the oedipal phase. Within this model, fear of castration is itself a death equivalent, a precursor of the fear of death occurring at a crucial phase in the psychological development of the child. This reversal of Freud's view, that death anxiety is a displacement of castration anxiety, has important implications for psycho-sexual development in childhood, adolescence, and later adult life, since it links the assertion of sexual identity not only to fear of castration but also to fear of death. Many young men risk death or deny its existence in order to assert their masculinity and to prove that they have the phallus. In this context, to be cowardly or impotent is a symbolic death, reflecting stasis and disintegration, while courage and potency reflect integrity, movement and vitality. Death is the ultimate separation, the final departure from all relationships, the disintegration of the mind and body and the ending of all movement and vitality leading to stasis. The image of the hero is he who is willing to risk or sacrifice his life but conquers death either in a literal or symbolic sense.

In the context of Lacanian theory, desire is structured in terms of possession (or not) of the phallus. The father's law of prohibition makes language a necessity; with the symbolic order, this language imposed by the father, comes the real, which escapes language. We might say that death anxiety is associated with the horror of the unsymbolisable real. Therefore to be the subject of desire—to be human—is to struggle constantly with the anxiety associated with death imagery. Similarly, in Lifton's theory, what keeps the human subject going is the struggle for symbolic immortality and vitality.

Humans achieve this symbolic immortality through a variety of modes. The desire to live on through one's children and grandchildren is a sort of "biological mode" associated with imagery of an endless continuous chain of biological attachment. In the theological mode there is belief in the literal survival of the soul after death. In the New Testament Christ says "He who believes in me will have life everlasting," and belief in the immortality of the soul seems to respond to one of man's deepest narcissistic needs, that his self will never be annihilated. The third mode of symbolic immortality is the creative: "I will live on in my work, my contributions to art, literature or science or in the positive influence I have on those around me." The fourth mode of symbolic immortality is related to our link with nature itself. The abundance of nature and the recurring cosmic cycles reassure man that the basis for daily life continues. The final mode of symbolic immortality is that of experiential transcendence. This is a state of intense psychic experience which may be produced by drugs or mystical states in which the individual has a sense that time itself has disappeared—a literal timelessness—and there is a sense of boundless and ecstatic participation.

In the traumatic situation—be it a concentration camp, torture, a road traffic accident, or a mugging—the individual encounters death. The situation may be so horrific that the threat of death constitutes the very fabric of the experience, or may be too sudden for the subject to be able to utilise his symbolic functions to cope with the threat of death. The death encounter in the traumatic situation seriously disrupts this ongoing effort of the self to symbolise its continuity and immortality and as a result the traumatised self is in a state of desymbolisation. In both Liftonian and Lacanian theory, trauma is an encounter with the real. In the context of trauma the real is linked to catastrophe and death and ultimately the experience of evil.

A case history may serve to illustrate these issues and to raise some questions about therapy:

A man in his forties, married with two children, and manager of an industrial centre, was closing the main door of the centre at night-time, in darkness. As he approached his car he was confronted by two men in balaclavas, holding sawn-off shotguns. They ordered him to open the door of the centre and instructed him to bring them to the control console for the alarm system. When they reached the console one of them put a gun to his knee and warned him that any mistake would lead to knee-capping (a punishment often used by guerilla or paramilitary groups; it involves shooting the victim in the backs of the knees and can lead to serious damage to the knee-joint). He disconnected the alarm without incident and thought, "If I cooperate they won't harm me." He was, however, aware that a large sum of money had been removed from the safe earlier that day and anxiously anticipated the disappointment and anger of the gunmen when this was discovered. The men led him towards the safe; they passed a desk on which lay a heavy paperweight. Fleetingly he thought that he could use the paperweight as a blunt instrument to overpower his assailants and prevent the robbery. This idea quickly gave way to the reality of the two guns pointing at him. When it came to unlocking the safe one of the gunmen placed a gun to his head. As he opened the safe he heard a click as the man set the firing mechanism of the gun. At this point the victim experienced mounting anxiety, thinking, "They're going to kill me. I don't want to die. I don't want to leave my wife and family." He described a feeling of extreme dread which was followed by a state of "not feeling anything, becoming more like a spectator." On discovering that the safe contained little money, the gunmen hit him several times with the butt of the gun and his injuries later required treatment in hospital.

In hospital he developed insomnia and nightmares about the hold-up, and during waking hours had frequent intrusive recollections of the event. During the night he would wake up suddenly with sensations of a gun being placed to his head. Similar feelings and sensations occurred during the day. He became hyper-alert, irritable, and sensitive to noise. He also became increasingly sensitive to any stimulus which reminded him of the hold-up, such as gunshot sounds on the television. He described feeling detached and withdrawn and was unable to respond with affection or warmth to family and friends. He was anxious and apprehensive, fearful of the dark, and suffered a general decline in energy level, libido and interest in hobbies and other activities. On several occasions recalling the hold-up incident he remarked that it was "as if it were really happening again as I speak of it." This suggests that the trauma itself is held in some form of "psychic suspension" which has a vivid quality of the "here and now." In psychiatric practice, this patient would be diagnosed as having typical features of post-traumatic stress disorder, according to DSM-IV criteria.[3] However Lifton's work enables the clinician to go beyond symptomatology and diagnosis to a deeper understanding of the life- and death-related issues in trauma.

Essential to Lifton's concept of trauma is the concept of the *death imprint*. If we return to our hold-up victim we can follow his initial defence against threat—"If I cooperate, they will not harm me"—to the idea of overcoming his assailants by using the paperweight on the desk as a weapon, to "Now they're going to kill me" when the gun was put to his head. It was at this moment that there was a radical intrusion of the image of death. The sense of personal invulnerability which is partly a denial that death is real is shattered and the self is permeated with fear of death. This moment is the coming together of the real threat in the hold-up situation and the residual anxiety from pre-existing, symbolic death encounters which threaten the self with disintegration. The patient's wishes "I don't want to die," and "I don't want to leave my family," reflect his reaction to unacceptable, premature and absurd death. The recurring dreams, nightmares and daytime intrusions of the trauma and the sensitivity to internal and external cues that symbolize or resemble the trauma could be considered as the ongoing internal psychological process of trying to overcome psychic numbing, to master the impact of the trauma and to attempt assimilation and integration of existing and pre-existing mental processes. The experience of forced inactivation—helplessness, symbolic castration and associated feelings of rage, guilt and impotence—pervade and dominate the victim's inner world. His inability and failure to have resisted or overcome his assailants create an ongoing process of repetition compulsion—a constant replaying of the traumatic scenario—in an attempt to absorb and master it.

The death imprint is part of the encounter with death—a death which has been survived. This survival requires a coming to terms with the experience of helplessness and powerlessness and an acceptance of the inner psychological change from anxiety, where the threat of death is anticipated to a giving up or surrender where the self is no longer able to hold itself together and the feeling state changes to one of passivity and progressive inhibition of mental function. To these feelings are added what Lifton calls "failed enactment." By this he means feelings of guilt and self condemnation for somehow failing to prevent the traumatic situation. In subsequent therapy sessions the patient described his fantasy, when passing the table with the heavy paperweight, of hitting the assailant on his left and somehow disarming the second assailant. This fantasy quickly gave way to the reality of two shotguns pointing at him and his knowledge that he was in the hands of dangerous gunmen. The image of resistance of being aggressively powerful, of being Superman, must give way to the image of powerlessness and castration. Here castration is impotence—a death equivalent which provokes a feeling of narcissistic rage, guilt, shame, helplessness and latent psychosexual difficulties. For this man neither fight nor flight were possible and the self had to call on a phylogenetically older psychological mechanism—to freeze or play dead, or in Lifton's terminology, psychic numbing.

Our hold-up victim describes feeling "nothing," like a "spectator." Lifton makes a distinction between repression and psychic numbing which he describes as a cessation of feeling. It is as though the psyche decides "If I feel nothing then death is not taking place." There is a process of mental dissociation. Feeling is dissociated from the cognitive awareness of the dread of anticipated real or symbolic death. The pretraumatic self with its biographical assets and liabilities in relation to life and death imagery tries to avoid disintegration and stasis by the adaptive use of psychic numbing. Not only is there cessation of feeling but psychic action with its constant creating and recreating of images undergoes progressive inhibition. There is a closing down of mental function.

The subject victim of trauma has a changed experience of self. The combination of death imprint, survival of the death encounter, failed enactment and psychic numbing has severely damaged the self process, leaving a depleted and desymbolized subject who finds it extremely difficult to trust other humans or the environment, which is often experienced as threatening or lethal. This clearly has important implications for therapy. Lifton describes this as leading to an expectation of what he calls counterfeit nurturance, a type of therapeutic forgery in which the subject finds it extremely difficult to form a trusting or positive transference to the therapist. It is as this point that the theoretical model held by the therapist, and the personality of the therapist comes into play. The traditional psychoanalytic model based on libido theory places special emphasis on early childhood trauma and particularly sexual trauma as both predisposing to and influencing the clinical picture in adult trauma. One could say that there is a risk that psychic trauma is replaced by psychic conflict and that this leads to a diminution or negation of the impact of the actual traumatic event in the perception of the therapist, and hence a possible failure to give full weight to the traumatic event itself. Lifton writes of the importance of bearing witness to the pain and suffering of the victim by a process of empathic participation in which the therapist remains open as opposed to closed and tries to recreate and symbolise the patient's traumatic narrative. Here openness to death related issues and how the therapist deals with his or her own death anxiety will have an important influence on the therapeutic process. In therapy, paradoxical anger and guilt towards the self progresses to anger directed at those responsible for the traumatic event. The manager described in the case history went through several months of struggling with dreams and fantasies of a vengeful and homicidal nature in trying to absorb and integrate his traumatic experience. There was an ongoing process of internal modification of his inner imagery to enable him to absorb and accept the trauma through an enlargement of his inner world.

A quest for meaning of necessity accompanies every therapeutic process which involves acceptance and working through the traumatic event and its concomitant death imagery. Any traumatic event raises questions about the meaning and value of human suffering. Lifton writes that "the death imprint is likely to be associated not only with pain but also with value—with a special form of knowledge and potential inner growth associated with the sense of having 'been there and returned.' " The death encounter undermines our magical sense of invulnerability by means of its terrible inner lesson that death is real, that one will oneself die—and this vies with our relief at no longer having to maintain that illusion.

Perhaps one can speak of varying degrees of knowing—insight and not-knowing. Via the traumatic event the victim has confronted the real in greater depth and this has illuminated the darkness or mystery of life but has not penetrated to the "not yet" which is part of the final transition from life into death. This "not yet, not-knowing" has the same time span as life itself and forms the basis for human hope or despair. Hope is the anticipation of fulfilment that in spite of death there is not only symbolic immortality but an openness to a transcendental reality. Despair is the anticipation of nonfulfilment, a nihilistic belief that on the other side of death there is nothingness.

Hope can be described as a trusting openness to the unforeseeable future which exceeds all expectations and calculations. Totalitarian ideologies such as the Marxist Utopia, Mao Tse-Tung's Continuous Revolution, or the Thousand-Year Reich all attempt to organize and close future time, and with it human freedom, creativity and hope. Personal death and confrontation with the real are denied. The natural aspiration for human hope is displaced and results in the creation of victimizers who claim absolute virtue and victims who are dehumanised and perceived as the embodiment of absolute evil. In killing their victims, the victimizers are killing death. In such ideologies the not-knowing is replaced by a claim to be all-knowing and to possess the absolute truth. The not-yet of the future is reduced to "doctrine over the person," and there is only one possible mode of being—to follow the ideological path.

The omnipotent claim to absolute knowledge, truth and virtue in confrontation with death and their personification in dictators has led to appalling human suffering in our time. The therapist, faced with the death anxiety of the patient, and indeed his own death anxiety, must avoid the position of the ideologist. Rather than possessing the Big Answer, he must, through his refusal of total knowledge, allow the patient to face the anxiogenic real.

The final lines of *The Protean Self* provide some hope in the face of the ever-present real: "By enabling one to transform discontinuity and pain, proteanism allows the traumatized to speak, and to be heard. It can give new voice and vitality to many who would otherwise be silent and deadened, and provide new byways to human connection. The protean path I describe, of individual people reaching toward global belonging, is a path of hope. One may experience that hope, and even a modest personal liberation, in consciously embracing that direction. The embrace is an act of imagination and, as such, a profound beginning."[4]

Notes

I would like to acknowledge Dr. Aisling Campbell, Newman Scholar in the Department of Psychiatry, University College, Dublin, and St. Vincent's Hospital, for her help in preparing this article.

1. Susanne Langer, *Mind: An Essay on Human Feeling,* two volumes (Baltimore: The Johns Hopkins University Press, 1972).

2. Jacques Lacan, "Function and Field of Speech and Language in Psychoanalysis," *Ecrits* (London: Routledge, 1977 [1953]).

3. American Psychiatric Association, *The Diagnostic and Statistical Manual of Mental Disorders,* 4th Edition, (Washington, D.C.: American Psychiatric Press, 1994).

4. Robert Jay Lifton, *The Protean Self* (New York: Basic Books, 1993), 232.

21

"How Pliant Is Science?"

Gerald Holton

At a time when it is fashionable to seek an escape from what is called elsewhere in this book the "straight jacket of a deadly modernism," a scientist is sometimes asked if there are now postmodern effects in science. The question obliges one, first of all, to think again about the old problems of periodization in the history of science. The existence of a significant postmodern turn in science would signal that science has lost its pliancy and is in the grip of some intellectual violence, passing through a discontinuity, a rupture of history, with "modern" behind us and "postmodern" right, left, and all before. Is this really the case? And if so, does it show up in the *content* of contemporary science—in the research journals, rather than in some of the current analyses of sociologists and philosophers or in those attention-seeking popularizations where we encounter the Gaia Hypothesis and the Anthropic Principle?

I

Trying to discern the arrival of a new age has of course long been a task that has attracted historians. Periodization, the arranging of the flow of events into separate eras, is a common tool, though applied more wisely from the safe distance of retrospection. That is how we got such schoolbook chapters as the Age of Reason, or the Progressive Era in America. An instructive example of that whole genre was provided by the American historian Henry Adams. At the beginning of this century, he had been impressed by the work of the chemist J. Willard Gibbs of Yale on the phase rule for understanding heterogeneous equilibria. Adams was also fascinated by the strange idea of some physicists of that day that the phase rule can serve, by analogy, as a means for putting into hierarchical order the following sequence: solid, fluid, gas, electricity, ether, and space, as if they formed a sequence of phases. Stimulated by such ideas, Adams believed that *Thought* itself, too, passed in time through different phases, each representing a different period. In his essay of 1909, *The Rule of Phase Applied to History*, Adams came to a remarkable conclusion about the imminent passing of modernity at that point: "The future of Thought," he wrote, "and therefore of History, lies in the hands of the physicist, and . . . the future historian must seek his education in the world of mathematical physics. . . . [If necessary] the physics departments will have to assume the task alone." Henry Adams' conclusion might fairly have been called in its own day an indication of what the postmodern age would look like. Today's formulation is likely to be exactly the opposite one.

I cite this example—and many more like it come to mind—to signal my methodological discomfort with trying to divide history into distinct "pre-" and "post-" periods. A less rigid and more workable notion is to recognize that at any given time and place, even while a civilization appears to be more or less in a settled state of dynamic equilibrium, there exist simultaneously several competing and perhaps even violently conflicting ideologies within the momentary heterogeneous mixture of outlooks. It is sometimes possible to identify one of these worldviews in retrospect as the most dominant one for a longer or shorter period; but what is more likely to be noted when seen in *real time* is that each of the different competing groups works fervently on raising its own ideology to a position where it would be accepted as the "taste of the time" or the "climate of opinion" which characterizes that particular age and region. And each group, at the same moment, as part of its agenda, *is also trying to delegitimate the claims of its main rivals*. Especially when the relatively stable equilibrium breaks down, the pandemonium of contrasting voices gets louder. Some partial victors rise to be major claimants above the rest, and one of them may even be generally recognized for a while as the embodiment of the new worldview or "sentiment" of the society. And in this constant seesaw of changing historic forces, mankind's inherent tendency toward over-ambition or one-sidedness may infect claimants—not excluding on occasion some scientists—and that in turn can generate in reaction the same sort of excess among the opposing claimants. Recognizing these facts is, in my view, central for understanding the oscillations in twentieth-century culture.

These excesses, when made in the name of either modernity or postmodernity, do not themselves establish unambiguously the validity of the notion of either one or the other. As Leszek Kolakowski remarked in his book *Modernity on Endless Trial*,[1]

"Let us accept our incurable ignorance of our own spiritual foundation and be satisfied with the survey of the surface of our 'modernity,' whatever the word might mean. Whatever it means, it is certain that modernity is as little modern as are the attacks on modernity. . . . I can well imagine Paleolithic nomads . . . predicting the imminent degeneration of mankind as a result of the nefarious invention of the wheel. . . . [p.3]

And he continues:

The clash between the ancient and the modern is probably everlasting and we will never get rid of it, as it expresses the natural tension between structure and evolution, and this tension seems to be biologically rooted; it is, we may believe, an essential characteristic of life. It is obviously necessary for any society to experience the forces both of conservation and of change. . . . [p.4] Modernity itself is not modern, but clearly the clashes about modernity are more prominent in some civilizations than in others and never have they been as acute as in our time. . . . [p.5]

He concludes:

Having no clear idea what *modernity* is, we have recently tried to escape forward from the issue by talking about *postmodernity* (an extension or an imitation of the somewhat older expressions *postindustrial society, postcapitalism*, etc.). I do not know what postmodern is and how it differs from premodern, nor do I feel that I ought to know. And what might come after the postmodern? The post-postmodern, the neo-postmodern, the neo-antimodern? [p.6]

II

These remarks are reminders of the need to examine whether there is a solid base behind the rhetoric about a periodization of modernity vs. postmodernity. But I must add that this skepticism cannot deny the reality of the resonant self-identification of individuals who personally opt for belonging firmly on either side of that uncertain divide. In science itself, this happens only rarely. But if the terminology had existed in the 1630s, the critics of Galileo's mechanics might have called that work *post*modern physics compared with the very competent mainstream Jesuit-scientists; and four decades later, Newton's readers might have hailed Sir Isaac as the conqueror over that same Galileo's *pre*modern physics.

Actually, the word scientists have employed for some time to denote an earlier stage of science is the ambivalent one, "classical," or if more clearly fruitful, "semiclassical." At any rate, the current research publications of physical scientists, to which I necessarily limit myself, are very disappointing when one searches in them for any conscious allegiance to what an avowed postmodernist—say, Zygmunt Bauman (in his *Intimations of Postmodernity*),[2] to choose just one example—might accept. Bauman's hopes may be kindled if he read the title of the physics paper, "Postmodern Quantum Mechanics,"[3] published recently by my colleague Professor Eric J. Heller, together with Steven Tomsovic of the University of Washington, in *Physics Today*, issued by the American Institute of Physics. But the paper turns out to be only about what they call "recent progress in semiclassical theory [which] has overcome barriers posed by classical chaos, and casts light on the correspondence principle." In fact, even without tracing chaos theory back to one of its real originators about 100 years ago, namely to Henri Poincaré in his *Celestial Mechanics*, Heller and Tomsovic end by sounding positively reactionary: "There is no doubt that the agenda of the old quantum theorists is active again. . . . Classical ideas pervade quantum mechanics. It is good to know how far they can really take us" (p.46).

From the Baumanian point of view, there is no trace in the research account of these physicists of what characterizes postmodernism—despite its title, there is nothing in the article about what Bauman calls "monopolistic" science, which he equates with totalitarianism (*Intimations*, pp. 71–72); they do not join in his praise of relativism as against universalism; there is no condemnation of what Bauman calls "monologism" (p.82ff); and they are apparently not even aware that, in Bauman's words, "we have abandoned the modernist conviction that only decisions standing up to the test of universal, objective reason are likely to lead to consequences which are useful and desirable" (p.85). In short our two physicists used the significant word in the title of their essay apparently in the spirit of playfulness, or by way of an inadequate analogy. They would no doubt be appalled by Jean-François Lyotard's misunderstanding of the key point of chaos theory (in his *The Postmodern Condition*),[4] i.e., by his failure to see that chaos theory deals with the search for order in the appearances of disorder, rather than the opposite.

What their article and thousands like it in the research science literature over the past three centuries do illustrate is the very opposite of any theory of history based on discontinuities and ruptures. Rather, they exhibit what I would call simply the *plasticity of science* (as against its supposed periodic fits of fragility or brittleness)—a pliancy which may be defined briefly by the ability of scientific theory and practice to evolve, even during periods of rapid advancement, by preserving enough coherence and commensurability between the earlier and the later formulation, thus avoiding the fragmentation of the mold, by allowing it to stretch into a new shape that has recognizable relations to the earlier one.

III

Let me illustrate this plasticity of science by reminding you of a few stations on the way to today's physical science. I think of Kepler as the first modern scientist because despite all his other preoccupations and allegiances it is he who made the decision to change the fundamental thematic notion for that field from the organismic to the physical. While working on the *Astronomia Nova* in 1605, Kepler lays out his program in a letter to his friend and patron Herwart von Hohenburg:

> I am much occupied with the investigation of the physical causes. My aim in this is to show that the celestial machine is to be likened not to a divine organism but rather to a clockwork . . . , insofar as nearly all the manifold movements are carried out by means of a single, quite simple magnetic force, as in the case of a clockwork all motions [are caused] by a simple weight. Moreover I show how this physical conception is to be presented through calculation and geometry.

In fact, Kepler is not able to show that this program works for him— his physics is too primitive in the details, and magnetism was of course the wrong horse to bet on. But he gave impetus to the subsequent search for one universal force law that explains the motions of the planets. Galileo, while deeply suspicious of his admiring but erratic colleague on the wrong side of the Alps, nevertheless pursued the same search in his own way, and began to think of gravity as the force that extended through the system, at least to the moon. And by further breaking the Aristotelian barriers between the terrestrial and celestial, he took the necessary next steps: secularizing science, submerging the qualitative in favor of the quantitative as the earmark of truth in physical science, and elevating experimental checks from illustrations of the value of a theory to the test of its *probability*.

At this early stage of the evolution of physical science, Galileo's published work was still narrative. Not until three decades later, in Newton's *Principia,* did the parsimonious style and axiomatic presentation, modeled on Euclid's geometry, take over—the sparse style of public science to which we are used today. In Galileo's books there was still no use of algebra, i.e., equations. He did not announce his famous law of free fall as we do in elementary physics, $s = 1/2 \, gt^2$. Rather, he made the mathematically equivalent, but seemingly quite mysterious, statement: "So far as I know, no one has yet pointed out that distances traversed during equal intervals of time, by a body falling from rest, stand to one another in the same ratio as the odd numbers beginning with unity."

To have put it in this way means that what counted for Galileo most was after all not the limited case of explaining the motion of a falling stone or a rolling ball, but the demonstration that terrestrial phenomena, of which these are examples, can be explained by the operation of *integers.* This is commensurable on one side with the number-physics of the Pythagoreans and neo-Platonists, and, on the other side, quite unexpectedly, with the quantum physicists in our century who, in the words of Niels Bohr, have assumed the task of building up "an understanding of the irregularities of nature upon the consideration of pure number."

We could similarly look at each of the next stages in the evolution of scientific practice by exfoliation and adaptation up to our day, as they developed against the background of a few constant themata. Going, so to speak, down the broadening river, from its sources to its current estuary, is one strategy for showing that a remarkable degree of continuity exists between seemingly disparate traditions in science. Time and time again a scientific practice or theory is enriched by adapting elements of other stages that may have been far removed in time, subject matter, and conceptual structure. (Of course the pursuit at times of a wrong idea—which is also part of the scientific enterprise—permits a similar tracing; failures, too, have parents as well as progeny.)

IV

But there is also another way to demonstrate the often hidden system of interconnections that link various scientific stages. Instead of going chronologically downstream, one can pick a particular scientific work and follow its antecedents upstream, thereby charting the system of "tributaries" that entered at various points. To speak operationally, one can select one scientific paper, and record the explicit and implicit citations found in it that indicate the resources that were used; then we can go to each of those cited or implied, earlier papers and look for works that are referred to there; and this process can be continued further back in time. This way of tracing resources results in laying bare the whole genealogical web of interconnections, the borrowing from earlier works, the interplay between applied and pure research, between different fields and sub-fields, and also between research traditions based on seemingly mutually hostile conceptual structures. The key to the success of this process lies in the adaptability of old knowledge to new purposes.

To exhibit this process in a concrete way, a small group of us has traced the genealogy of one particular work. The case we chose was the rather spectacular discovery of high-temperature superconductivity by K. Alex Müller and his former student J. Georg Bednorz in 1986, for which they were awarded the Nobel Prize in Physics in 1987. As one fully expects, one finds all the debts to previous, unsuccessful attempts to discover high-temperature superconductivity, and more broadly to the tradition of ordinary superconductivity research going back to Kamerling Onnes. But equally important to the final result were many earlier advances, in distant fields that one could have hardly expected to lend themselves so readily to the job at hand in 1986. Somehow the earlier achievements turned out to be waiting for uses that had not yet been dreamt of.

To mention just a few, almost at random: In choosing the Ba-La-Cu-O compound, which first yielded the desired result, Müller and Bednorz relied in good part on reasoning based not only on the Bardeen-Cooper-Schrieffer (BCS) theory of superconductivity of 1957, but also on the theories of solid state going back to Jahn and Teller's theorem in quantum chemistry of 1937, and Landau's idea of polarons of 1933. The production of the experimental results in 1986 depended crucially on the adaptability or plasticity of earlier, separately originated items, from an IBM-PC for automated control and data-acquisition, to techniques of cooling whose principles go back to the Joule-Thomson experiment of 1853.

The methods of measurement and observation marshaled for the critical Müller-Bednorz experiment show an impressive variety and ancestry: the temperature was determined by means of resistance thermometry, whose historical roots lie in Humphry Davy's discovery in 1821 that electrical resistance is temperature-dependent. The magnetic susceptibility of the sample was measured in part by using the Josephson effect of 1962. The measurement of resistance relied on the usual techniques of electric circuitry, whose principles include Ohm's law (1826); the structure of the sample was analyzed with x-ray diffractometry, the rudiments of which were developed by Bragg and Bragg in 1913, building on von Laue's work on x-rays in 1912.

The whole map of this river system ending at the Müller-Bednorz estuary spans over two centuries, and the sources of the tributaries lie in fields as diverse as material science, physical chemistry, solid-state physics, statistical mechanics, crystallography, quantum mechanics, low-temperature physics, electromagnetic theory, and electronics. And of course at another level, a similar network of borrowings and adaptations can be drawn for the development of the social system of science operative in this case, the evolution of criteria of trust in data, the growth of teamwork, the old and ever-changing story of patronage and funding. All this contradicts the popular image of such work as a "revolutionary breakthrough," made by these two men alone.

V

Here one may well ask: What is there about the physical sciences which makes them, at any stage of their—let us say—momentary modernity, so plastic or adaptable for use in the next stage of their modernity, under circumstances that could hardly have been predictable? Perhaps a deeply believing realist might have the easiest answer to this hard question. Such persons are now rare, but they might find some support in certain surprising and still insufficiently explained historical facts. One is that two quite different lines of work, starting from different theoretical presuppositions, sometimes can be shown to be at bottom just two different views of the same matter. A classic case in point was the demonstration of the equivalence of apparently opposing theories, the matrix mechanics of Heisenberg and the wave mechanics of Schrödinger. What looked like contradiction was dissolved, to everyone's surprise.

Another fact that probably does not puzzle believing realists is the well-known simultaneity of certain scientific discoveries, theoretical or experimental, by persons or teams that had not been in contact with one another, and who were working under different social or cultural conditions within which they might have been thought to be constructing their results. A famous example is the development of quantum field theory through renormalization, achieved separately by Julian Schwinger in America and by Sin-Itiro Tomonaga, then rather isolated in wartime and postwar Japan. A less well-known illustration comes from the First International Conference on Atomic Energy in Geneva in August 1955. After several years of enforced scientific isolation for Soviet scientists, there was a sudden thaw in the Cold War behavior of the West and the East. At that point scientists from both sides met and gave talks on their respective experimental results—for example on the sensitive matter of the low-energy cross-sections of uranium and other elements, obtained and jealously guarded in secret work on each side of the iron curtain. It was a rather emotional occasion when the projected graphs showed that the curves of data by the Russians and the Americans coincided remarkably. (I won't enter here into the question of why the curves shown by the British were not quite so good.) Some sociologists and anthropologists have chosen to dwell almost exclusively on the passing controversies and differences among scientists. But at the end of the day it is also necessary to look at coincidences of results. Thus Sharon Traweek's book *Beamtimes and Lifetimes. The World of High Energy Physicists,*[5] about the differences between Japanese and American physics teams, would have been even better if it had even a single graph of the entirely comparable results which the respective labors of these different communities have produced.

But there remains another possible place to look for postmodern effects in research science. For is it not true that some highly respected working scientists, such as Howard Georgi and Philip Anderson, would be satisfied with a stratified, let us say "pluralistic," physics, one in which each of the strata has its own set of basic laws? And does this not contradict the more established program of working toward one "foundational," unified physics, a vision which has motivated most major physical scientists from Newton to Faraday, from Maxwell to Einstein, and to our day, as in the writings of Steven Weinberg, who speaks of "Newton's dream to understand all of nature"[6] in one coherent way? Is there not here a moment of conflict (so welcome a research site for postmodernists) between those who can revel in diversity *versus* those who pursue what Isaiah Berlin called the Ionian Fallacy, the legacy of Thales of Miletus, who taught us to look for the One in the Many?

Yet, if that is what postmodernism in science now amounts to, it is indeed a poor shadow of what passes for the real thing outside the lab. If one looks at the totality of physical scientists, it is true that the narrow-focused splitters outnumber the horizon-seeking lumpers in practice. But that, too, is an old story, as confirmed by a glance at the publications of the Academies ever since the seventeenth century. Those who do not feel threatened by finding irreducible diversity at the base of things might be represented by J. J. Thomson, no radical, who remarked in his 1909 presidential address to the British Association that "The sum of knowledge is . . . a diverging not a converging series." And in any case, evidence for nature's holism has come to us mostly indirectly, through seemingly narrow concerns. As Victor Weisskopf put it, it was the study of the twists of frog muscle that led to the laws of electricity, which then were found to be at the basis for the structure of matter. The detour through diversity has often paid off even for unifiers. It is not by accident that in the "Table of Categories" in Kant's *Critique of Pure Reason* the first two of his fifteen categories are *Unity* and *Plurality*.

My own gut sympathies do in fact lie more with the unifiers. Yet as a historian of science, I believe that those who dwell on today's version of the controversy between foundationalists and pluralists in science miss the vital role which the simultaneous existence of both parties plays, and always has played, in the progress of a science. I mentioned earlier that Kolakowski correctly pointed to "the natural tension between structure and evolution," and held that it may not only be biologically rooted but even an essential characteristic of life. In the same way, science needs and depends critically on the conscious dialogue between the lumpers and the splitters, the unity-seekers and their antithematic opposites, the diversifiers. Even *that* dialogue has been part of science's astonishing commensurability.

This has never been put better than by one of our great science synthesizers of the early nineteenth century, Hans Christian Oersted, who shall have the last word today with an observation as true now as it was then:

> One class of natural philosophers have always a tendency to combine the phenomena and to discover their analogies; another class, on the contrary, employ all their efforts in showing the disparities of things. Both tendencies are necessary for the perfection of science, the one for its progress, the other for its correctness. The philosophers of the first of these classes are guided by the sense of unity throughout nature; the philosophers of the second have their minds more directed towards the certainty of our knowledge. The one are absorbed in search of principles, and neglect often the peculiarities, and not seldom the strictness of demonstrations; the other consider the science only as the investigation of facts, but in their laudable zeal they often lose sight of the harmony of the whole, which is the character of truth. Those who look for the stamp of divinity on every thing around them, consider the opposite pursuits as ignoble and even as irreligious; while those who are engaged in the search after truth, look upon the other as unphilosophical enthusiasts, and perhaps as phantastical contemmers of truth. . . . This conflict of opinions keeps science alive, and promotes it by an oscillatory progress.

Notes

1. Leszek Kolakowski, *Modernity on Endless Trial* (Chicago: University of Chicago Press), 3–6.

2. Zygmunt Bauman, *Imitations of Postmodernity* (London and New York: Routledge, 1992).

3. Eric J. Heller and Steven Tomsovic, "Postmodern Quantum Mechanics," *Physics Today*, 46, 7 (July 1993), 38–46.

4. Jean-Francois Lyotard, *The Postmodern Condition* (Minneapolis: University of Minnesota Press, 1984).

5. Sharon Traweek, *Beamtimes and Lifetimes. The World of High Energy Physics* (Cambridge: Harvard University Press, 1988).

6. Steven Weinberg, *Dreams of a Final Theory* (New York: Pantheon Books, 1992).

22

Confidentiality: In the College Presidential Search Process and Beyond

David Riesman

When the *Festschrift* editors asked me for a contribution, they also said that the volume was going to be kept confidential from Robert Jay Lifton, and this word, "confidentiality," gave me a clue as to my own possible contribution. I was immediately reminded of Bob Lifton's encouragement to my wife Evelyn and me to publish the diaries we severally had kept during a two-month stay as guests of International House of Japan in the fall of 1961. For Evelyn, this was part of a habit of keeping a diary that went back to her childhood; for me, it was part of my more recently developed pattern of recording interviews and other events with prospective bearing on my research. Bob Lifton assured us that the Japanese we had met and about whom we had written would not have the same obsession with privacy characteristic of Americans. What we then did was to change the names and some identifying details and send draft copies to our interlocutors in Japan, none of whom objected. (We subsequently discovered that they would have preferred us not to disguise names.) Our book, *Conversations in Japan: Modernization, Politics, and Culture,* was published in 1967, with no Japanese objections of which we were aware, other than our decision to disguise people's names. In 1965, from January through June, we had been at the University of Sussex, then one of the new British universities, and again we had kept diaries and notes. And it was inconceivable then as it is at this writing that one could publish something about living people in the United Kingdom, any more than we could do so vis-à-vis living Americans. Robert Lifton had helped teach us something significant about cultural differences, with respect to privacy and publicity.

Confidentiality in Fieldwork

Questions concerning confidentiality have been salient throughout my life as a scholar. My preference has always been for field research, and the "field" that was most accessible to me in terms of language and relative ease of access and comprehension has been that of higher education. This has meant that in writing, alone or with colleagues, about particular institutions I have made it a practice to share what I wrote with those I had interviewed, and share observations also with institutional officials. In some instances, the outcome was that I could publish my observations provided that I made certain modifications in the text. In other instances, and these have been common, I disguise names and locations of institutions, even though I recognize that an ingenious detective could almost certainly locate and identify institutions that I had disguised only superficially.[1]

In 1980, I began to work with Judith Block McLaughlin, then as a graduate student and soon as a colleague at the Harvard Graduate School of Education, in studying searches for college and university presidents throughout the United States. One of our principal concerns has been whether or not the search process can be kept confidential, partly in order to have more candid discourse among members of the search committee, and partly in order to be able to recruit top academic officers, primarily sitting presidents, who cannot afford a charge of institutional disloyalty if they become candidates without actually being chosen as presidents.

Freedom of Information and Sunshine Laws

In academic settings, search committees now are reasonably representative of campus constituencies. They serve for this trip only. Confidentiality allows the members of the committee to be candid with each other concerning what the institution needs and what candidates offer. Confidentiality also provides potential candidates with opportunities to explore the possibility of moving to a presidency without jeopardizing their local situation on charges of disloyalty.

What we might term the microscopic issues of confidentiality in academic settings are played out on a larger, noisier stage in the United States as a whole where, on the one hand, American individuals' obsession with privacy has increased along with a level of distrust that often verges on paranoia, while simultaneously the press and other media have been insisting on "the public's right to know" in an almost plebiscitary insistence that everyone should be able to take part in the political process by, so to speak, sitting in on what is going on. The Freedom of Information Act at the federal level is one example of this pressure for publicity, understandable in the light of Watergate and ensuing scandals, but also potentially hazardous to American foreign policy, which is at risk anyway from the realization by non-Americans that Americans may be obsessed with privacy for themselves but are given to gossip and can often not be trusted with state secrets. Every state in the union has an open meeting, or as it is referred to in some states, a sunshine law, requiring that public bodies open their proceedings to the media or to any interested bystander. The press and its juridical advocates who push in particular cases for the opening of meetings or records have not in this way won the trust of the American people, but to put it crudely, are the prostitutes to bring Americans the goodies we enjoy even as they earn our disrespect. Those seeking access, for whatever reason, have had at their disposal governmental and private legal entrepreneurs eager to comply.

The False Glare of "Sunshine"

By the time, fifteen years ago, that Judith Block McLaughlin and I began studying searches for college and university presidents at all sorts of institutions in the public and private sectors, these procedures were no longer handled by informal action among a handful of trustees. Partly in response to the revolts against authority in the 1960s, faculty members and also in most instances students were added to search committees in which board members were often a minority. What had been a taken for granted presumption of confidentiality among gentlemen in an earlier day became an often inflammatory issue over the last quarter century. Moreover, in the public sector, where eighty percent of students are educated, state open meeting and sunshine laws are increasingly invoked by the press to gain entrée to a search. The idea that this supposed democratization will get rid of the "old boy network" has proved fallacious. No state is more proud of its sunshine law than Florida, whose officials like to refer to themselves as operating in the Sunshine State. But in the university system, the result has been searches more politicized and in many ways less open than before the zealous application of the Sunshine Law to the presidential search process. This occurs because sitting presidents, with negligible exceptions, do not want to be candidates and exhibit publicly their disloyalty—and then lose. This is what happened to John DiBiaggio, when he was president of the University of Connecticut and was recruited by the former chancellor as a candidate for the presidency of the University of Florida, winning strong faculty support but losing out in the end precisely to the "old boy network" when Marshall Criser, an alumnus of the College and the Law School and a former Regent, a practitioner-entrepreneur in Palm Beach, was chosen as President. And DiBiaggio had to find an escape from the University of Connecticut, where his disloyalty was venomously reprobated. Only in complete confidentiality arranged by a search consultant was he able to be named president of Michigan State University and escape near-certain dismissal at Connecticut. The chairman of the Department of Communications at the University of Florida is one of many academics in the field of mass communications who passionately favors sunshine laws, believing that they serve the interests of the people. But Jack Wheat, a Tallahassee correspondent for *The Miami Herald*, has written effectively about the negative consequences of the Florida "openness," which leads neither to public trust nor to any serious participation on the part of a particular campus.

"Sunshine" in Michigan

The press sees itself as acting in the public interest when it insists that no public decisions should be made "behind closed doors"—where of course scurrilous things do sometimes go on, much as they do when doors are open—but the interest, even the prurient interest, on the part of readers may in the case of searches for university presidents be only fitfully present. When the University of Michigan Board of Regents began a search for a successor to departing president Harold Schapiro, who had assumed the presidency of Princeton University, the Regents insisted on the constitutional status of the university as a basis for conducting proceedings indeed behind closed doors, while *The Ann Arbor News* brought suit in order to have access not only to meetings but to all the paperwork that commonly surrounds a search. The search went ahead with a moderate but jeopardized degree of confidentiality, a situation that made some sitting presidents unwilling to participate, and the Regents ended up with Vice President and Provost James Duberstadt, who was simply promoted to the presidency.

At this point, *The Ann Arbor News* won its suit, with the result that an enormous array of materials became public, including the notes of participants and in one case the diary of one of the Regents. The names of prospects strewn about in this fashion included a very large number of sitting presidents who would never have dreamed of becoming candidates even had the search guaranteed confidentiality (which by the nature of human beings, can never be done) who were embarrassed at their present locales, not only by suspicions of potential disloyalty, which in a country given to such high levels of distrust is almost standard, but also with news of not such agreeable things said about them in the discourse reported in the papers that were publicized.

The most dramatic stories had to do with the candidacy of Vartan Gregorian, who was at the time president of the New York Public Library and who was the favorite of alumni, faculty, and students, who supported his candidacy with enthusiasm. However, the news also came out that one of the Regents, Dean Baker, had telephoned Gregorian to say that, far from supporting his candidacy, he was passionately opposed to it, and had sworn to make life miserable for him regardless of whatever policies and measures he would propose to strengthen and lead the University of Michigan. Gregorian withdrew from the search. When all the papers came out, the press and others declared that, had the search been in the public arena, "We could have had Gregorian!"

I had known Gregorian for twenty-five years, and I wrote to him to say that I was certain that he would not have been a candidate had the search been public, and that the statements by many that had the search not been concealed, Gregorian would have been a willing candidate, were fallacious. On November 15, 1994, Gregorian wrote me to say that he had seriously considered the University of Michigan out of his belief in the importance of public higher education, and because there was such near-unanimity of support for him, including the Governor, former President Gerald Ford, and many who would have been his colleagues within the University of Michigan administration. He assured me that, indeed, I was not mistaken: he would never have become a candidate had there not been the promise of confidentiality, a promise kept to him by Brown University, which soon recruited him for its Presidency. Dean Baker's opposition was only a minimal factor in leading Gregorian to withdraw his candidacy, when he came to recognize the limited resources that the state of Michigan provided to assist the University, which includes not only Ann Arbor, but also the campuses at Flint and Dearborn; moreover, Michigan would accept only a third of its entering students from outside the state. The Regents had deep ideological differences and personality conflicts, and they did not confine themselves to setting the larger policy but often interfered with the internal management of the University. Thus, while Dean Baker's antagonism was surely no help in his potential recruitment, it was not a major factor in leading him to withdraw.

The Decline of Institutional Loyalty

The loss of authority is often accompanied by the decline or disappearance of institutional loyalty. People like to regard themselves as "agin the system." When, now some years ago, the Regents of the State University of New York system were conducting a search for a new Chancellor to replace Clifford Wharton, Jr., the chairman of the Board asked all the members of the search committee to agree to maintain confidentiality. However, the student who had been elected to the Board concluded that his appropriate loyalty was to his fellow students, or perhaps to their newspapers, and revealed the Regents' choice prematurely, to the dismay of other members of the Board.

The Bennington College Story

It is not only in searches that loss of collegiality and institutional loyalty can prove calamitous. A 1986 episode in the history of Bennington College is an illustration. The College has lived for years on the brink of financial collapse. It has virtually no endowment—a matter at the outset of principle. Its tuition has been the highest in the country and, no longer a woman's college, its enrollments have fallen even while the number of faculty has remained relatively high. In that situation some dozen years ago, the board of trustees decided that they had to take drastic steps if the College was to escape bankruptcy. Faculty members insisted on being included in the deliberations, and they were. After the very first such meeting, when there was serious discussion of large cuts in the faculty, one of the faculty participants went to *The Bennington Banner* with an inflammatory story about the destruction of Bennington that portended. The story was picked up by *The Brattleboro Reformer* and by *The Boston Globe,* and the program for restructuring Bennington College was abandoned. This is one of many examples of the lack of ability to maintain confidentiality in the face of polemical antagonisms.

In 1994, President Elizabeth Coleman and members of the Board of Trustees decided on a drastic restructuring that was believed, in my judgment appropriately, as essential if Bennington College were to survive.

Faculty members on five-year rolling contracts were let go; departments were abolished to be replaced by interdisciplinary divisions; foreign language programs were eliminated, with students finding foreign language instruction elsewhere in the Southern Vermont area. When this dramatic plan was put into effect in June, 1994, dismissed faculty members understandably sought legal counsel and are planning to bring suit, by charging that improper procedures were used in releasing them. Many faculty members assumed in this and in other comparable crises that, if only the trustees were up to their job, they could all rest comfortably, and with increased emoluments. Bennington College's survival hangs in the balance as I write these lines in the fall of 1994.

What seems paradoxical in America is that the seal of confidentiality has become fragile even while we Americans are obsessed with our demands for privacy. Many people who are not at evident risk for criminal attack have unlisted telephone numbers. Survey researchers find that Americans are today less ready than they were a generation ago to respond to questionnaires, sometimes understandably and sometimes maniacally, fearing some kind of hoax or sales pitch or whatever. Women confide in other women in some measure, but men in their relations to one another, even if they are pals, rarely confide matters of deep concern to them. To put the matter most dramatically, people want assurances that nothing in their own lives will be exposed to others beyond the minimum requisite for education and further advancement. Often they guard even trivial matters about themselves. The world they envisage is even more hostile than the world actually around them, and then is refracted in their own attitudes. To put the matter grossly, individuals believe that whatever is known about them should be kept in complete confidentiality, but they have a right to know as citizens and employees about the lives and deeds of others. Just as Evelyn and I could not publish our diaries of the United Kingdom in the way we were able to do vis-à-vis Japan, so it would not occur to us that Evelyn's diaries or my private commentaries about our American lives could be appropriately published, at least until well sorted out and censored, and after our deaths.[2]

Many Americans believe that they are entitled to confidentiality and privacy in all their exchanges and dealings while those others, university officials, government officials, more or less public figures of any sort, are subject at all times to "the public's right to know" irrespective of the actual harm done by such disclosure. (American foreign policy itself suffers by the lack of trust non-American officials often have in the confidentiality of their exchanges with American diplomats and negotiators.) The press and the other media, which are often the vehicles for disclosure and which pride themselves on pursuing what they regard as the public's interest in seeking disclosure, do not win public trust as a result; in a way, they are like the prostitutes whom individuals may enjoy and yet whom they despise: those who bring the news are regarded as no better, and often even a bit worse, than those who make it.

Jack Wheat covers higher education for *The Miami Herald* from a base in Tallahassee, and is a remarkable reporter for believing that Florida's Sunshine Law actually damages the search process and limits potential outcomes—he is unusual in not taking for granted the press's supposed mandate to enforce what is only superficially Sunshine. What has actually occurred in the Florida State System searches has been an arrangement between the higher education Chancellor in Tallahassee, the state capital, and the particular solicited candidate assuring this person that he or she will have no real competition. Sitting presidents turn down the hazards of a Florida search and leave the choice to fall on local state politicians, as most recently in selections for the presidency of the University of South Florida and of Florida State University, both government officials without particular experience in higher education. These outcomes can hardly help but increase already all-too-widespread public cynicism.

Issues in the Presidential Search

As I have already indicated, confidentiality is an issue not only vis-à-vis the candidates but vis-à-vis the discourse concerning them. For example, suppose that as now frequently happens a black candidate is on the list. In public, especially white males will be extremely cautious in expressing any criticisms, for fear of being charged with racism and/or sexism. In private, misgivings can be shared. This is all the more important today, when search consultants make it part of their sales pitch that they will help the institution find women and minority candidates, but they do not tell the institution that, once chosen, it is extremely difficult to let such incumbents go, out of fear of the charge of racism and/or sexism. In fact, it is rare today to find a search committee which does not have at least one woman as a member, and also a black person. In a Williams College search some years ago, faculty chose as its representatives the three men who then headed the divisions of humanities, natural sciences, and social sciences, and a woman had to be found to be added to the mix. Such outcomes are frequent.

Yet to apply Affirmative Action criteria to the choice of a college or university president runs hazards in addition to the likelihood that such a person cannot easily be got rid of. It tends to break the link to alumni, perhaps especially those alumni, often the most generous, who are avid football, basketball, or hockey fans. Even in coed institutions, it has been in the past male donors and mobilizers of other donors who have predominated in philanthropy toward the institution. To choose a woman somewhat curtails the sense of connection to the institution, even if the woman takes an active interest in sports and their advancement. In state university systems, the system itself will tend to see to it that one or another locale will have a black and also a female president, because the main source of support comes from the state and not from the alumni of that particular place.

More generally, what has happened in the search process is that presidents do not come from the immediate locale, and rarely are alumni of the institution where they are chosen. Searches are national, and while there is some tendency in the South to choose people from the South, this is by no means guaranteed. Someone can be brought to Virginia Polytechnic Institute and State University from a northern state institution. For institutions that aim to be national, this mode of selection is not problematic. For those, and these are still the majority, which cultivate a local clientele, nationalizing the search can jeopardize the close connection of person and place.

James O. Freedman is a New Hampshire native who went to Harvard College and then Yale Law School. After having been Dean of the Law School at the University of Pennsylvania, he became President of the University of Iowa and from there moved to the presidency of Dartmouth College. At Dartmouth, being a Harvard College alumnus is a negative asset, because of the tendency of Harvard College undergraduates to look down on the presumably nonintellectual Dartmouth undergraduates. Being a New Hampshire native in no way prepared Freedman for the idiosyncratic culture of Dartmouth College, for example, the intense wish that it remain a *College,* so that when he referred to "Dartmouth University," far from complimenting people, he infuriated them. The presidency at Iowa in no way prepared him for Dartmouth, particularly since he had a staff at Iowa which he could not match at more intimate Dartmouth College. The search consultant, almost omnipresent William Bowen of Heidrich & Struggles, was no help at all in alerting Freedman to the specific concerns and even anxieties of Dartmouth College alumni, many of whom on retirement moved to the Hanover Inn, rather than to Florida, in order to maintain their links to the College.

The chair of the search committee which chose Freedman left the board when Freedman became president, so that the latter lacked the mentorship which continuity on the board might have provided for him. It is in such situations that I have suggested that new presidents need what I sometimes refer to as a "court jester" to help them appreciate the idiosyncracies of their position and their place. Confidentiality permitted the recruitment of Freedman, but of course could play no part in his habituation to the new setting.

The maintenance of confidentiality requires a concern for the group. It requires subordination of one's own desire for réclame through publicity to the interests of the group and even to the overriding role of the search committee chair. This kind of subordination to group norms is antithetical to current extravagances of American anarchic individualism. But it is essential if the search process is to reach optimal goals, rather than to recruit mediocre candidates who are only minimally threatened by having their names exposed or even are required to get out of the situations where they currently are because of poor performance there. Indeed, it has been astonishing to me to see how many presidents have been chosen who had performed badly at their previous institutions, which were eager to get rid of them. Of course, confidentiality does not assure the benign outcome of a search, but lack of confidentiality limits both the range of candidates who may be considered and the level of discourse used by the search committee in reflecting on the prospects at hand. Members of a search committee may behave in the group better than they do in ordinary settings, and much worse, depending in part on the degree of confidentiality and in considerable part on leadership. Size is also germane. It is hard to keep a group in focus which numbers more than twenty, although a chairman of remarkable capacity can manage a group as large as twenty-five or thirty, but that is rare. Groups sometimes are too small: they cannot provide a range of viewpoints or access to a variety of potential candidates. They also are likely to lack legitimacy because they represent too few members of the choosing institution. In these matters, a degree of balance is requisite which is not a quality often sought in American extravagant individualism. With confidentiality as a protection, members of a search committee can rise above themselves and above the constituencies they were chosen to represent and seek the beneficence of the institution as a whole. More commonly, in the absence of confidentiality and in the absence of a sense of responsibility to the whole on the part of individual committee members, the search ends up with not necessarily the lowest common denominator but with someone who is high in the calculation of a particular search committee member but does not attract or represent the search committee as a whole. Such prospects will have only a fragmentary hold in their new locales, although with good luck they may establish themselves de novo by their own exertions.

As I hope I have made clear, there is no absolute link between the quality and confidentiality of a search and the quality and endurance of the person chosen. "Bad" searches can produce remarkably good candidates and vice-versa. But in general, it is fair to say that good searches are likely to produce superior candidates. There is, however, a link between the preoccupation of many with their own privacy while at the same time they believe that they have the "right to know" when it concerns other people who might have a position of responsibility. They do not trust people chosen from their own ranks, nor do they have a high regard for the mass media which bring the "news" of what is actually or supposedly going on. This suggests something about the vulnerability of Americans today, of which they are aware in the economic arena but perhaps less so in the broader public arena to which they apply the simple prescription of distrust and are so deeply cynical that it actually makes people gullible—gullible to those who play upon the cynicism and suggest "remedies," whether these be term limits or other seemingly simple but dangerous prescriptions to respond to the distrust. Presidential searches can then be seen as a microcosm of this larger constellation of misgivings, whose origins lie both within the individual psyche and the social constellations within which people live.

Notes

I am indebted to the Markle Foundation for their support of my research on confidentiality in relation to the media.

1. For a fuller discussion, see my essay, "Ethical and Practical Dilemmas of Fieldwork in Academic Settings: A Personal Memoir," in Robert K. Merton, James Coleman and Peter Rossi, eds., *Qualitative and Quantitative Social Research: Papers in Honor of Paul F. Lazarsfeld* (New York: Free Press, 1979).

2. It has been astonishing to me that one of the top CIA officials dealing with the Soviet Union, Aldrich Ames, was for many years a counter-spy, who betrayed to the Soviet Union individuals (some of whom he had himself recruited) who were spying on behalf of the United States. His sudden lavish wealth, his various unscheduled travels—these excited doubts among a few, but when these were raised, they were quickly quashed. Here is a remarkable case of extravagant trust, a lack even of the most obvious precautions, against a continuing series of what were in many cases lethal betrayals.

Shame and Public Life

Jean Bethke Elshtain

Reading Robert Jay Lifton's *The Nazi Doctors*, one is ashamed—ashamed at the horrific deed-doing here on display; ashamed that those committed to healing, men and women, convinced themselves that it was noble to kill; ashamed at the knowledge that atrocities each day are perpetrated on our fragile globe. Lifton points out that the Nazis "mounted a consistent attack upon what they viewed as exaggerated Christian compassion for the weak individual instead of tending to the health of the group, of the *Volk*." Lifton's searing examples of ideologically motivated "compassion" that killed put errant shamelessness on display, much to our shame as human beings. The perverse socio-political "therapy" of what Lifton calls Nazi bio-politics is a stirring reminder, and an indictment, of a time and a place now a half-century old but very much part of our present past. The scene of one Dr. Pfannmüller, "fat" and "grinning," holding aloft a "whimpering skeleton" of a child, proclaiming as a real accomplishment that "this one" had only "two or three more days," is a snapshot of hell.

In line with Lifton's project, I will offer up the meditations of the German theologian and anti-Nazi martyr, Dietrich Bonhoeffer, on why shame is necessary, necessary not just "in private" but to public life as well. One of the reasons Bonhoeffer was so repulsed by Nazism was precisely because of its aberrant shamelessness. Nazi ideology dictated erasing any barrier between public and private, between that which should be open to public scrutiny and definition and that which should not. The horrific denouement of an ideology that required breaching the boundary of shame was the shamelessness of death camps where human beings were robbed of dignity, stripped of privacy, deprived, therefore, of an elemental freedom of the body in life and of the respect we accord the bodies of the dead after life is no more. Scenes of starved, naked bodies, piles and piles being shoved by bulldozers into lime pits is a nigh inexpressible instance of shamelessness, with the dead reduced to anonymous carcasses.

279

As a political philosopher, it has been one of my tasks to explore the relation between public and private, categories and spheres of life that are always defined and understood in relation to one another. I have been touched by much of Lifton's work because he, too, is always working this boundary, or traversing this borderland. If one looks to the derivation of private, it means "not open to the public" and public, by contrast, is that "of or pertaining to the whole, done or made in behalf of the community." In part, these contrasts derive from the Latin origins of public, *pubes*, the age of maturity when signs of puberty begin to appear: then and only then does the child enter, or become qualified for, public things. Similarly, *publicus* is that which belongs to, or pertains to "the public," the people. But there is another meaning: public as open to scrutiny; private as that not subjected to the persistent gaze of publicity. Here we glimpse matters not wholly revealed for we always look through a glass darkly in the realm of human affairs. This barrier to full revelation is necessary in order to preserve the dignity and possibility of different sorts of relationships and different orders or spheres of existence: the citizen and the mother; the friend and the official, and so on.

In his great and difficult text, *Letters and Papers from Prison,* written after his arrest by the Gestapo, Bonhoeffer reflects on what he calls "The sense of quality." He notes that at times "it may have been the business of Christianity to champion the equality of all men; its business today will be to defend passionately human dignity and reserve." I take this to be a recognition of the need for shame. Human dignity and reserve need their champions today, perhaps more than ever, in a time and a place when shamelessness is trumpeted as a sign of free expression; when rectitude appears to have gone into hiding. I will take as my texts Bonhoeffer's Biblical study of "Creation and Fall" and his exploration of the theme of shame in the *Ethics.* He asks us to consider why shame exists, for initially, in the Garden, "the man and his wife were both naked, and were not ashamed." Shame enters with knowledge. But it is knowledge of a particular kind, awareness of "our division," of humankind's recognition of its own evil. In the now lost "unity of unbroken obedience man is not ashamed. . . . Shame only comes into existence in the world of division. Knowledge, death, sexuality—here . . . we are dealing with the connexion between these three primaeval words of life." If we pretend to a primordial wholeness that no longer exists, we fall into a form of self-idolatry: we make believe that we are pre-lapsarians, that we are once again innocents in the Garden, that we have known no evil.

But evil will have its due, Bonhoeffer argues. It is our task to prevent it from having its day. And central to that task is a recognition of shame and the limits to human self-striving and self-overcoming that recognition affords. Shame is not "good in itself," Bonhoeffer insisted, and to argue in that way is "moralistic, puritanical, totally unbiblical." Rather, shame "must give reluctant witness to its own fallen state." From its division, humankind covers itself. Man "without a limit, hating, avidly passionate, does not show himself in his nakedness." The human being hates this limit. He—and she—would overcome it. Rather than witness to our fallen state, we are seduced by arrogant anthropocentrism and by a totalist politics that promises a Garden beyond good and evil as its culminating point. But first we must expose everything; we must ferret out all enemies; we must destroy all that stands in our way or in the way of thousand-year Reichs or classless societies where all division has been eradicated. We fall prey to deadly bio-politics, for example, as we engineer ways to get the "unworthy" out of sight and out of mind. Bonhoeffer, however, insists that we ongoingly give witness to that which torments us—our knowledge of division. He deepens this insistency in his finished *Ethics* and ties his argument explicitly to the hubris of political or public overcoming, arrogant anthropocentrism that requires a norm of shamelessness in order for human beings to carry out the dirty work, dirty no more, or so is the claim, because the ruthless deed-doer knows no evil. They have overturned all received values. Humility is servility in their eyes. Recognition of limits, cowardice. Decency, gullibility. Skepticism, treason. In a world in which all barriers to action and expression have been crushed, we are no longer open to Bonhoeffer's quiet but firm recognition when he writes: "The peculiar fact that we lower our eyes when a stranger's eye meets our gaze is not a sign of remorse for a fault, but a sign of that shame which, when it knows that it is seen, is reminded of something it lacks, namely, the lost wholeness of life, its own nakedness."

We *must*, Bonhoeffer insists, enter the public sphere—the world of publicity—with a mask, but not a mask of deceit; rather, one of rectitude that alone permits us to be for the other, to respect the other as we can from beneath our mask of "longing for the restoration of lost unity." Precisely because we give voice to our own division, we can recognize the integrity—the stubborn reality—of the other before us. Human beings must live "between covering and discovering, between self-concealment and self-revelation, between solitude and fellowship." This "in between" is similarly reflected in politics, the realm of secular affairs, where we both cover and dis-cover, where we protect and promote, where we can engage and can withdraw. Should politics claim the totality of us, that is a claim based on a unity we have lost; it is a claim that promotes violent impositions, often in the name of progress. This "dialectic of concealment and exposure" simply is the human condition. We cannot will or wish our way out of it. Those who try bring destruction on themselves and others. They must deify man and this "is the proclamation of nihilism. With the destruction of the biblical faith in God and of all divine commands and ordinances, man destroys himself. There arises an unrestrained vitalism which involves the dissolution of all values and achieves its goal only in the final self-destruction, in the void."

The radical, argues Bonhoeffer, and Nazis were nothing if not radical, although Bonhoeffer includes the zealous French Revolutionaries and Marxist ideologues committed to a teleology of violence in his indictment, always hates the created world. "The radical cannot forgive God His creation. He has fallen out with the created world. . . . It is replaced by bitterness, suspicion, and contempt for men and the world." Making of human projects an absolute leads humanity into the abyss. "Our responsibility is not infinite; it is limited," Bonhoeffer insisted again and again. For the human being is "appointed to the concrete and therefore limited responsibility which knows the world as being created, loved, condemned and reconciled by God. . . ." The world, in a sense, discloses what our responsibility should be in a concrete way, not through an unlimited and abstract benevolence, nor an equally unlimited, abstract and altogether deadly militance. Hence Bonhoeffer's condemnation of the ideologue, the one who "sees himself justified in his idea." He—the ideologue—looks into the mirror of the self and declares it good. He cannot *see* the starving child he holds aloft and chortles over. But the responsible person recognizes "not my will but Thine be done" and this acceptance of limits paradoxically frees us to serve God and our neighbor in a way that is "not unlimited and arrogant but creaturely and humble."

Interestingly, a very different witness to the torment of our century—Albert Camus—worked out his own way to Bonhoeffer's themes. He, too, insisted that "we all carry within us our places of exile, our crimes and our ravages. But our task is not to unleash them on the world; it is to fight them in ourselves and others." This is a plea for rectitude; this is an insistence that we not pitch ourselves into shamelessness. For the integrity of public and private life are destroyed if we do. Camus, too, criticizes the regicides of the French Revolution for they were also deicides—they were killing not just the king but God, for only then could they eradicate the barrier to totalistic politics represented by a God who knows our shame and who urges us to its recognition. Camus renounced the claims of politics to aspire to the absolute. Yet a third witness, Hannah Arendt, argued that "the only reasonable hope for salvation from evil and wickedness at which men might arrive in this world and even by themselves, without any divine assistance" is the imperfect working of government, the flawed actions of citizens among citizens, citizens mindful of human limits who seek partial redemption only: political hope by contrast to earthly salvation.

The trouble with those who go into the "school of revolution," as Arendt puts it, is that they claim perfect knowledge. They can see into the future. They know beforehand the course "a revolution must take." But this is a "grandiose ludicrousness," Arendt avers, for its automatic adherence to the claims of revolutionary necessity is compulsive, unlike the uncoerced actions and reactions of citizens doing the work of practical politics as concrete care for the person before me. "Since the days of the French Revolution," writes Arendt, "it has been the boundlessness of their sentiments that made revolutionaries so curiously insensitive to reality in general and to the reality of persons in particular, whom they felt no compunctions in sacrificing to their 'principles', or to the course of history, or to the cause of revolution as such." Politics without limits is evil for it ignores human distinctiveness in favor of wholly abstract construals. *In concretissimo*—not dead abstractions but concrete realities, the human being before us—that must compel our attention and it cannot if we are self-absorbed, self-obsessed, riding the stormy tides of political excess.

When the shameless speak of necessity they compare it to a torrent, a compulsion governed by historic laws that are irresistible. When those aware of the barrier of shame—and here I return to Bonhoeffer—speak of necessity they write out of sorrowful recognition. For such a one understands that "no law can compel the responsible man to take any particular decision in the face of such necessities," such necessities being a reaction to a time and place where the order of things is upended; where the state overruns its legitimate bounds; where the relative order of this earth is dispelled. But in breaking a law to try to put things right, the responsible agent recognizes his or her own guilt. He or she can do no other. This action is always "performed wholly within the domain of relativity, wholly in the twilight which the historical situation spreads over good and evil." This is not, Bonhoeffer assures us, a demand that "ethics and ethicists . . . intervene continuously in life." No, let us hope not, for their vocation is to "draw attention to the disturbance and interruption of life by the 'shall' and the 'should' which impinge on all life from its periphery."

The ethical marks boundaries—boundaries of shame and shamelessness; boundaries of public and private; boundaries of intimacy and publicity. This is political philosophy, here indebted to Bonhoeffer's theology, as a *via negativa*, that which the state or political actors are *not* permitted to do. In her last works before her death, the political theorist Judith Shklar wrote of a "liberalism of fear." She claimed that political philosophers had concentrated overmuch on grand and abstract articulation of total systems of justice. Far better, she argued, to look concretely at injustice, at Nazi doctors, for example, at all the many specific moments of unjust behavior or laws or actions or polities and assess what one might conclude from this unblinkered evaluation of human affairs. We require, it seems, perhaps now more than ever, *barriers to action* as much or more than we require incitements to action. That is why we must always ask what is being called upon or called up in us when we are asked to endorse this or to promote that. With Bonhoeffer, we respond: "What is to come?" We acknowledge our fearfulness but we do not fall into cowardice. Knowingly, we place ourselves on the edge and resist the temptation to capitulate to passivity, on the one hand, restless and reckless activity, on the other.

"Our conclusion," writes Bonhoeffer, "must be that action which is in accordance with Christ is action which is in accordance with reality. This proposition is not an ideal demand, but it is an assertion that springs from the knowledge of reality itself. Jesus Christ does not confront reality as one who is alien to it, but it is He who alone has borne and experienced the essence of the real in His own body." It was this Christian compassion—of which Lifton has written—that the Nazis aimed to kill. That so many nominal Christians went along is an enduring shame. Bonhoeffer, by contrast, who split from the official Church to help form the Confessing Church, faithful to the Gospel, opposed to Nazism, notes that as we tend to "concrete interventions in the visible world, and it is certain that hunger and satisfaction of hunger are concrete and visible matters," these matters are given shimmering vitality because they gesture toward the ultimate from that realm which can only aspire to the penultimate. Recognition of shame, of our division and our fallenness, releases us for concrete intervention even as it chastens our claims to possess the ultimate.

Now I readily admit that it is very difficult to mount a defense of the necessity for shame in today's world. But it makes sense, even amidst the hub-bub and the hurly-burly and the frenetic demands of the present to think about shame and shamelessness. Shame or its felt experience as it surrounds our body's functions, passions, and desires requires symbolic forms, veils of civility that conceal some activities and aspects of ourselves even as we boldly and routinely display and reveal other sides of ourselves when we take part in public activities in the light of day for all to see. When one opens one's body up to publicity, and when intimate life is put on display, one not only invites, one actively seeks the exploitation of one's own body. For one has withdrawn the body's intimacy from interpersonal relations and exposed it to an unknown audience who will make of it what they will. Thus one may become an occasion for scandal or abuse or even violence toward others through one's own relentless self-exposure.

This is the scandal of the present and it reminds us, as I indicated earlier, that shame is central to safeguarding the freedom of the body; hence, to help keep alive our freedom to act responsibly, to be for others. Small wonder, then, that so many philosophers and theologians and political theorists have found in shame a vital and powerful feature of our human condition that we would overturn at our peril. Shamelessness is rarely on display so violently and pitilessly as in the case of the Nazi doctors. But we must tend to our own versions of it as part of our concrete obligation as citizens, whether we are, with Bonhoeffer, Christians or not. To take up this burden is not, as Dietrich Bonhoeffer rightly insists, to embrace duplicity and disguise; rather, it means holding on to that concealment necessary to a rich personal life and to human dignity in order that one might know and thus work to attain that which is at once self-revelatory and public, central to human solidarity and fellowship, to what is in common.

I want to conclude with a poem that, in its tender specificity and incarnational concreteness, reminds me of Bonhoeffer and evokes, as well, Lifton's love of his Wellfleet dunes. The poem speaks to recognitions that are made possible—recognition of joy in the beauty of the world and the creative capacities of human beings—*only* because, in our shame, we know the boundaries of our own limits. Then and only then can we respect that which is.

> Blue herons that fish in silence,
> webs that sag with dew,
> old pines in mist,
> the snow at sea,
> and hues as they merge in evening,
> rain on mossed rocks,
> and crackling flames,
> and a breeze touched with brine,
> and leaf-stained light in autumn,
> Gandhi, Bach, Monet, Maria,

and a stream pool laved with pollen,
the surf as it lathers
and then hisses on the beaches,
the twilight, the stillness
:these things

Fred Dings

Index

About the Contributors

Norman Birnbaum is University Professor at Georgetown University Law Center and author of *Searching for the Light: Essays on Thought and Culture* and *The Radical Renewal: The Politics of Ideas in Modern America.*

Peter Brooks is Tripp Professor of Humanities at Yale University and author of *Body Work: Objects of Desire in Modern Narrative* and *Reading for the Plot: Design and Intention in Narrative.*

Cathy Caruth is associate professor of English and comparative literature at Emory University and author of *Unclaimed Experience: Trauma, Narrative, and History,* and editor of *Trauma: Explorations in Memory.*

Mary Ann Caws is Distinguished Professor of Art History, Comparative Literature, and French at the Graduate Center of the City University of New York and author of *Art of Interference: Studied Readings in Verbal and Visual Texts* and *Women of Bloomsbury: Virginia, Vanessa and Carrington.*

Joshua Dorban is a clinical psychologist and lecturer in the Department of Behavioral Sciences, Sackler School of Medicine, Tel Aviv University. He is a candidate at the Jerusalem Institute of Psychoanalysis.

John S. Dunne is O'Brien Professor of Theology at the University of Notre Dame. He is the author of many books, including *The Way of All the Earth, Time and Myth, Reasons of the Heart,* and most recently *Love's Mind.*

Jean Bethke Elshtain is Laura Spelman Professor of Social and Political Ethics at the University of Chicago and author of *Women and War* and *Democracy on Trial.*

Cynthia Fuchs Epstein is Distinguished Professor of Sociology at the Graduate Center of the City University of New York and author of *Women in Law* and *The Anxious American* (forthcoming).

Lillian Feder is Distinguished Professor Emerita of English, Classics, and Comparative Literature at the Graduate School of the City University of New York, and author of *Madness in Literature and Ancient Myth in Modern Poetry.*

Larry Friedman is professor of history at Indiana University, Blooming-ton, and author of *Menninger: The Family and the Clinic, Gregarious Saints: Self and Community in American Abolitionism*, two other historical volumes, and an impending biography of Erik Erikson.

Todd Gitlin, who this fall becomes professor of culture and communica-tion at New York University, is the author of several books on politics, society, and culture, including *The Whole World Is Watching, Inside Prime Time,* and *The Sixties: Years of Hope, Days of Rage*, as well as a novel, *The Murder of Albert Einstein*. His new book, *The Twilight of Common Dreams: Why America Is Wracked by Culture Wars* will be published this November. He is a columnist for the *New York Observer.*

David G. Goodman is professor of Japanese literature in the Department of East Asian Languages and Culture at the University of Illinois/Ur-bana-Champaign, and author of *After Apocalypse: Four Japanese Plays of Hiroshima and Nagasaki.*

Judith Lewis Herman is associate clinical professor of psychiatry at the Cambridge Hospital, Harvard Medical School. She is the author of *Fa-ther-Daughter Incest* and *Trauma and Recovery.*

Gerald Holton is Mallinckrodt Professor of Physics and professor of the history of science at Harvard University and author of *Thematic Origins of Scientific Thought; Kepler to Einstein* and *Science and Anti-science.*

Frances Degen Horowitz is president of the Graduate School and Uni-versity Center, the City University of New York. A psychologist in infant behavior and development, she is the author of more than 100 articles, as well as *Exploring Developmental Theories: Toward a Structural/Behavioral Model of Development*, and editor of *The Gifted and the Talented: Develop-mental Perspectives.*

Betty Jean Lifton is a writer, psychologist, lecturer, and adoption coun-selor. She is the author of *Journey of the Adopted Self: The Quest for Whole-ness, Lost and Found: The Adoption Experience, The King of Children: A Biogra-phy of Janusz Korczak, A Place Called Hiroshima* (with the photographer Eikoh Hoseo), and numerous books and plays for children.

Phyllis Palgi is professor of anthropology at the Sackler School of Medi-cine, Tel Aviv University, and has written widely in the fields of ethno-medicine, death studies, and immigrant adjustment. Between 1953 and 1981 she served as the first government anthropologist in the Depart-ment of Health in Israel.

David Riesman is Henry Ford II Professor of Social Sciences Emeritus at Harvard University and the country's most eminent sociologist. His most famous book is *The Lonely Crowd.*

Richard Sennett is University Professor of Humanities and professor of history and sociology at New York University and author of *The Fall of Public Man* and *Flesh and Stone: The Body and City in Western Civilization.*

Margaret Thaler Singer is emeritus professor of psychology at University of California, Berkeley, and author of *Cults in our Midst.*

Lionel Tiger is Charles Darwin Professor of Anthropology at Rutgers University. Among his books are *Men in Groups, The Manufacture of Evil: Ethics, Evolution and the Industrial System,* and *The Pursuit of Pleasure.*

Paul L. Wachtel is Distinguished Professor of Psychology at the City College of New York and the Graduate Center of the City University of New York, and author of *Therapeutic Communications and The Poverty of Affluence.*

Noel Walsh is professor and chair of the Department of Psychiatry at St. Vincent's Hospital, Dublin. He has lectured widely on Lacanian theories of psychotherapy, death studies, and the social and cultural meanings of psychoanalysis.

About the Editors

Charles B. Strozier is professor of history at John Jay College and the Graduate Center, City Unversity of New York, where he is also codirector of the Center on Violence and Human Survival. He is a practicing psychoanalyst and senior faculty member of the Training and Research Institute in Self Psychology in New York City. He is the author of *Lincoln's Quest for Union: Public and Private Meanings* (Basic Books), collaborator with Heinz Kohut, *Self Psychology and The Humanities: Reflections on a New Psychoanalytic Approach* (Norton Publishing Company), and editor (with Daniel Offer) of *The Leader: Psychohistorical Studies* (Plenum Press). Two books are in preparation: *Heinz Kohut and the Self: Psychoanalysis at the Millennium,* and an edited volume (with Michael Flynn), *Two Thousand: Essays on the End* (New York University Press).

Michael Flynn is lecturer of psychology at York College, the City University of New York, and associate director of the Center on Violence and Human Survival, John Jay College, City University of New York. He is a psychotherapist in private practice specializing in the treatment of victims and perpetrators of physical and sexual violence. He is editing (with Charles Strozier) *Two Thousand: Essays on the End* (New York University Press).